Curso tercero

Workbook

for a Third Course

in Spanish

MARVIN WASSERMAN
Former Chairman, Department of Foreign Languages
Susan E. Wagner High School
Staten Island, New York

CAROL WASSERMAN, Ph.D.
Adjunct Assistant Professor of Spanish
Borough of Manhattan Community College
New York City

When ordering this book, please specify:
either **R 502 W** or CURSO TERCERO/WORKBOOK

Dedicated to serving

AMSCO

our nation's youth

AMSCO SCHOOL PUBLICATIONS, INC.
315 Hudson Street/New York, N.Y. 10013

ISBN 0-87720-541-8

PRINTED IN THE UNITED STATES OF AMERICA

Preface

CURSO TERCERO is a workbook for students who have had two years of high school Spanish. Since the Spanish curriculum varies from school to school, some teachers may find this book just as useful in their second-year classes. CURSO TERCERO completes the sequence begun with our workbooks *Curso primero* and *Curso segundo*.

The text is divided into three sections: Grammar, Activities, and an Appendix. Part 1, **Grammar**, consists of 18 chapters in which the "rules" of Spanish grammar taught in most three-year courses are clearly explained in short units. Many of these "rules" are directly reinforced by practice. Each chapter concludes with a set of summary exercises. As in *Curso segundo*, the entire course can be mastered in small steps.

Part 2, **Activities**, consists of several kinds of exercises that provide extensive practice in the four basic skills: speaking, listening, reading, and writing. The passages in the Listening- and Reading-Comprehension units were excerpted from essays or articles in popular Spanish and Latin-American periodicals. Most of the activities in the units titled "Practice in Speaking" and "Writing Practice" follow the models of current comprehensive three-year examinations.

The **Appendix** provides a review of grammar topics taught in Levels I and II, such as conjugations, Spanish numerals, and weather expressions. Since these topics need not be taught again in a third-year course, they are not included among the 18 chapters of Part 1. Thus, greater attention can be given in Part 1 to the complexities of Spanish usage that are often overlooked in the first two years. The student who has forgotten the forms of **saber** in the imperfect subjunctive or needs to recall how **gustar** is used will find such information in the Appendix.

Other distinctive features in CURSO TERCERO are:

1. Ten illustrated essays about interesting places and customs in the Hispanic world.
2. A more thorough treatment of the ways in which possession is expressed in Spanish.
3. A chapter on the various ways in which *to be* is expressed in Spanish (a matter not limited to the use of **ser** and **estar**).
4. A discussion of the difficulties in choosing between the imperfect and the preterite of **ser** or **estar**.
5. A chapter on the various uses of the infinitive.
6. A comprehensive treatment of the uses of the subjunctive.

The chapters in CURSO TERCERO are arranged topically to permit the teacher to follow any order suitable to the objectives of the course and the needs of the students. This flexibility is facilitated by the detailed table of contents at the front of the book and the comprehensive index at the back.

—The Authors

Acknowledgments

Grateful acknowledgment is made to the following sources for permission to print adaptations of copyrighted articles.

Tiempo Madrid, Spain	pages 203–204, items 2, 3, 4 205–206, items 1, 2 213, item 1
Muy Interesante revista de divulgación científica y cultural Madrid, Spain	page 204, items 5, 6, 7 206, item 3 207–208, item 6 211, item 6 219, item 4 220, item 5 222, items 1, 2 223, item 2 226–227, item 2
Geomundo U.S.A.	page 205, item 10 216, item 6
Américas U.S.A.	page 212, item 7
Revista de Geografía Universal *Edición Argentina* Buenos Aires, Argentina	page 208, item 7
Historia y Vida Barcelona, Spain	pages 209–210, items 2, 3 213–214, items 2, 3 217, item 1
El Comercio Lima, Peru	page 215, item 5
Hombre de Mundo U.S.A.	page 221, item 6
Hombre de Mundo Quito, Ecuador	pages 225–226, item 4
revista *Aventura* Madrid, Spain	page 224, item 1

Contents

Part 1–Grammar

Part 2—Activities

Appendix

Part 1
Grammar

1 The Present Tense

Review the conjugations of verbs in the present tense on pages 237–240.

1 The Spanish present tense may express either of two English tenses: the simple present (*I speak*) or the present progressive (*I am speaking*). The first denotes an action that occurs regularly, the second, an action that is occurring "now" or in progress.* Which English translation is the appropriate one depends on the context:

—¿Qué **haces** los sábados?	"What *do you do* on Saturday?" (= every Saturday)
—**Hago** mis tareas, juego al tenis, . . .	"I *do* my homework, I play tennis, . . ."
—¿Qué **haces** ahora?	"What *are you doing* now?"
—**Escribo** una carta.	"I *am writing* a letter."

Using the Present to Express the Near Future

2 In both Spanish and English, the present tense is often used to signify that an action will take place in the near future:

Mañana **vamos** al cine.	Tomorrow we are going to the movies.
Te **veo** más tarde.	I'll see you later.
Esta noche **cenamos** en un restaurante español.	Tonight we're eating (we will eat) in a Spanish restaurant.

. . . and to Ask for Instructions

3 The present tense is generally used in Spanish to ask for instructions:

¿Qué **hago** ahora?	What shall I do now?
¿Adónde **llevo** el libro?	Where shall I take the book?

*Many people who learn English as a foreign language have trouble mastering the difference between the present and the present progressive. Beginners sometimes confuse the two tenses: "I go to the store now"; "I am leaving the house every morning at 8:00." Can you explain why such an error might be made by a student of English whose native language is Spanish?

___ EJERCICIOS _____

A. VERBOS REGULARES

Substituya el verbo subrayado por la forma correspondiente del verbo entre paréntesis y escribala en la linea a la derecha. (Replace the underlined verb with the corresponding form of . . .)

1. (beber) ¿Cuántas veces al día <u>toma</u> Ud. café? _____
2. (comprar) ¿Qué <u>venden</u> en esa tienda? _____
3. (bajar) Por esa escalera se <u>sube</u> muy fácilmente. _____
4. (responder) ¿Cómo <u>contestamos</u> a esa pregunta? _____
5. (vivir) Mi madre <u>trabaja</u> en el centro. _____
6. (explicar) ¿Cómo te <u>describo</u> ese libro? _____
7. (llegar a) Mañana <u>partimos para</u> Madrid. _____
8. (deber) ¿<u>Deseas</u> ver esa película? _____
9. (escuchar) No <u>comprendéis</u> mi pregunta. _____
10. (regresar) ¿A qué hora <u>volvemos</u> a casa esta noche? _____

En los ejercicios **B** a **D,** complete las oraciones con las formas apropiadas de los verbos entre paréntesis.

B. VERBOS QUE CAMBIAN LA VOCAL RADICAL (stem-changing verbs)

1. (nevar) La radio dice que _____ en Chicago ahora.
2. (volar) ¿A qué altura _____ nuestro avión?
3. (oler) Esas rosas _____ muy bien.
4. (sentirse) ¿Cómo _____ tú esta tarde?
5. (servir) ¿Qué se _____ en ese restaurante esta noche?
6. (morirse) Esta mañana yo casi _____ de hambre.
7. (perder) Vas a _____ el autobús si no corres.
8. (empezar) ¿A qué hora _____ la clase de español?
9. (soler) Mi padre _____ llegar a casa a las seis de la tarde.
10. (sonreír) Chica, estás muy bonita cuando _____ .

C. VERBOS IRREGULARES

1. (decir) ¿Qué me _____ acerca de tu problema?
2. (venir) El tío Esteban no _____ esta noche a cenar.
3 & 4. (reconocer, ser) Yo no _____ a ese hombre. ¿Quién _____?
5. (ir) ¿Adónde _____ vosotras esta tarde?
6. (estar) Ellos _____ en Barcelona este verano.

7. (dar)   ¿Qué te _____ yo en tu cumpleaños?
8. (oír)   Cada noche nosotras _____ el mismo programa de radio.
9. (hacer)   ¿Y yo? ¿Qué _____ con todo esto?
10. (ser)   Tú _____ mi mejor amigo.

D. VERBOS CON CAMBIO ORTOGRÁFICO (verbs with spelling changes)

1. (seguir)   Mis amigos _____ los mismos cursos este semestre.
2. (dirigir)   ¿Quién _____ la orquesta este año?
3. (fingir)   Yo siempre _____ no conocer a esas personas.
4. (proteger)   Yo _____ a mis hijos cuando es necesario.
5. (exigir)   Ese trabajo _____ mucha paciencia.
6. (vencer)   Yo nunca _____ a mi primo en el tenis.
7. (extinguir) Los bomberos _____ el fuego con mucha rapidez.
8. (conseguir) Si yo _____ mi pasaporte a tiempo, puedo ir a España con ustedes.
9. (escoger)   ¿Qué _____ tú del menú?
10. (torcer)   Yo te _____ el brazo si no me obedeces.
11. (enviar)   ¿Qué tipo de regalo me _____ tú en mi cumpleaños?
12. (continuar) El artículo _____ en la próxima página.
13. (construir) ¿Qué _____ esos trabajadores en esa calle?
14. (graduarse) Yo me _____ el año que viene.
15. (conducir) Mi padre me dice que yo _____ el carro muy bien.

E. Conteste en oraciones completas:

1. *a.* ¿Piensa su familia comprar un ordenador (una computadora)?

_____

   b. ¿Qué tipo de ordenador piensan ustedes conseguir?

_____

   c. ¿Por qué?

_____

2. ¿A qué altura vuela un jet* en un vuelo transatlántico?

_____

3. *a.* En su clase de español, ¿cuándo corrige el profesor (la profesora) a los alumnos?

_____

   b. ¿Le (La) corrige Ud. a él (a ella) algunas veces?

_____

*The English word *jet* (for jet airplane) is commonly used in Hispanic countries, although the "correct" Spanish expression is *avión a reacción* or *avión a chorro*.

4. *a.* ¿Cómo se consigue una licencia de conducir?

   _____

   b. ¿Cuándo va usted a conseguirla?

   _____

5. *a.* ¿A qué centro comercial va usted a menudo?

   _____

   b. ¿Cuántas tiendas tiene?

   _____

   c. ¿Cuál es su tienda favorita?

   _____

   d. ¿Por qué?

   _____

6. *a.* Al llamar a un amigo por teléfono, ¿cómo lo saluda Ud.?

   _____

   b. Y cuando él responde, ¿qué le dice a Ud.?

   _____

7. *a.* ¿Qué tipo de música oyen Uds. en su clase de música?

   _____

   b. ¿Les gusta?

   _____

8. *a.* ¿A qué hora se acuesta Ud. los sábados?

   _____

   b. ¿Y los días de entre semana?

   _____

9. ¿Con qué se enciende un cigarrillo?

   _____

10. *a.* ¿Qué hace Ud. cuando le duele la cabeza?

    _____

    b. ¿Consulta Ud. alguna vez a algún médico?

    _____

    c. Y ¿qué le dice el médico?

    _____

11. ¿Cómo se despide Ud. de un amigo al salir de su casa?

    _____

12. *a.* ¿Se fían los profesores de sus alumnos durante un examen?

    _____

    b. ¿Por qué?

    _____

13. *a.* ¿Se gradúa Ud. mañana?

    _____

b. Si no, ¿cuándo se gradúa, entonces?

_____

14. *a.* Cuando Ud. entra en la cafetería de su escuela durante la hora del almuerzo, ¿a cuántas personas reconoce Ud.?

_____

b. ¿Cuántas personas lo (la) reconocen a Ud.?

_____

15. ¿Le da Ud. una propina a su profesor* de español después de la lección?

_____

16. Cuando Ud. va a la playa, ¿qué pone en su maletín?

_____

17. ¿Pierde Ud. mucho peso cuando juega al tenis?

_____

18. ¿Se ríen mucho sus compañeros de clase cuando su profesor* cuenta un chiste?

_____

19. ¿Cómo se divierten Uds. los domingos por la tarde?

_____

20. ¿Se despierta Ud. o sigue Ud. durmiendo cuando su profesor* le hace una pregunta?

_____

F. Aquí están algunas *respuestas*. ¿Cuáles son las preguntas? Escriba una pregunta para cada respuesta.

EJEMPLO: Tomo la cena a las ocho. $\begin{cases} \textit{¿A qué hora toma Ud. la cena?} \\ \qquad\qquad \text{O:} \\ \textit{¿Qué hace Ud. a las ocho?} \end{cases}$

1. Quiero dar un paseo.

_____

2. No, no nos acordamos de ella.

_____

3. Nuestra profesora nos corrige.

_____

4. Elegimos otro presidente cada cuatro años.

_____

5. Se divierten jugando al béisbol.

_____

6. Nos sentamos en el autobús sólo cuando hay suficientes asientos para las personas mayores.

_____

7. Te traigo un bonito regalo.

_____

*See the footnote on page 31.

8. Estoy enferma.

_____

9. No lo sé.

_____

10. Le pertenece a mi hermano.

_____

11. Se construye en aquella calle.

_____

12. Sí, papá, siempre guío con cuidado.

_____

13. No, porque nos sentimos muy mal esta noche.

_____

14. Sí, los entiendo a Uds. perfectamente.

_____

15. Lo veo todas las noches en el Canal 4.

_____

G. Traduzca al español:

1. George, will I see you* at the basketball game?

_____

2. They generally watch television in the evening after dinner. (Use *soler* (*ue*) + *inf.*, to be in the habit of, accustomed to.)

_____

3. She is getting her driver's license next week.

_____

4. How tall is your brother? ("How much does your brother measure?")

_____

5. The inhabitants of that town are fleeing from the hurricane.

_____

6. Who is directing the school orchestra this semester?

_____

7. At what time are they having lunch tomorrow? (Use the verb *almorzar*.)

_____

8. Where does your uncle work in the city?

_____

9. I propose John for the job.

_____

10. What shall I bring to the party tonight?

_____

*In this book, assume that the pronoun *you* is the familiar singular if the person is addressed by his or her first name.

11. I don't deserve a good mark on this test.

_____

12. Is there room for me ("Do I fit") in your car, or shall I walk?

_____

13. When are you (*Uds.*) going to the theater?

_____

14. Susan, I'm offering you two tickets to tonight's rock concert ("concert of rock music"). Do you want them, or shall I give them to someone else?

_____

_____

15. Is he coming to our barbecue next Sunday?

_____

16. What university does your sister attend?

_____

17. I know them, but I don't know their address yet.

_____

18. At what time do you (*Ud.*) wake up on Sunday? (= every Sunday)

_____

19. How much does that computer cost?

_____

20. Are your parents having a good time in Spain this summer?

_____

21. I never fall asleep in my Spanish class.

_____

22. How often ("How many times") does your father repeat the same advice?

_____

23. Some students don't contribute very much to the discussions in class.

_____

24. Mr. Smith's lessons don't vary too much from term to (*en*) term.

_____

25. "Is it raining now?" "No, I think it's beginning to snow."

_____

2 The Preterite Tense

Review the conjugations of verbs in the preterite tense on pages 240–242.

1 The preterite is generally the equivalent of the English past tense:

—¿**Viste** el programa anoche?   "Did you see the program last night?"

—Sí, lo **vi**. También **llamé** a mi primo, y **charlamos** por una hora.   "Yes, I saw it. I also called my cousin, and we chatted for an hour."

—¿Qué **hizo** Ud. ayer por la mañana?   "What did you do yesterday morning?"

—**Fui** al centro donde **compré** varias cosas.   "I went downtown where I bought several things."

2 The preterite often occurs with phrases that tell us at what point in the past an action ended: **ayer** (yesterday), **anoche** (last night), **la semana pasada** (last week), **hace un mes** (a month ago), etc. Whenever the preterite is used, a phrase of that kind is either expressed or implied. Keep this in mind when you are uncertain as to which tense—the preterite or the imperfect (see chapter 3)—is the most likely equivalent of the English past tense.

Verbs with Special Meanings in the Preterite

3 The following verbs often have special meanings in the preterite tense:

CONOCER

Conocí a José en Madrid.   I *met* Joseph in Madrid. (I *made his acquaintance*.)

PODER

Pudieron terminar la obra.   They *managed to* finish the work.

QUERER

Mi hermana **no quiso** vernos anoche.   My sister *refused to* see us last night.

SABER

> **Supe** que habían llegado tarde.   I *learned* (*found out*) that they had arrived late.

TENER

> Esta mañana **tuvimos** una tarjeta postal de Enrique.   This morning we *got* (*received*) a postcard from Henry.

To express their more usual meanings in the past (I *knew* Joseph, they *could* (*were able to*) finish..., my sister *didn't want* to see us, etc.), the imperfect tense is most often used. See chapter 3.

___ EJERCICIOS ___

A. Complete la oración con el pretérito del verbo entre paréntesis.

1. (comenzar) ¿Cuándo _____ a nevar anoche?

2. (decir) Chica, tú no me _____ la verdad.

3. (poder) Yo no _____ ver el partido a causa de la lluvia.

4. (ser) Esa autora _____ muy famosa en el siglo XIX.

5. (almorzar) Hoy yo _____ muy temprano.

6. (dormir) El niño _____ diez horas anoche.

7. (hacer) ¿Qué _____ ella por la madrugada?

8. (vivir) Mis abuelos _____ en Puerto Rico hace 20 años.

9. (servir) ¿Qué te _____ ellos en su casa anoche?

10. (sacar) Ayer yo _____ tres libros de la biblioteca.

11. (estar) ¿Y tú? ¿Dónde _____ anoche con tus amigos?

12. (venir) ¿A qué hora _____ Uds. esta mañana?

13. (traducir) Ayer en la clase de español los alumnos _____ al inglés dos párrafos de *Don Quijote*.

14. (tropezar) Hace una hora que yo _____ con mi profesor en el centro comercial.

15. (oír) ¿Qué clase de música _____ Ud. en el concierto anoche?

16. (acordarse) Parece que ellos no _____ de nosotros.

17. (sentarse) ¿Dónde _____ todos en el salón?

18. (sentirse) Adolfo _____ muy mal ayer por la tarde.

19. (irse) Mis parientes _____ hace una hora.

20. (morirse) La pobre vieja _____ la semana pasada.

B. Complete la segunda oración de cada par con el pretérito del verbo subrayado.

1. ¿Cuándo <u>vienes</u> a ver la colección?

   ¿_____ a verla esta mañana?

2. ¿A qué hora <u>almuerza</u> ella esta tarde?

   ¿_____ ella tarde hoy?

3. Este semestre <u>leemos</u> una novela completa en la clase de español.

   El semestre pasado _____ una obra teatral.

4 & 5. Nuestro profesor <u>corrige</u> cada falta que <u>hacemos</u>.

   Ayer también _____ las faltas que _____.

6. Mi padre <u>exige</u> mucho de toda la familia.

   Anoche _____ demasiado de mi hermano Paco.

7. Nunca <u>llego</u> a tiempo a la escuela.

   El año pasado nunca _____ tarde.

8. ¿Qué <u>pueden</u> Uds. ver desde aquí?

   ¿Qué _____ oír desde tan lejos?

9 & 10. ¿<u>Corren</u> o <u>andan</u> Uds. por el parque en la tarde?

   ¿_____ o _____ Uds. a la escuela esta mañana?

11. ¿Qué nos <u>traen</u> mañana para la fiesta?

   ¿Nos _____ algo bueno anoche?

12 & 13. No <u>creemos</u> todo lo que <u>oímos</u> en la televisión.

   No _____ lo que _____ ayer en la radio.

14. Mi madre <u>consigue</u> buenas gangas en el supermercado.

   Ayer no _____ nada bueno.

15. ¿Cuánto dinero <u>piden</u> por el ordenador?

   En esa tienda _____ más de mil dólares.

16. ¿Adónde <u>prefieres</u> ir hoy?

   Ayer _____ quedarte en casa.

17. Aquí se <u>construye</u> un rascacielos de setenta pisos.

   El año pasado se _____ otro edificio menos alto.

18. La clase nunca se <u>ríe</u> de los chistes del profesor.

   Anoche mi familia se _____ toda la noche de ese programa.

19. ¿Quién <u>pone</u> las cintas en la grabadora?

   ¿Quién las _____ allí hace una hora?

20 & 21. Siempre <u>cuelgo</u> mi ropa en el armario cuando <u>llego</u> a casa temprano.

   Ayer no la _____ en él porque _____ muy tarde.

22 & 23. Hoy no <u>quiero</u> jugar al tenis porque <u>hace</u> mal tiempo.

   Ayer no _____ salir de casa porque _____ mucho viento.

24 & 25. <u>Parece</u> que no <u>hay</u> nadie aquí en este momento.

   Le _____ que tampoco _____ nadie aquí anoche.

C. Conteste en oraciones completas:

1. *a.* ¿Adónde hizo Ud. su viaje más reciente?

   _____

   b. ¿Quiénes le (la) acompañaron?

   _____

   c. ¿Cuál fue el motivo del viaje?

   _____

   d. Después de llegar a su destino, ¿por cuánto tiempo se quedó allí?

   _____

2. *a.* ¿Qué aprendieron Uds. ayer en la clase de español?

   _____

   b. ¿Lo comprendió Ud. perfectamente?

   _____

   c. ¿Lo presentó bien el profesor?

   _____

   d. ¿Sacó Ud. apuntes durante la clase?

   _____

3. *a.* ¿Cuándo fue la última vez que Ud. fue a una fiesta?

   _____

   b. ¿Fue Ud. solo(-a) o acompañado(-a)?

   _____

   c. ¿Dónde tuvo lugar la fiesta?

   _____

   d. ¿Se divirtió Ud. allí?

   _____

   e. ¿Por qué? (o ¿por qué no?)

   _____

4. *a.* ¿Qué le dijo Ud. esta mañana a su madre (padre) cuando salió de casa?

   _____

   b. ¿Qué le contestó a Ud. su madre (padre)?

   _____

   c. ¿A qué hora salió Ud. de casa?

   _____

5. *a.* ¿Cómo se sintió Ud. el primer día de clases?

   _____

   b. ¿Estuvo Ud. satisfecho(-a) con todos sus profesores?

   _____

   c. ¿Por qué? (o ¿por qué no?)

   _____

    d. ¿Cuántos profesores dieron clases interesantes el primer día?

    _____

6. *a.* ¿Cuántas horas durmió Ud. anoche?

    _____

    b. ¿Durmió Ud. más tiempo el sábado por la noche?

    _____

    c. ¿Hizo Ud. algo interesante durante el fin de semana?

    _____

    d. ¿Pudo Ud. hacer todas sus tareas sin dificultad?

    _____

7. *a.* ¿A qué hora se levantó Ud. ayer por la mañana?

    _____

    b. ¿Qué hizo Ud. para prepararse para el día?

    _____

D. Escriba preguntas que se puedan contestar usando toda la información contenida en la oración.

      EJEMPLO: Busqué a Carlos en la sala para hablar con él.
          a. *¿Qué hizo Ud. en la sala?*   (Busqué a Carlos.)
          b. *¿Dónde buscó Ud. a Carlos?*   (en la sala)
          c. *¿Para qué buscó Ud. a Carlos?*   (para hablar con él.)

1. Me encontré con Susana en la esquina después del concierto.

    a. _____

    b. _____

2. Mis abuelos llegaron a casa a las ocho de la mañana.

    a. _____

    b. _____

    c. _____

3. Mi tío me mandó cien dólares porque se los pedí.

    a. _____

    b. _____

    c. _____

4. Mi padre vino tarde porque tuvo que quedarse en la oficina hasta las siete.

    a. _____

    b. _____

5. La policía fue llamada para detener al ladrón.

    a. _____

    b. _____

6. Fuimos a Colombia en avión.

   a. _____

   b. _____

7. Recibí una calculadora de bolsillo en mi cumpleaños.

   a. _____

   b. _____

8. Benito Pérez Galdós escribió ochenta novelas.

   a. _____

   b. _____

   c. _____

9. Escogimos el otro televisor porque nos pareció mejor.

   _____

10. Los soldados lucharon muy valientemente para ganar la batalla lo más pronto posible.

    a. _____

    b. _____

    c. _____

E. Traduzca al español:

1. *a.* Where did your friends go yesterday afternoon?

   _____

   b. They went downtown to get new clothes.

   _____

2. *a.* What did you do in school today, Johnny?

   _____

   b. I didn't do anything special ("exceptional").

   _____

3. *a.* To get to school, did you walk or take the bus?

   _____

   b. We walked because the bus didn't come.

   _____

4. *a.* I looked for my sister but she wasn't there.

   _____

   b. Where was she?

   _____

5. *a.* Did you (*Ud.*) read the magazine that I brought you?

   _____

   b. No, I didn't read it because I lost my eyeglasses.

   _____

6. *a.* What did your parents give you for your birthday, Jane?

   _____

   b. They gave me an electric typewriter that cost $350.

   _____

7. *a.* How long (*Cuánto tiempo*) did Mary sleep this afternoon?

   _____

   b. She slept for three hours, and when she got up she did her homework.

   _____

8. I felt very sick after the party. Did you (*Uds.*) feel sick too?

   _____

9. "Where did Charles put his coat?" "He put it in my room on the bed."

   _____

10. *a.* My father refused to give me the car last night.

    _____

    b. Why? Did he need it?

    _____

    c. No; he didn't trust me.

    _____

11. *a.* Where did you (*tú*) meet that pretty girl?

    _____

    b. I met her at the dance last night.

    _____

12. *a.* How did he find out that he passed the exam?

    _____

    b. The teacher greeted him with a smile this morning.

    _____

13. *a.* Did your brother go skiing yesterday?

    _____

    b. Yes; he fell several times and hurt himself. (Use the expression *hacerse daño*.)

    _____

14. *a.* What did they say about last night's meeting?

    _____

    b. They said that too many members were absent.

    _____

15. *a.* Last night I started to play chess with George. (Use the expression *ponerse a*.)

    _____

    b. I played all night and never went to bed.

    _____

16. *a.* Who played the piano at the wedding?

    _____

b. I played the piano and my sister played the clarinet.

_____

17. One witness lied at the trial. The other witnesses told the truth.

_____

18. *a.* Did they visit their grandparents last summer?

_____

   b. Yes, they spent three weeks with them. They had a very good time. (Use the expression *divertirse mucho.*)

_____

19. *a.* Did you (*Uds.*) manage to finish your work?

_____

   b. Yes; we finished it in three hours.

_____

20. *a.* How many television programs did you (*vosotros*) see last night?

_____

   b. We didn't watch television because we had to clean the house.

_____

CHAPTER 3
The Imperfect Tense

Review the formation of the imperfect tense on pages 242–243.

1 Both the preterite and the imperfect are past tenses. The preterite tells us that an action or event ended in the past, whereas the imperfect describes what *was happening* or *used to happen*. Although the two tenses differ in meaning, they may often have the same English translation:

Ayer Pablo **salió** de casa a las ocho.

Todos los días Pablo **salía** de casa a las ocho.

Yesterday…
Paul left the house at 8 o'clock.
Every day…

2 The imperfect tense is used as follows:

A. To express a regular or habitual action, often equivalent to English *used to…* or *would…* (= used to):

Todas las noches, después de la cena, **mirábamos** la televisión.

Every night after supper we watched (would watch, used to watch) television.

Ella **cocinaba** y yo **lavaba** los platos.

She cooked (would cook) and I washed (would wash) the dishes.

B. To describe what *was happening*, often equivalent to English *was (were)… -ing:*

La banda **tocaba** un tango pero sólo dos parejas **bailaban.**

The band was playing a tango but only two couples were dancing.

C. To express clock-time in the past:

Eran las ocho cuando salieron.

It was eight o'clock when they left.

D. To describe an action that was interrupted by an occurrence expressed in the preterite:

Preparaba la comida cuando Laura llegó.

She was preparing dinner when Laura arrived.

¿Qué **hacías** cuando te llamé?

What were you doing when I called you?

Note the following patterns:

Yo **trataba** de dormir cuando **sonó** el teléfono.	I was trying to sleep when the telephone rang.
Mientras **sonaba** el teléfono, **fui** a buscar mis zapatillas.	While the telephone rang (was ringing), I went to look for my slippers.
Mientras yo **buscaba** mis zapatillas, el teléfono **dejó** de sonar.	While I was looking for my slippers, the telephone stopped ringing.

E. With **ser** and **estar** to describe persons or situations:

Eran pobres pero felices.	They were poor but happy.
La casa **estaba** en una colina.	The house was on a hill.

F. In narrative style, to describe people, scenes, or situations:

Ese día **hacía** mucho calor. Todo el mundo **estaba** en la playa. Los niños **construían** castillos de arena mientras sus padres **descansaban** debajo de sus sombrillas.	It was very warm that day. Everybody was at the beach. The children built sand castles while their parents relaxed under their beach umbrellas.

3 Part D, above, showed how the preterite and imperfect tenses differed by using them together in the same sentence. Note two other possibilities:

a. Two actions occur at a specific time in the past (one morning); therefore, both are in the preterite:

Esta mañana Marta se **levantó** tarde y se **vistió** rápidamente.	This morning Martha got up late and dressed quickly.

b. Two continuous actions occur at the same time in the past; therefore, both are in the imperfect:

Mientras Marta se **vestía, escuchaba** la radio.	While Martha got dressed, she listened to the radio.

Using the Imperfect to Express States of Mind

4 Verbs that express beliefs, desires, or other states of mind—such as **creer, pensar, querer,** and **saber**—are generally used in the imperfect tense when referring to the past:

Yo **creía** que ella era muy bonita.	I thought that she was very pretty.
Sabíamos que **querían** vender su casa.	We knew that they wanted to sell their house.

Verbs That Have Different Meanings in the Preterite and Imperfect Tenses

5 As we saw in chapter 2, the verbs **conocer, poder, querer, saber,** and **tener** have special meanings in the preterite. Thus, their more general meanings in the past tense should be expressed by the imperfect. Note the differences in meaning:

¿Conociste a Pedro en Buenos Aires?	Did you meet (= make the acquaintance of) Peter in Buenos Aires?
¿Conocías a los amigos de Pedro?	Did you know Peter's friends?

Using the Imperfect and Preterite Tenses with *Ser* and *Estar*

6 To express the past, **ser** and **estar** may be used in the imperfect or the preterite. The imperfect describes persons or situations, the preterite treats such descriptions as facts that are "past and gone." Which tense to use depends more on feeling or intuition than logic. Use the imperfect tense unless you wish to make it especially clear that whatever "was" is now a thing of the past. Compare:

En aquel entonces ella **era** reina de España.	At that time she was Queen of Spain. (narrative style)
Ella **fue** reina de España en el siglo XV.	She was Queen of Spain in the 15th century. (She is no longer queen.)
Estaban en casa todas las tardes.	They were at home every afternoon. (regularly)
Estuvieron en casa hasta las dos.	They were at home until two o'clock. (They are no longer there.)

___ EJERCICIOS ___

A. Complete la segunda oración de cada par con la forma del imperfecto del verbo subrayado.

1. ¿Dónde <u>están</u> todos tus amigos ahora?

   ¿Dónde _____ todos tus amigos cuando los llamé?

2. Ayer <u>vi</u> una película buena.

    Yo siempre _____ buenas películas en el Cine Ritz.

3. Anoche <u>fuimos</u> a ver una función musical.

    Cuando vivíamos en Los Angeles, todos los sábados _____ a un concierto.

4. Ella <u>anduvo</u> a casa muy rápidamente anoche.

    Ella _____ por nuestra calle cuando la vimos.

5. ¿<u>Leíste</u> el artículo que te recomendé?

    ¿_____ el periódico cuando te llamé por teléfono?

6. La semana pasada <u>llovió</u> sin parar.

    _____ mientras estábamos en el centro.

7. Anita y yo <u>somos</u> buenos amigos.

    Siempre _____ buenos amigos cuando íbamos a la escuela juntos.

8. Generalmente <u>juegan</u> al tenis en el verano.

    Por lo general _____ al tenis cuando hacía buen tiempo.

9. ¿A qué hora <u>salió</u> Jacobo de casa esta mañana?

    ¿A qué hora _____ Jacobo cuando vivía en Nueva York?

10. Anoche me <u>acosté</u> temprano.

    Todas las noches me _____ a la misma hora.

11. Mientras yo miraba la televisión, me <u>dormí</u>.

    Cada vez que miraba la televisión, me _____.

12. Siempre <u>bailamos</u> cuando hay buena música en la radio.

    Siempre _____ a la música de la orquesta.

13. No <u>tengo</u> mucho que decir en este momento.

    Yo nunca _____ mucho que decir cuando estaba en la clase.

14. ¿Qué hora <u>es</u>?

    ¿Qué hora _____ cuando se fueron?

15. A menudo <u>voy</u> a casa de mis abuelos.

    A menudo _____ a visitarlos cuando tenía tiempo libre.

16. <u>Creemos</u> que <u>pueden</u> hacer el trabajo con facilidad.

    _____ que _____ hacerlo fácilmente.

17. ¿Cómo te <u>sientes</u> en nuestra casa?

    ¿Cómo te _____ en casa de tus suegros?

18. ¿Dónde nos <u>sentamos</u> en el teatro?

    Antes siempre nos _____ en el fondo.

19. Esta mañana se <u>levantaron</u> temprano y se bañaron inmediatamente.

    Mientras se _____, decidieron bañarse.

20. ¿Quién <u>fue</u> Presidente en el año 1932?

    Dicen que ese Presidente _____ un buen político.

En los ejercicios **B** a **E**, escriba la forma apropiada de cada verbo, eligiendo el pretérito o el imperfecto según el sentido del pasaje.

B. El sol _____ mientras Carmen _____ a la parada del
　　　　　1. brillar　　　　　　　　　　　　2. acercarse

autobús. Ella _____ diez minutos hasta que por fin _____ el
　　　　　3. esperar　　　　　　　　　　　　　　　　4. venir

autobús. Cuando _____ al centro, _____ muy cansada pero
　　　　　　5. llegar　　　　　　　　　6. estar

_____ comprar unas cosas. _____ en el centro una hora y media
　7. querer　　　　　　　　　　8. quedarse

pero no _____ nada. Cuando _____ volver a casa, ya era tarde.
　　　　9. comprar　　　　　　　　　10. decidir

C. —Hola, José, ¿adónde _____ tú cuando te _____ en la
　　　　　　　　　　　1. ir　　　　　　　　　　　2. ver

esquina?

—Yo _____ al centro, pero nunca _____ allí porque
　　　3. ir　　　　　　　　　　　　4. llegar

_____ a llover y no _____ paraguas. Por eso _____
　5. empezar　　　　　　　6. tener　　　　　　　　　　7. volver

a casa. Cuando _____, _____ con mis primos Juan y Carolina,
　　　　　8. entrar　　　　9. encontrarse

quienes _____ sentados en la sala. Ellos me _____ que me
　　　10. estar　　　　　　　　　　　　　11. decir

_____. Mientras tanto _____ la lluvia, y yo les
　12. esperar　　　　　　　　13. cesar

_____ si _____ salir conmigo. Me _____ que no
　14. preguntar　　　15. querer　　　　　　　　16. contestar

_____ posible porque _____ otros planes para la tarde. Ellos
　17. ser　　　　　　　　　18. tener

_____ de mí y _____.
　19. despedirse　　　　20. irse

D. Esta mañana yo _____ de casa y _____ a la estación del
　　　　　　　　1. salir　　　　　　　　2. encaminarse

metro. Mientras _____, _____ por la calle mucha gente.
　　　　　3. caminar　　　　4. pasar

_____ un tiempo espléndido y no _____ ganas de ir a la escuela.
　5. hacer　　　　　　　　　　　　6. tener

Sin embargo, _____ necesario. Por fin _____ a la estación donde
　　　　　7. ser　　　　　　　　　　8. llegar

_____ muchas personas. Allí _____ a mi amigo Antonio, quien me
　9. haber　　　　　　　　10. ver

_____ calurosamente y me _____ cómo _____. Le
　11. saludar　　　　　　　　12. preguntar　　　　　13. estar

_____ que _____ bien. Los dos _____ un rato hasta
　14. contestar　　　15. sentirse　　　　　　16. charlar

que _____ el tren. Nosotros _____ al tren que
　　17. venir　　　　　　　　18. subir

_____ su ruta a la escuela. El viaje _____ demasiado corto y
　　　19. empezar　　　　　　　　　　　　　　　　　　　　　　　20. ser

pronto _____ a nuestro destino. Al salir de la estación, _____ con
　　　　　　21. llegar　　　　　　　　　　　　　　　　　　　　　　22. tropezar

algunos amigos nuestros, y juntos _____ hacia la escuela. Yo
　　　　　　　　　　　　　　　23. andar

_____ que _____ a ser un día muy largo y aburrido.
　　24. pensar　　　　　　　　25. ir

E. Como esta mañana _____ buen tiempo y yo no _____ que ir
　　　　　　　　　　　　1. hacer　　　　　　　　　　　　　　　　2. tener

al trabajo, yo _____ dar un largo paseo por la ciudad. Antes de salir de casa,
　　　　　　　3. decidir

_____ a mi amigo Guillermo para ver si él _____ acompañarme.
　　4. llamar　　　　　　　　　　　　　　　　　　　　　　　5. querer

Como él no _____ ocupado y _____ unas horas libres,
　　　　　　　6. estar　　　　　　　　　　7. tener

_____ mi invitación.
　　8. aceptar

Guillermo y yo _____ en la esquina de la avenida Columbus y la calle 78,
　　　　　　　　9. encontrarse

donde _____ nuestro paseo. Mientras _____ por las calles del
　　　　10. empezar　　　　　　　　　　　　　　　　11. andar

vecindario, _____ pasar a la gente y _____ mirando los
　　　　　　12. ver　　　　　　　　　　　　　　13. divertirse

escaparates de las tiendas. También _____ los menús de algunos restaurantes—
　　　　　　　　　　　　　　　　14. leer

ya _____ en el almuerzo—pero _____ seguir nuestro camino y
　　15. pensar　　　　　　　　　　　　　16. decidir

comer más tarde.

Al pasar nosotros por una tienda popular de ropa, le _____ a Guillermo si
　　　　　　　　　　　　　　　　　　　　　　17. preguntar

_____ entrar. El _____ que sí, y en seguida _____.
　　18. desear　　　　　　　19. decir　　　　　　　　　　　　　　20. entrar

¡Qué magnífica colección de ropa _____! Yo _____ comprar casi
　　　　　　　　　　　　　　　　21. haber　　　　　22. querer

todo lo que _____, pero eso _____ imposible. Yo
　　　　　　23. ver　　　　　　　　　24. ser

_____ una chaqueta roja de cuadros y un par de pantalones negros. Todo esto
　25. escoger

_____ más de ciento cincuenta dólares. Yo se los _____ al
　26. costar　　　　　　　　　　　　　　　　　　　　　　27. pagar

dependiente con mi tarjeta de crédito, y salimos de la tienda.

Al poco rato _____ enfrente del Museo de Historia Natural. En ese momento,
　　　　　　28. encontrarse

Guillermo me _____ que _____ hambre, y él _____
　　　　　　29. decir　　　　　　　30. tener　　　　　　　　31. sugerir

un restaurante pintoresco no lejos del museo. _____ allí en cinco minutos.
　　　　　　　　　　　　　　　　　　　　32. llegar

Como _____ temprano, no _____ muchas personas en el
       33. ser   34. haber

restaurante. El camarero nos _____ una mesa al lado de una ventana por
                              35. ofrecer

donde _____ mirar afuera. Del menú _____ dos sándwiches y
       36. poder   37. escoger

dos tazas de café. Cuando _____ de comer, _____ la cuenta y la
                          38. terminar   39. pedir

_____ en seguida. Le _____ una propina generosa al camarero y
40. pagar   41. dejar

_____ para seguir nuestro paseo.
42. salir

   Regresando al museo, vimos que _____ abierto al público.
                                  43. estar

_____ entrar para ver las nuevas exhibiciones. Todo _____ muy
44. decidir   45. ser

interesante, especialmente los dinosaurios que todavía me _____. Después de
                                                          46. fascinar

pasar unas dos horas admirando las maravillosas cosas del museo, yo _____ el
                                                                    47. mirar

reloj. Ya _____ tarde. _____ que dejar el museo para volver otro
          48. ser   49. tener

día. Esta visita nos _____ mucho.
                     50. gustar

F. Conteste en oraciones completas:

1. ¿Quiénes estaban en casa ayer cuando Ud. volvió de la escuela?

   _____

2. ¿Cuántos años tenía su madre cuando Ud. nació?

   _____

3. Cuando sus padres eran jóvenes, ¿tenían los mismos lujos que Ud. tiene ahora?

   _____

4. ¿Dónde estaba Ud. ayer por la tarde?

   _____

5. ¿Qué hora era cuando Ud. y sus amigos llegaron a la escuela esta mañana?

   _____

6. ¿Qué tiempo hacía cuando Ud. se levantó ayer por la mañana?

   _____

7. ¿Sabía Ud. hablar inglés cuando tenía un año de edad?

   _____

8. ¿Qué hacía Ud. esta mañana mientras estaba en el autobús o el metro camino de la escuela?

   _____

9. Cuando Ud. era muy joven, ¿iba con frecuencia a las discotecas?

   _____

10. ¿Cuánto costaba una computadora personal cuando Ud. era niño(-a)?

_____

11. ¿A qué escuela primaria asistía Ud. cuando era niño(-a)?

_____

12. ¿A qué velocidad volaban los aviones transatlánticos en 1950?

_____

13. *a.* Cuando sus abuelos tenían su edad, ¿podían mirar la televisión?

_____

    b. ¿Cómo se divertían en casa?

_____

14. En el siglo XIX, ¿cómo iba un viajero de Nueva York a Londres?

_____

15. Antes de inventarse el teléfono, ¿qué medios de comunicación existían?

_____

G. Traduzca al español:

1. *a.* Where were you (*Uds.*) going when we saw you?

_____

    b. We were going to the park to play baseball, but we never got there because it began to rain and we didn't have umbrellas.

_____

_____

2. It was 2:30 when the basketball game started.

_____

3. I thought they were at home when I called them, but no one answered the phone.

_____

4. We used to be good friends, but something happened and the friendship ended.

_____

5. *a.* I spent last summer at that hotel.

_____

    b. How was the food there? ("Did one eat well there?")

_____

    c. It wasn't very good. ("One did not eat very well.") And they served us such small portions (*raciones*).

_____

6. Michael, did you know where your son was last night?

_____

7. I couldn't get to school on time because the bus was always late ("always arrived late").

_____

8. My uncle used to be a good driver but he had a serious accident, sold his car, and refused to drive afterwards. (serious = *grave*)

   _____

   _____

9. While we ate, we talked about the day's activities.

   _____

10. *a.* They couldn't send us the bill because the computer broke down.

    _____

    b. When the computer was out of order ("did not function"), no one in the office was able to work.

    _____

11. School was very boring today; we didn't learn anything new.

    _____

12. *a.* What time was it when the explosion occurred?

    _____

    b. It was one o'clock and there was nobody in the building.

    _____

    c. The firemen arrived at 1:10 and put out the fire in twenty minutes.

    _____

13. When I was in the hospital, I received cards every day from my friends and relatives.

    _____

    _____

14. *a.* How long did you spend at the mall this afternoon?

    _____

    b. We spent three hours there.

    _____

    c. While we were there we met our Spanish teacher, who was buying a new dress.

    _____

    _____

15. *a.* My uncle lived in Barcelona for ten years.

    _____

    b. He had many friends while he lived there.

    _____

    c. When he left, he promised to get in touch (*ponerse en contacto*) with them.

    _____

    _____

16. *a.* When my father attended college, he joined a fraternity. (to join = *hacerse socio(-a) de*)

    _____

    b. While he was a member of the fraternity, he took part in many interesting activities.

    _____

    _____

17. *a.* Last night we went to a concert of rock music and had a good time.

_____

_____

   b. While the stars sang and played, many spectators danced in the aisles.

_____

_____

   c. They finally got tired and sat down.

_____

18. *a.* She said that she knew my friend Frank.

_____

   b. She met him one summer during a trip to Spain.

_____

19. *a.* When I got to the bus stop, the bus was already pulling away. (to pull away, withdraw = *alejarse*)

_____

   b. But I didn't have to wait long; the next bus came in five minutes.

_____

20. *a.* We went to pick up our tickets, but the box office was closed when we got there.

_____

_____

   b. We returned early the next day because we wanted to get good tickets.

_____

Las Cataratas del Iguazú

Entre las maravillas del mundo están las Cataratas del Iguazú, situadas en medio de la selva, en la parte del Río Iguazú que forma la frontera entre el Brasil y la Argentina. Cada país ha hecho un parque nacional alrededor de estas cataratas, y en ambos lados del río es posible llegar frente a ellas. En el lado argentino se camina por pasarelas (catwalks) y en el brasilero por senderos. En el lado brasilero es posible también tomar un helicóptero y gozar de una vista panorámica de las cataratas.

Lo más impresionante de las cataratas es "la Garganta del Diablo", una nube perpetua de espuma que brota a una altura de 150 metros (500 pies).

Encima de las cataratas principales el Río Iguazú alcanza una extensión de cuatro kilómetros (2,5 millas) mientras se lanza hacia un precipicio de 60 metros (200 pies).

CHAPTER 4
The Future and the Conditional

Review the conjugations of verbs in the future tense and the conditional on pages 243–244.

The Future Tense

1 English expresses the future tense by using the helping verbs *shall* and *will*. In Spanish, the future tense is expressed by adding certain endings to the infinitive or a modified form of the infinitive.

¿Cuándo **tendremos** nuestro examen?	When will we have our exam?
La semana próxima **visitaré** a mis abuelos.	Next week I shall visit my grandparents.

Using the Future Tense to Express Probability in the Present

2 The future tense in Spanish is often used to express the probability of some occurrence or situation in the present. When used in a question, it is generally translated by "I wonder . . .":

—¿Dónde **estarán** mis guantes?	"I wonder where my gloves are. (Where can my gloves be?)"
—**Estarán** en tu cuarto.	"They are probably (They must be) in your room."
—¿Por qué **saldrá** ahora?	"I wonder why he is leaving now."
—**Tendrá** que coger el próximo autobús.	"He probably has to catch the next bus."

29

The Conditional

3 The English conditional is formed with the helping verb *would*. Spanish forms the conditional in the same way as the future tense: by adding certain endings to the infinitive or a modified form of the infinitive. Note that verbs with irregular stems in the future have the same irregular stems in the conditional.

—¿Qué **harías** con tanto dinero?   "What would you do with so much money?"

—Yo **viajaría** por el mundo entero.   "I would travel all over the world."

Using the Conditional to Express Probability in the Past

4 Just as the future tense may express wonderment or probability in the present, the conditional may express the same mood when referring to the past:

—¿Cuántos años **tendría** esa mujer?   "I wonder how old that woman was."
—**Tendría** por lo menos 90 años.   "She must have been (was probably) at least 90 years old."

—¿**Sería** interesante la conferencia?   "I wonder if the lecture was interesting."

—No, **sería** muy aburrida.   "No, it was probably (must have been) very boring."

___ EJERCICIOS _____

A. Complete la segunda oración de cada par usando el verbo subrayado en el tiempo futuro (si la oración empieza en el presente) o en la forma del condicional (si la oración empieza en el pasado).

EJEMPLOS: Dicen que lloverá mañana.
          Dijeron que ____*llovería*____ pronto.

          Pensaban que llegaríamos tarde.
          Piensan que ____*llegaremos*____ temprano.

1. Prometo que lo haré dentro de cinco minutos.

   Prometí que lo _____ lo más pronto posible.

2. Dijeron que vendrían a las cinco.

   Dicen que _____ a las ocho de la mañana.

3. Julio escribió que nos <u>enviaría</u> el paquete en seguida.

   María escribe que lo _____ mañana.

4. Yo sé que tú <u>tendrás</u> las cintas.

   Él sabía que tú _____ los discos.

5. El alcalde declara que <u>habrá</u> un estado de emergencia en la ciudad.

   El Presidente declaró que _____ un cambio en la economía.

6. El meteorólogo pronosticó que <u>nevaría</u> en el fin de semana.

   El periódico pronostica que _____ esta noche.

7. Juramos que te <u>ayudaremos</u> con tu problema.

   Jurábamos que te _____ a buscar el reloj.

8. Mis padres dijeron que <u>harían</u> un viaje por España.

   Mis abuelos dicen que _____ un viaje a Puerto Rico.

9. Pienso que esas pinturas <u>valdrán</u> por lo menos medio millón de dólares.
   Pensaba que estas joyas _____ una fortuna.

10. Ellos creían que tú <u>sabrías</u> la respuesta.

    Los profesores creen que tú _____ las respuestas.

B. Conteste en oraciones completas:

1. ¿Cuánto dinero tendrá Ud. en el banco el año próximo?

   _____

2. ¿Cómo se divertiría Ud. en una discoteca?

   _____

3. ¿Cuántos años tendrá su profesor* de español?

   _____

4. ¿Qué edad tendría Julio César cuando murió?

   _____

5. ¿Qué se pondrá Ud. si hace frío mañana?

   _____

6. ¿Se quejaría Ud. de una nota de 96 en su clase de español?

   _____

7. ¿A qué país le gustaría a Ud. viajar?

   _____

8. ¿Qué hará Ud. esta noche entre las ocho y las nueve y media?

   _____

*If a noun has a masculine and a feminine form, the masculine form may be used to designate a person of either sex. The person asking question 3 uses the masculine form *profesor* because he or she doesn't know whether your teacher is a man or a woman. If your teacher is a woman, the form you use in your answer would be "mi *profesora.*"

9. ¿Quién vendrá a su casa este fin de semana?

_____

10. ¿Sabría Ud. reparar un reloj roto?

_____

11. ¿Quiénes lo (la) acompañarán a Ud. a la escuela mañana?

_____

12. En su opinión, ¿quién será el próximo presidente de los Estados Unidos?

_____

13. ¿Sería Ud. un buen alcalde (una buena alcaldesa) de su ciudad?

_____

14. ¿A cuántas millas de la Tierra estará el planeta más cercano?

_____

15. ¿Cuántas estrellas habrá en el cielo? ¿Podría Ud. contarlas?

_____

C. Aquí están algunas *respuestas.* ¿Cuáles son las preguntas? Escriba una pregunta para cada respuesta.

        EJEMPLO: Volveré a casa.   *¿Qué harás después de las clases?*

1. Estaré allí para las ocho de la noche.

_____

2. Yo le diría la verdad.

_____

3. Tendrá al menos cincuenta años.

_____

4. Serían las diez de la mañana.

_____

5. Yo les escribiría que los echo de menos.

_____

6. Podré hacerlo si tengo tiempo.

_____

7. Yo compraría un coche caro y un yate.

_____

8. Me las lavaré con agua y jabón.

_____

9. Nos pondremos un traje de baño.

_____

10. Nos sentaríamos delante para ver mejor.

_____

D. Traduzca al español:

1. *a.* At what time will your brother come to the meeting this evening?

_____

b. He'll be there at about half past seven.

_____

2. *a.* Would she drive her mother's car to go to the mall?

_____

   b. No, she wouldn't drive it without her permission.

_____

3. *a.* Why wouldn't John play tennis with his sister?

_____

   b. He wouldn't want to beat the girl in every game. (to beat = *ganar*)

_____

4. *a.* I wonder how old that man is.

_____

   b. He must be at least 75 years old.

_____

5. *a.* I wonder who those people were.

_____

   b. They were probably friends of my uncle.

_____

6. *a.* How many people will there be at the conference next week?

_____

   b. I think there will be at least a thousand people.

_____

7. *a.* Our teacher promised that he would not give us an exam next week.

_____

   b. Would he keep his promise?

_____

8. *a.* I wonder how much money he has in the bank.

_____

   b. He must have a fortune.

_____

9. *a.* I wonder where they put my books.

_____

   b. They probably put them in the bookshelf.

_____

10. *a.* Some day these coins will be worth a fortune.

_____

   b. I wonder how much they are worth now.

_____

11. *a.* Adam says he will bring the tape recorder if you want it.

_____

b. Did he say he would bring his tapes too?

_____

12. *a.* My brother thinks that he will go to a good college next September.

_____

    b. Would his friend Joe (*Pepe*) go to a different college?

_____

13. *a.* Susan, will you go shopping with us tomorrow afternoon after school (*después de las clases*)?

_____

    b. I would go with you, but I would have to clean my room first.

_____

14. *a.* Did she say that she would be able to go with us to the movies tonight?

_____

    b. She won't be able to go because she will have to study for her exams.

_____

15. *a.* Would you (*Uds.*) buy a color television set instead of a black-and-white set?

_____

    b. I would prefer to buy stereo components.

_____

16. *a.* Will that witness tell the truth at the trial or will he lie?

_____

    b. I believe he'll lie. He wouldn't tell the truth.

_____

17. *a.* Where will you (*tú*) go on your trip next summer?

_____

    b. I would go to Spain and Portugal but I won't have enough money.

_____

18. *a.* I wonder if our teacher is absent today.

_____

    b. He's probably here; he's never absent.

_____

19. *a.* At what time will your father leave his office this afternoon?

_____

    b. I think he'll leave before five o'clock.

_____

20. *a.* I wonder if he knew all the answers to today's test.

_____

    b. He probably knew most of the answers, but not all (of them).

_____

El Lago de Titicaca

Titicaca, el lago sagrado de los incas, está situado entre el Perú y Bolivia a una altura de 3825 metros (12.580 pies) sobre el nivel del mar. Tiene 176 kilómetros (110 millas) de largo y 64 kilómetros (40 millas) de ancho. Las islas más conocidas de este lago son las del Sol y la Luna. Según una leyenda, en la Isla del Sol se fundó el imperio de los incas. Allí el Dios Sol creó a Manco Cápac, el primer inca, y a Mama Ocllo, su mujer-hermana. El Rey Sol mandó a los dos a la Tierra con una vara de oro. Ellos comenzaron a buscar un sitio de tierra fértil donde hincar la vara. Por fin llegaron al cerro de Huanacauti del Valle Fértil del Cuzco, donde la vara de oro se hundió muy fácilmente en la tierra. En este sitio del Perú fundaron el imperio de los incas.

A lo largo de las orillas de este lago, las culturas pre-hispánicas desarrollaron sus civilizaciones avanzadas.

Puno (el Perú)

En el famoso altiplano del sur del Perú a una altura de 3800 metros (12.500 pies) sobre el nivel del mar está situada la ciudad de Puno, conocida por numerosas fiestas que se celebran allí casi cada mes del año. Desde Puno se pueden hacer excursiones al Lago Titicaca, especialmente a las islas flotantes de Uros, donde vive una tribu de unos 600 pescadores indios. Éstos son conocidos por las totoras (reeds) que utilizan para construir sus casas, barcos y balsas (rafts). Al norte de Puno se encuentran las tumbas de Sillustani llamadas *chullpas*. Estas *chullpas* son torres de adobe o piedra de unos 7,5 metros (25 pies) de alto. La más alta mide un poco más de 12 metros (40 pies). En estas *chullpas*, probablemente construidas por los indios *collas* antes de la llegada de los incas, se enterraban no sólo los muertos sino también todo lo que éstos pudieran necesitar en "el otro mundo": esposas, criadas, comida, bebidas y ropa. La mayor parte de las *chullpas* fueron destruidas por los españoles después de la conquista.

Suriqui (Bolivia)

En esta pequeña isla, en la parte boliviana del lago, los habitantes construyen las famosas *totoras* (reedboats) por métodos que datan más de mil años. Dos hermanos de Suriqui construyeron la famosa balsa en la cual el noruego Thor Heyerdahl hizo su expedición a través del Océano Atlántico en 1970.

Tiquina (Bolivia)

En el lado boliviano del Lago Titicaca está el Estrecho de Tiquina, que separa la parte norte del lago, llamada Chucuito, de otro lago que se llama Hiñay Marca. Los coches pueden cruzar este estrecho en unas barcas pequeñas construidas y dirigidas por los indios mismos. En los dos lados del Estrecho están los pueblos pintorescos de San Pedro y San Pablo.

Copacabana (Bolivia)

A unos 48 kilómetros (30 millas) del Estrecho de Tiquina, en la península de Copacabana en el Titicaca, se encuentra un santuario religioso famoso que atrae a muchos peregrinos. El pueblo está situado a orillas de una hermosa bahía, y tiene una iglesia renacentista y la milagrosa imagen original de la Virgen morena de Copacabana.

Tiahuanaco (Bolivia)

Al extremo sur del Lago Titicaca, a 71 kilómetros (43 millas) de La Paz, se encuentran las ruinas de una civilización preincaica, la de los *aimaraes*, la cual data del año 700 después de Cristo. Esta tribu fue sometida por los incas en el siglo XV. Allí en Tiahuanaco se pueden ver monumentos, acueductos, templos y piedras monolíticas de gran tamaño. Entre éstos se destaca la famosa "Puerta del Sol", un gran bloque de piedra que pesa unas diez toneladas, con la figura del dios Viracocha en el centro. Según la tradición, es allí donde se fundó la ciudad de La Paz.

CHAPTER 5

The Compound Tenses

Review the past participles and the conjugations of **haber** on pages 244–245.

1 A Spanish compound tense consists of a form of **haber** + the past participle of the verb used in that tense. The most common compound tenses are the present perfect, pluperfect, future perfect, and conditional perfect. These are similar to their English equivalents in structure and meaning. Note, for example, the following compound forms of **hablar:**

present perfect:	**he hablado**	I have spoken
pluperfect:	**había hablado**	I had spoken
future perfect:	**habré hablado**	I will (shall) have spoken
conditional perfect:	**habría hablado**	I would have spoken

The Present Perfect

2 The present perfect, which is formed with the present tense of **haber,** often denotes an action or event in the recent past that continues into the present or has just ended:

¿**Has visto** esa película?   Have you seen that film?

Sí, la **he visto** dos veces.   Yes, I have seen it twice.

Hemos ido al cine a menudo.   We have gone to the movies often.

The Pluperfect

3 The pluperfect tense, which is formed with the imperfect tense of **haber,** denotes an action that occurred before another action in the past, which is understood or expressed in the preterite or imperfect:

Ella dijo que **había llegado** tarde.   She said that she had arrived late.

¿Qué **habían comido** ellos en el restaurante?   What had they eaten in the restaurant?

The Future Perfect

4 The future perfect, which is formed with the future tense of **haber,** expresses an action or event that *will have occurred* before some other future action or event:

Para las diez **habré terminado** mi trabajo.	By ten o'clock I will (shall) have finished my work.
¿**Habrá salido** antes de llegar nosotros?	Will he have left by the time we get there?

The Conditional Perfect

5 The conditional perfect, which uses the conditional form of **haber,** expresses what *would have happened* (but didn't):

¿Qué **habrías hecho** tú sin nuestra ayuda?	What would you have done without our help?
Yo **habría llamado** a la policía.	I would have called the police.
Yo no **habría querido** hacer otra cosa.	I would not have wanted to do anything else.

Using the Future Perfect and the Conditional Perfect to Express Probability

6 Like the simple future and the conditional (chapter 4), the future perfect and the conditional perfect are often used to express probability or wonderment:

—¿Qué **habrá hecho** ese hombre?	"I wonder what that man has done."
—¿Quién sabe? **Habrá cometido** algún crimen.	"Who knows? He may have (must have) committed some crime."
—¿A qué hora **habrían traído** la comida?	"I wonder at what time they had brought the food."
—La **habrían traído** durante la tarde.	"They had probably brought it during the afternoon."

7 Note the differences in tense and meaning:

PRESENT

Pablo **trabaja** aquí.
Paul works here.

PRESENT PERFECT

Pablo **ha trabajado** aquí.
Paul has worked here.

IMPERFECT

Pablo **trabajaba** aquí.
Paul used to work here.

PLUPERFECT

Pablo **había trabajado** aquí.
Paul had worked here.

FUTURE AS "PROBABILITY"

Pablo **trabajará** aquí.
Paul must work (probably works) here.

FUTURE PERFECT AS "PROBABILITY"

Pablo **habrá trabajado** aquí.
Paul must have (probably has) worked here.

CONDITIONAL AS "PROBABILITY"

Pablo **trabajaría** aquí.
Paul probably worked here.

CONDITIONAL PERFECT AS "PROBABILITY"

Pablo **habría trabajado** aquí.
Paul had probably worked here.

Further examples—note the different meanings of the future and future perfect of **ser** as expressions of wonderment:

—¿Quién **será** ella?
—**Será** abogada.

"I wonder who she is."
"She must be (is probably) a lawyer."

—¿Quién **habrá sido** ella?
—**Habrá sido** abogada.

"Who could she have been?"
"She must have (may have) been a lawyer."

8 Nothing comes between the form of **haber** and the past participle. Thus, (*a*) object pronouns precede **haber** (as in "le ha escrito") and (*b*) in questions, the subject follows the participle (as in "¿han comido **los chicos**?").

__ EJERCICIOS __

Complete la oración, usando el verbo entre paréntesis.

A. PRESENT PERFECT

EJEMPLO: (hablar) Roberto _____*ha hablado*_____ del asunto.

1. (comer) Creo que ellos _____ en aquel restaurante.

2. (volver) ¿A qué hora _____ ella esta mañana?

3. (escribir) Mi hermano no nos _____ todavía.

4. (morir) En el incendio _____ cincuenta personas.

5. (llegar) La secretaria dice que los clientes _____ ya.

6. (recibir) ¿Tú no _____ mi carta todavía?

7. (levantarse) ¿Por qué _____ tú tan temprano?

8. (ponerse) Mi madre _____ su vestido nuevo.

9. (hacer) ¿Qué _____ el nene con sus juguetes?

10. (irse) Nosotros _____ ya del edificio.

B. PLUPERFECT

EJEMPLO: (hablar) Roberto ___*había hablado*___ del asunto.

1. (estacionar) Yo le dije a mi padre que Uds. _____ el coche en el garaje.

2. (traer) Creía que ella y yo _____ los discos.

3. (hacerse) Mi hermano José _____ un ingeniero famoso.

4. (salir) ¿A qué hora _____ ellos de la escuela?

5. (acostarse) Nosotros _____ a las tres de la madrugada.

6. (romper) El policía dijo que mi hermano _____ el escaparate de la tienda del Sr. López.

7. (vestirse) Yo creía que tú _____ ya.

8. (ponerse) Estábamos seguros de que ellos _____ el abrigo antes de salir de casa.

9. (decir) Parecía que ella no _____ la verdad acerca del incidente de ayer.

10. (vender) Yo sabía que vosotros _____ el coche para comprar otro.

C. FUTURE PERFECT

EJEMPLO: (hablar) Roberto ___*habrá hablado*___ del asunto.

1. (enseñar) Mi profesora nos _____ todos los tiempos compuestos para fines de esta semana.

2. (estar) ¿Dónde _____ mis hijos?

3. (comer) Los niños _____ todos los sandwiches porque no queda ninguno.

4. (escribir) ¿ _____ tú todas las tarjetas antes de medianoche?

5. (hacer) Para el sábado nosotros _____ todas las tareas.

D. CONDITIONAL PERFECT

EJEMPLO: (hablar) Roberto ___*habría hablado*___ del asunto.

1. (leer) Yo _____ todas las novelas, pero no las pude encontrar en la biblioteca.

2. (decir) Sé que ella me _____ todos los detalles, pero ya era tarde y teníamos que volver a casa.

3. (ser) Ese hombre _____ uno de los ladrones mencionados en el periódico.

4. (abrir) ¿A qué hora _____ ellos su tienda el día del huracán?

5. (recibir) "¿Recibieron el telegrama tus abuelos?" "Lo _____ dos días después de que lo envié."

E. Conteste en oraciones completas:

1. *a.* ¿Le ha traído Ud. un regalo hoy a su profesor de español?

   _____

   b. ¿Le ha traído su profesor un regalo a Ud. hoy?

   _____

2. ¿Cuántos libros habrá leído Ud. para el domingo próximo?

   _____

3. ¿Sabía Ud. que los Vikingos habían visitado a Norteamérica cuatro siglos antes de Cristóbal Colón?

   _____

4. ¿Ha tenido su familia buena suerte en la lotería recientemente?

   _____

5. *a.* ¿Habría trabajado Ud. veinte horas al día para conseguir suficiente dinero para comprar un coche?

   _____

   b. Si no, entonces ¿cuántas horas habría trabajado?

   _____

6. ¿Cuántos coches habrán pasado por su calle durante las últimas dos horas?

   _____

7. ¿Se ha acostado Ud. jamás después de las tres de la madrugada?

   _____

8. ¿Cuántas veces ha hablado Ud. hoy en su clase de español?

   _____

9. ¿Sabía Ud. que había nevado mucho en las Montañas Rocosas durante el invierno pasado?

   _____

10. ¿Qué ropa se ha puesto Ud. esta mañana?

    _____

11. *a.* ¿Les ha dicho Ud. jamás una mentira a sus padres?

    _____

    b. ¿Le han dicho sus padres jamás una mentira a Ud.?

    _____

12. Hoy día, ¿habrían muerto muchos enfermos sin la ayuda de los antibióticos?

_____

13. *a.* ¿Qué problema ha resuelto Ud. recientemente?

_____

  b. Y ¿cómo lo ha resuelto?

_____

14. ¿Habría descubierto Colón el Nuevo Mundo sin la ayuda de la reina Isabel?

_____

15. ¿Cuántas composiciones habían escrito Uds. en su clase de inglés hasta finales del mes pasado?

_____

F. Traduzca al español:

1. *a.* Where have they been for so many hours?

_____

  b. They've been at the theater watching ("seeing") a play.

_____

2. *a.* Michael, I thought you had already gone to bed.

_____

  b. No, I had not gone to bed because I still had work to do.

_____

3. *a.* Our Spanish teacher will have taught us all the tenses by the end of this week.

_____

  b. Will you (*Uds.*) have learned them all by then?

_____

4. *a.* What would she have done without her father's help?

_____

  b. She would have had a lot of trouble ("difficulty").

_____

5. *a.* Louis says that he has seen that movie already.

_____

  b. Have you (*tú*) seen it yet?

_____

6. *a.* I knew that they had enjoyed themselves at the party.

_____

  b. I wouldn't have enjoyed myself there.

_____

7. *a.* She must have fallen on the ice while she was skating.

_____

b. Had she fallen before?

_____

8. *a.* I wonder if they have brought the tapes from the concert.

_____

b. I think they haven't brought them this time.

_____

9. *a.* He had probably eaten downtown that day.

_____

b. I wonder if he had been with his friends.

_____

10. *a.* It is obvious (*evidente*) that you (*Ud.*) have smoked too many cigarettes.

_____

b. I would have smoked more, doctor, but I couldn't stop coughing.

_____

11. *a.* I would have liked to see that television program last night.

_____

b. Had your parents seen it?

_____

12. *a.* Will they have returned before midnight?

_____

b. I think they've returned already.

_____

13. *a.* Caroline, do you know whether my father has bought a computer?

_____

b. He hasn't bought it yet.

_____

14. *a.* She said she had put on her new suit for the interview.

_____

b. What would you (*Ud.*) have put on?

_____

15. *a.* Mary, have you written yet to your grandparents in Florida?

_____

b. I would have written to them, but I had forgotten their address.

_____

CHAPTER **6**

The Present Participle (El Gerundio) and the Progressive Tenses

Review the formation of the present participle (the Spanish *gerundio*) on pages 245–246.

The Progressive Tenses

1 The *gerundio* is equivalent to the English present participle, which ends in *-ing*. The gerundio may be used with any tense of **estar** to form a progressive tense:

PRESENT PROGRESSIVE

—¿Qué **estás leyendo?**   "What are you reading?"
—**Estoy leyendo** una novela.   "I am reading a novel."

IMPERFECT PROGRESSIVE

Ellos **estaban mirando** la televisión cuando entré.

They were watching television when I came in.

PRETERITE PROGRESSIVE

Los chicos **estuvieron tocando** un disco tras otro hasta que los vecinos se quejaron.

The boys were playing one record after another until the neighbors complained.

FUTURE PROGRESSIVE

Mañana a esta hora **estaremos volando** a México.

Tomorrow at this time we shall be flying to Mexico.

The present progressive and the imperfect progressive are the most common.

44

The Simple and Progressive Tenses Compared

2 *a.* A simple tense can often be interchanged with the corresponding progressive tense to express the same meaning:

$$\left\{\begin{array}{l}\text{¿Qué \textbf{hace}}\\\text{¿Qué \textbf{está haciendo}}\end{array}\right\}\text{su padre}$$

ahora?

What is your father doing now?

$$\text{Mis hermanos}\left\{\begin{array}{l}\textbf{jugaban}\\\textbf{estaban jugando}\end{array}\right\}$$

al tenis cuando empezó a llover.

My brothers (*or* brother and sister) were playing tennis when it began to rain.

The progressive tenses emphasize the "ongoing" quality of an action, expressing it as a process taking place at a given moment.

b. The verbs **ir** and **venir** are generally not used with **estar** to form progressive tenses:

¿Adónde **ibas** cuando te vi? Where were you going when I saw you?
Vengo a ayudarlos. I am coming to help you.

$$\left\{\begin{array}{l}\textit{Seguir}\\\textit{Continuar}\end{array}\right\} + \textit{Gerundio}$$

3 The verb **seguir** or **continuar** followed by the *gerundio* means *to continue* or *keep on* (*doing something*):

Sigan Uds. **estudiando.**

Continue (Keep on) studying. (Continue to study.)

Continuaron andando por el caminito.

They continued (kept on) walking (They continued to walk) along the path.

Other Uses of the *Gerundio**

4 The *gerundio* can be used as an adverb meaning *by . . .-ing:*

---

*Do not confuse the *gerundio* with the English gerund, which is used as a verbal noun. It is usually translated by the Spanish infinitive:

Smoking is dangerous to your health = **El fumar** es peligroso para la salud.
Swimming is a good exercise = **El nadar** es un buen ejercicio.

Trabajando ganarás dinero.   By working you will earn (some) money.

5 It can also be used as a participle in the sense of *while . . .-ing:*

Saliendo de la escuela, me encontré   Leaving (As I was leaving) school, I met
con Juana.   Jane.

___ EJERCICIOS _____

A. Conteste la pregunta usando el tiempo progresivo correspondiente.

EJEMPLOS: ¿Qué estudias ahora?

Estoy estudiando el español.

¿Qué tocaba Martín en el concierto?
Estaba tocando el clarinete.

1. ¿Dónde duermen ellos ahora?

   _____

2. ¿Qué vendían en esa tienda?

   _____

3. ¿De dónde traías los discos?

   _____

4. ¿Dónde jugaréis mañana por la mañana?

   _____

5. ¿Qué pedías a la camarera?

   _____

6. ¿Qué aprende Ud. en su clase de matemáticas?

   _____

7. ¿Qué cintas tocaban Uds. en la fiesta?

   _____

8. ¿Qué leerás en la biblioteca?

   _____

9. ¿Qué nos dirían Uds. acerca de la situación?

   _____

10. ¿Con quién bailarás esta noche?

    _____

B. Aquí están algunas *respuestas.* ¿Cuáles son las preguntas? Escriba una pregunta para cada respuesta, usando el tiempo progresivo correspondiente.

EJEMPLO: Yo dormía.   *¿Qué estabas haciendo cuando te llamé?*

1. Miro la televisión.

   _____

2. No, juego al ajedrez.

_____

3. Pasábamos el tiempo en el salón de juegos.

_____

4. Los lleva a la biblioteca.

_____

5. En la primera competición cantaremos tres canciones.

_____

6. Subo al cuarto piso.

_____

7. Piden vino tinto con queso.

_____

8. Sí, nos divertimos mucho allí.

_____

9. Los traigo para la fiesta.

_____

10. Corro porque necesito ejercicio físico.

_____

C. Usando un gerundio, cambie la oración según el ejemplo.

> EJEMPLO: Si estudias, aprenderás mucho.
> _Estudiando aprenderás mucho._

1. Si Uds. cantan con nosotros, se divertirán mucho.

_____

2. Si vendemos la casa, ganaremos suficiente dinero.

_____

3. Si tienes dinero, podrás viajar a España.

_____

4. Si voy a los cines españoles, aprenderé más español.

_____

5. Si duermes ocho horas, te sentirás mejor por la mañana.

_____

D. Escriba otra oración que tenga el mismo significado, usando un gerundio.

> EJEMPLO: Mientras yo andaba por la calle, me encontré con mamá.
> _Andando por la calle, me encontré con mamá._

1. Mientras íbamos a la piscina, vimos que empezaba a llover.

_____

2. Mientras miraba la televisión, me dormí.

_____

3. Mientras bailaba con ella, le pisé el pie tres veces.

_____

4. Mientras traía las cintas a casa, me caí en la calle.

_____

5. Mientras yo cocinaba la comida, me quemé el dedo.

_____

E. Traduzca al español, usando tiempos progresivos donde sea posible.

 1. "What were they doing when you came in?" "They were playing cards."

_____

 2. "Where is she going tonight?" "She is going to the discotheque with Jane."

_____

 3. "Is he bringing the tapes now?" "Yes, he's bringing them all."

_____

 4. *a.* By sleeping all night, you'll wake up refreshed.

_____

   b. Reading near the open window, you (*tú*) will catch a cold.

_____

 5. *a.* Going to the store, I met three friends.

_____

   b. Coming home, they met us on the corner.

_____

 6. *a.* They will continue to run in the marathon every year.

_____

   b. By running every day, you (*Uds.*) will keep in good shape.

_____

 7. *a.* What is mom serving for dinner?

_____

   b. Chicken with rice. She is serving the main dish now.

_____

   c. She was serving the salad when you arrived.

_____

 8. *a.* Would they be walking through the park at this hour?

_____

   b. No, they would be driving their motorcycles.

_____

 9. "I'm going to sleep now." "At what time will you (*Ud.*) be getting up?"

_____

10. *a.* My parents are having a very good time in Spain this summer. (Use the verb *divertirse.*)

_____

   b. Were you (*tú*) having a good time at the party last night?

_____

Las Islas Galápagos

En el Océano Pacífico, a 600 millas (960 kilómetros) al oeste del Ecuador, están las Islas Galápagos, un grupo de trece islas mayores y docenas de islas pequeñas. Estas islas tienen un área de 3000 millas cuadradas (unos 4800 kilómetros cuadrados). Fueron descubiertas por el explorador Tomás de Berlanga en 1535. Las islas llevan su nombre por los enormes galápagos (tortoises) que se encontraban allí. Por desgracia, los galápagos están casi extintos, víctimas de los piratas, balleneros (whalers) y petroleros (oil men) que los mataban para comerlos.

Se cree que las islas se originaron hace más de tres millones de años por erupciones volcánicas, y que los galápagos y las iguanas son descendientes de animales prehistóricos.

En las Galápagos viven especies de plantas, peces y reptiles que no se encuentran en ninguna otra parte del mundo. En estas islas se han conservado también cantidades de flora y fauna muy extrañas y raras.

En el año 1835, Charles Darwin, el famoso naturalista inglés, exploró estas islas. A Darwin le fascinaron la flora y fauna del archipiélago, y todo lo que vio allí le ayudó a formular su teoría sobre la evolución de las especies: en el transcurso de millones de años, sólo pudieron sobrevivir aquellas especies de plantas y animales que pudieron adaptarse a los cambios en su ambiente.

Actualmente el archipiélago es un parque nacional donde se protegen todos los animales, reptiles y aves. Se limita el número de turistas que pueden visitar las islas, y no se permite ni tocar ni dar de comer a los animales. Todavía se pueden ver los galápagos que se colocan sobre las rocas como si estuvieran tomando baños de sol.

Se ha dicho que las Islas Galápagos son un verdadero parque zoológico extravagante.

CHAPTER 7

Using the Subjunctive after Certain Verbs and Impersonal Expressions; The Subjunctive in Various Tenses

Review the formation of the present subjunctive on pages 246–247.

The Subjunctive in *Que* Clauses

1 Some verbs often have an infinitive object; for example, **querer:**

Elena quiere **salir.**   Helen wants to leave.

This Spanish sentence and its English equivalent have the same structure: subject/verb/infinitive. Unlike Spanish, however, the English infinitive may acquire a subject of its own, as in

Helen wants *me* to leave.

where the subject of *to leave* is the pronoun *me.* (It's "me" that would do the "leaving," not Helen.) In Spanish, the infinitive **salir** would be replaced by a **que** clause:

Elena quiere **que yo salga.**   (Literally: Helen wants that I leave.)

Similarly,

Esperamos **llegar** a tiempo.   We expect to arrive on time.
  But:
Esperamos **que usted llegue** a   We expect *you* to arrive on time.
  tiempo.

This chapter and parts of chapter 8 will deal with the subjunctive in **que** clauses.

Using the Subjunctive after Certain Verbs

2 The subjunctive is used after verbs that express a wish or preference, such as **desear, querer, preferir, insistir (en):**

Desean que yo **vea** el programa.   They want me to watch the program.
¿Por qué **insistes en** que ella **vaya**   Why do you insist on her going with
  contigo?   you?

Practice A: Complete the *que* clause in the second sentence with the subjunctive form of the verb used as infinitive object in the first sentence.

> EXAMPLE: No deseo comprar ese vestido.
>   No desea que tú *compres* esa falda.

1. ¿Qué quieres hacer?

   ¿Qué quieres que yo _____?
2. ¿Prefieren Uds. vender su casa?

   ¿Prefieren Uds. que ellos _____ su tienda?
3. Queremos aceptar su invitación.

   Queremos que Uds. _____ nuestro regalo.
4. Insisto en salir ahora mismo.

   Insisto en que Ud. _____ en seguida.
5. Deseamos aprender el subjuntivo.

   Deseamos que ella _____ a patinar.

3 The subjunctive is used after verbs or idioms that express feelings, such as **alegrarse de,** to be glad; **esperar,** to hope; **sentir,** to be sorry; **temer,** to fear; **tener miedo (de),** to be afraid:

Me alegro de que **sigas** ese curso.   I'm glad that you are taking (will take)
                                                 that course.

Esperamos que Uds. **lleguen** tem-   We hope that you arrive (will arrive)
  prano.   early.

Note that the present subjunctive may be used to express the present or the future.

Practice B: Complete the *que* clause with the subjunctive form of the verb used in the preceding sentence.

> EXAMPLE: Tengo miedo de salir de mi casa.
>   Tengo miedo de que ellos *salgan* tarde.

1. Nos alegramos de tener un automóvil nuevo.

   Nos alegramos de que él _____ un coche grande.

2. Sentimos oír la mala noticia.

   Sentimos que ellos _____ la noticia en estas circunstancias.

3. Esperan volver antes de las ocho.

   Esperan que nosotros _____ temprano esta noche.

4. Temo cruzar la calle cuando hay tanto tráfico.

   Temo que tú _____ esa avenida sin esperar la luz verde.

5. ¿Se alegran Uds. de estudiar español?

   ¿Se alegran Uds. de que yo _____ francés?

4 The subjunctive is used after verbs that express commands, requests, permission, and related meanings, such as **decir,** to tell (someone to do something); **dejar,** to let, allow; **mandar,** to order; **pedir,** to ask, request; **permitir,** to permit; and **prohibir,** to forbid, prohibit. These verbs generally take an indirect object pronoun **(me, te, le, nos, os, les).** They can be divided into two groups:

a. Verbs that *must* take a **que** clause: **decir** and **pedir.**

Dígale a ella que **lleve** el vestido azul.	Tell her to wear the blue dress.
Nos piden que **traigamos** el dinero.	They ask us to bring the money.

b. Verbs that may take either an infinitive object or a **que** clause: **dejar, mandar, permitir,** and **prohibir.**

No les permito **fumar.** No les* permito **que fumen.**	I do not permit them to smoke.
Mis padres no me dejan **salir** de casa **(que salga** de casa) sin haber tomado el desayuno.	My parents don't let me leave the house without having had breakfast.

Practice C: Complete the Spanish sentence with a verb in the subjunctive or the infinitive form—whichever is appropriate.

> EXAMPLE: Tell them to come.
> Dígales que *vengan.*

1. Tell her to go home.

   Dígale a ella que _____ a casa.

2. She is asking me to take her to the dance.

   Me pide que la _____ al baile.

3. The boss is ordering us to work three hours more. (2 ways)

   El jefe nos manda _____ tres horas más.

   Or: El jefe nos manda que _____ tres horas más.

*The object pronoun in the main clause may be omitted: **No permito que fumen.**

4. They forbid us to wear blue jeans in school. (2 ways)

Nos prohíben _____ bluejeans en la escuela.

Or: Nos prohíben que _____ bluejeans en la escuela.

5

The subjunctive is used after verbs or expressions of doubt, uncertainty, or denial, such as **dudar,** to doubt; **no estar seguro(-a),** not to be sure; **no creer,** not to believe; and **negar,** to deny:

Dudo que **hagan** eso.	I doubt that they are doing (will do) that.
No creo que **lleguen** tarde.	I don't believe (think) they will arrive late.
Niegan que **sea** necesario.	They deny that it is (will be) necessary.

6

Dudar and **negar** are followed by the indicative when used negatively:

No dudo que **harán** eso.	I don't doubt that they will do that.
No niegan que **será** necesario.	They don't deny that it will be necessary.

7

Creer, used affirmatively, is followed by the indicative:

Creo que **irán** a casa.	I believe (think) that they will go home.

In questions, however, it may be followed by either the indicative or the subjunctive, depending on the degree of uncertainty in the mind of the speaker:

a. ¿Cree Ud. que **van** a casa?
b. ¿Cree Ud. que **vayan** a casa? } Do you think they are going home?

Question *a* is a simple request for information. Question *b* asks, in effect, "Do you suppose they are going home? (I have my doubts.)"

Practice D: Complete the Spanish sentences.

1. I don't think (believe) she'll drive tonight.

   No creo que ella _____ esta noche.
2. I think he'll spend a lot of money.

   Creo que _____ mucho dinero.
3. We doubt that they will want to come.

   Dudamos que _____ venir.

4. We do not doubt you will want to go.

   No dudamos que Ud. _____ ir.

5. He denies that she is his friend.

   Niega que _____ su amiga.

6. He does not deny that she is a teacher.

   No niega que _____ profesora.

7. We are sure he has the tickets.

   Estamos seguros de que _____ los billetes.

8. We are not sure she has the money.

   No estamos seguros de que _____ el dinero.

9. Do you think Mary is bringing the photos? *(The speaker doubts it.)*

   ¿Crees que María _____ las fotos?

10. Do you think she will show us the letter? *(simple request for information)*

    ¿Crees que ella nos _____ la carta?

The Subjunctive after Impersonal Expressions

8 The subjunctive is used after impersonal expressions such as:

es dudoso, it is doubtful	**más vale** } it is better
es importante } it is important	**es mejor** }
importa	
	es necesario, it is necessary
es imposible, it is impossible	**es posible,** it is possible
es lástima, it is a pity	**es probable,** it is probable

If no new subject is introduced, the expression is followed by an infinitive.

Es imposible llegar temprano.
It is impossible to arrive early.

Es imposible que lleguemos temprano.
It is impossible for us to arrive early.

Es mejor decir la verdad.
It is better to tell the truth.

Es mejor que digas la verdad.
It is better for you to tell (that you tell) the truth.

Practice E: Combine the two sentences as shown in the example.

EXAMPLE: Usted viene aquí. Es importante.
Es importante que usted venga aquí.

1. Ya no tenemos dinero. Es lástima.

2. Irán al cine. Es probable.

_____

3. Pablo saldrá bien en el examen. Es dudoso.

_____

4. Mañana lloverá. Es posible.

_____

5. Compre usted ese disco. Es necesario.

_____

Impersonal Expressions That Do Not Take the Subjunctive

9 Impersonal expressions that express certainty are followed by the indicative:

es evidente, it is evident   **es verdad,** it is true   **es cierto,** it is certain

Es verdad que ella **trabaja** allí.   It is true that she works there.
Es cierto que **tienen** el dinero.   It is certain that they have the money.

10 If these expressions are used negatively, they are followed by the subjunctive:

No es verdad que ella **trabaje** allí.   It is not true that she works there.
No es cierto que **tengan** el dinero.   It is not certain that they have the money.

Practice F: Express in Spanish.

1. It is possible that they will take the train.

_____

2. It is true that she is not rich.

_____

3. It is not evident that he has talent.

_____

4. It is important for us to see that program this afternoon.

_____

5. It is not true that they always come late.

_____

The Subjunctive in Various Tenses

Review the formation of the imperfect, present perfect, and pluperfect subjunctives on pages 248–249.

11 If the **que** clause refers to the past, its verb may take three possible subjunctive forms:

Me alegro de $\begin{cases} \text{que } \textbf{hayan venido.} \\ \text{que } \textbf{vinieran.} \\ \text{que } \textbf{hubieran venido.} \end{cases}$ I'm glad $\begin{cases} \text{that they have come.} \\ \text{that they came.} \\ \text{that they had come.} \end{cases}$

The tenses of the subjunctive are:

PRESENT SUBJUNCTIVE

Temo que **vayan** sin nosotros.

No creemos que **tengan** tan mala suerte.

Es posible que no **puedan** ir al concierto.

I am afraid they are going (will go, may go) without us.

We don't think they are (will be) so unlucky.

It is possible that they cannot (will not be able to) go to the concert.

PRESENT PERFECT SUBJUNCTIVE

Esperamos que **hayan visto** la película.

Dudo que **haya dicho** la verdad.

We hope that they have seen the movie.

I doubt that he has told the truth.

IMPERFECT SUBJUNCTIVE

Temían que no **volviera (volviese)** a tiempo.

Negaba que ellos **fueran (fuesen)** sus amigos.

Era imposible que **hiciera (hiciese)** la tarea.

They were afraid that he would (might) not return on time.

He denied that they were his friends.

It was impossible for him to do the task.

PLUPERFECT SUBJUNCTIVE

Me alegraba de que **hubieran (hubiesen) traído** los regalos.

No estaba segura de que **hubiera (hubiese) pedido** el libro.

I was glad that they had brought the gifts.

I (*f.*) was not sure that he had asked for the book.

12 If the main clause expresses a wish, request, or indirect command, its tense will determine the tense of the verb in the **que** clause. (*a*) If the main clause is in the present or future tense, the verb in the **que** clause is in the present subjunctive; (*b*) if the main clause is in the preterite or the imperfect, the verb in the **que** clause is in the imperfect subjunctive.

    a. La directora les **dice** que **entren** en su despacho.
        The principal tells them to come into her office.

    b. La directora les **dijo** que **entraran** en . . .
        The principal told them to come into . . .

    a. ¿Qué **quieren** Uds. que **hagamos?**
        What do you want us to do?

    b. ¿Qué **querían** Uds. que **hiciéramos?**
        What did you want us to do?

    a. ¿Qué me **pides** que **traiga** a la fiesta?
        What are you asking me to bring to the party?

    b. ¿Qué me **pediste** que **trajera** a . . .?
        What did you ask me to bring . . .?

13 If the verb in the main clause is in the conditional form, the verb in the **que** clause will be in the imperfect subjunctive:

    No les **pediría** que **salieran (saliesen)** tan pronto.
        I would not ask them to leave so soon.

Practice G: Complete the Spanish translations.

1. I'm telling them to come into my office.
   Les digo que entren en mi despacho.
   I told them to come into my office.

   Les dije _____.

2. They don't think I have drunk too much wine.
   No creen que yo haya bebido demasiado vino.
   They didn't think I had drunk too much wine.

   No creían _____.

3. It was necessary for them to study a lot.
   Era necesario que estudiasen mucho.
   It is necessary for them to study a lot.

   Es necesario _____.

4. It was a pity that she had been sick.
   Era lástima que ella hubiera estado enferma.
   a. It is a pity that she has been sick.

   Es lástima _____.

   b. It is a pity that she was sick.

   Es lástima _____.

5. They asked me to play soccer with them.
   Me pidieron que jugara al fútbol con ellos.
   They are asking me to play soccer with them.

   Me piden _____.

6. I doubt that they will bring enough money.
   Dudo que traigan suficiente dinero.
   a. I doubt that they have brought enough money.

   Dudo _____.
   b. I doubt that they brought enough money.

   Dudo _____.

7. Did you want us to see that movie?
   ¿Quería Ud. que viéramos esa película?
   Do you want us to see that movie?

   ¿Quiere Ud. _____?

8. They will not permit us to smoke in their house.
   No nos permitirán que fumemos en su casa.
   a. They would not permit us to smoke in their house.

   No nos permitirían _____.
   b. They denied that we had smoked in their house.

   Negaron _____.

9. I prefer that you accompany me to the store.
   Prefiero que me acompañes a la tienda.
   I preferred that you accompany me to the store.

   Preferí _____.

10. It is doubtful that they will be able to come tomorrow.
    Es dudoso que puedan venir mañana.
    a. It was doubtful that they could come yesterday.

    Era dudoso _____.
    b. It was doubtful that they had been able to come the other day.

    Era dudoso _____.

11. I was not sure that they were coming on time.
    No estaba segura de que vinieran a tiempo.
    a. I am not sure that they will come on time.

    No estoy segura _____.
    b. I am not sure that they have always come on time.

    No estoy segura de que siempre _____.

12. They want you to be generous.
    Desean que seas generoso.
    They wanted you to be generous.

    Deseaban _____.

13. Is it possible that they have seen the exhibit?
    ¿Es posible que hayan visto la exhibición?
    Was it possible that they had seen the exhibit?

    ¿Era posible _____?

14. They denied that she knew how to dance.
Negaban que supiera bailar.

   a. They will deny that she knows how to dance.

   Negarán _____.

   b. They don't deny that she knows how to dance.

   No niegan _____.

15. I hope that you will be here early.
Espero que estés aquí temprano.

   I hoped that you would be here early.

   Esperaba _____.

___ EJERCICIOS _____

A. Cada pregunta tiene la respuesta indicada entre paréntesis. Conteste la pregunta usando la forma apropiada del subjuntivo.

> EJEMPLO: *a.* ¿Qué quieres que yo haga? (traer los paquetes)
> *Quiero que traigas los paquetes.*
>
> *b.* ¿Qué querían Uds. que yo hiciera? (traer el correo)
> *Queríamos que trajeras el correo.*

1. *a.* ¿Qué le pide Ud. a ella que haga? (bailar conmigo)

   _____

   b. ¿Qué le pidió a él que hiciera? (bailar con otra chica)

   _____

2. *a.* ¿Qué prefieren Uds. que hagamos? (salir en seguida)

   _____

   b. ¿Qué preferían Uds. que hiciéramos? (salir de paseo)

   _____

3. *a.* ¿Qué me dices que haga? (venir con nosotras)

   _____

   b. ¿Qué me dijiste que hiciese? (venir lo más antes posible)

   _____

4. *a.* ¿Qué le permiten Uds. que haga? (ir al concierto)

   _____

   b. ¿Qué le permitieron Uds. que hiciese? (ir al cine)

   _____

5. *a.* ¿Qué quieren ellas que tú hagas? (ver la película)

   _____

   b. ¿Qué quisieron ellas que tú hicieras? (ver ese programa de televisión)

   _____

B. Complete la respuesta según se indica entre paréntesis, usando el subjuntivo.

> EJEMPLOS: ¿Esperan Uds. que volvamos temprano? (quedarse en la ciudad)
>
> No, esperamos que Uds. _____*se queden en la ciudad*_____.
>
> ¿Sentiste que yo no pudiera ir a la fiesta? (estar enferma)
>
> Sí, y yo también sentí que _____*estuvieras enferma*_____.

1. ¿Temían ellos que ella no quisiera ir al centro comercial? (querer acompañarla)

   No, temían que nosotros no _____.
2. ¿Es necesario que yo tome la medicina? (descansar mucho)

   Sí, y también es necesario que tú _____.
3. ¿Era posible que hubieran llegado tarde? (haber notado su llegada)

   Sí; y era posible que Ud. no _____.
4. ¿Me pediste que fuera a la tienda? (comprar unos comestibles)

   Sí, y también te pedí que _____.
5. ¿Nos permitirán que tomemos cerveza en la fiesta? (beber vino)

   No, pero permitirán que vosotros _____.

C. Conteste la pregunta con una oración completa, usando el subjuntivo.

1. ¿Qué prefiere Ud. que le den sus padres en su cumpleaños?

   _____
2. ¿Se alegró su profesor de que Ud. viniera a la clase hoy?

   _____
3. ¿Le permitirán a Ud. sus padres que viaje a España el verano próximo?

   _____
4. ¿Cree Ud. que su profesor de español le dé un regalo mañana?

   _____
5. ¿Fue necesario que Ud. se quedara en casa todo el día?

   _____
6. ¿Tiene Ud. miedo de que caiga una bomba atómica sobre su escuela?

   _____
7. ¿Niegan sus amigos que Ud. sea la mejor persona del mundo?

   _____
8. ¿Es necesario que los niños vayan a la escuela los sábados?

   _____
9. ¿Cuándo le prohíben sus padres que mire la televisión?

   _____
10. ¿Cuándo les dicen los profesores a los estudiantes que estudien más?

    _____
11. ¿Por qué no les permiten a Uds. que fumen en la escuela?

    _____

12. ¿Sería posible que Ud. y sus amigos fuesen a un concierto de música rock el domingo próximo?

_____

13. ¿Le permitió Ud. jamás a un profesor que fuera a su casa para hablar con sus padres?

_____

14. ¿A qué hora le dicen sus padres que se acueste los sábados?

_____

15. ¿Duda Ud. que haya una tercera guerra mundial?

_____

D. Here is a conversation between Pedro and Elena, who are classmates at school. What will they say when they discuss the same subject at their high-school reunion ten years later? To find out, rewrite this dialogue so that it refers to the past. Hint: Start by changing each verb in the main clause to the imperfect tense.

PEDRO: Siempre quieres que estudiemos juntos para los exámenes.

ELENA: ¿No te gusta mi compañía?

PEDRO: Sí, pero no me gusta que tu hermanito ponga la televisión mientras estudiamos. ¿No puedes decirle que la apague?

ELENA: A menudo estudiamos hasta muy tarde. ¿Esperas que el chico pase toda la noche sin mirar la televisión?

PEDRO: Es lástima que Juanito no tenga su propio televisor.

ELENA: Tiene uno en su cuarto pero no funciona.

PEDRO: Pues, no importa. Tú sabes que siempre me divierto cuando estudio contigo en tu casa.

ELENA: ¿Y no te alegras también de que siempre haya pasteles y helado en mi nevera?

PEDRO: Sí, por eso temo que vayamos a engordar mucho. Pero ¡al menos nos ayuda a estudiar!

E. Traduzca al español:

1. I hope that my cousins will visit us soon.

_____

2. We hoped that those famous singers would come to our town.

_____

3. Is it possible that we will be able to live on the moon in ("within") a few years?

_____

4. I'm glad that they came to the conference but I don't think they heard much; the microphone wasn't working ("functioning").

_____

_____

5. My brother doubted that I would want to listen to his tapes.

_____

6. My parents will not believe that we have done our homework.

_____

7. Did your father let you drive the car last night?

_____

8. Does your sister let you use her typewriter?

_____

9. The principal ordered them to leave his office at once.

_____

10. My teacher insists that we speak Spanish in class all the time.

_____

11. What do you want me to bring to the party?

_____

12. Would they want us to pay for the refreshments?

_____

13. We are sorry that she hasn't been able to see you, Charles.

_____

14. She said she was sorry that you (*tú*) hadn't seen the film.

_____

15. What did you (*Ud.*) ask them to do?

_____

16. I'm telling you (*pl.*) to stay home tonight.

_____

17. Will it be necessary for us to get up early tomorrow morning?

_____

18. Was it important for her to write this letter?

_____

19. It is true that they have escaped from prison.

_____

20. It is not true that he has stolen the jewels.

_____

21. We were afraid that you had gotten lost.

_____

22. I'm afraid that he won't be able to find our house.

_____

23. Tell her to go downtown with you, Mrs. Mendoza.

_____

24. Ask them to show us the slides of their trip.

_____

25. They said it was certain that he had arrived home before midnight.

_____

8

Other Uses of the Subjunctive

Conjunctions That Take the Subjunctive

1 The subjunctive is used after the following conjunctions:

antes (de) que, before
con tal que, provided that
en caso de que, in case

para que, in order that
sin que, without

Salieron **antes de que llegara.**

Te prestaré el carro **con tal que** lo **devuelvas** mañana.

Mi madre nos preparó unos sandwiches **en caso de que tuviéramos** hambre.

Anoche volvimos a casa muy tarde **sin que** mi padre lo **supiera.**

They left before he arrived.

I'll lend you the car provided you return it tomorrow.

My mother prepared some sandwiches for us in case we were (got) hungry.

Last night we got home very late without my father's knowing it.

Practice A: Change the tense of the subjunctive as shown in the examples.

EXAMPLES: Antes de que lleguen, terminaremos el partido.

Antes de que _____*llegaran*_____, terminamos el partido.

Prometieron acompañarnos al centro con tal que trajéramos las cintas.

Prometen acompañarnos al centro con tal que _____*traigamos*_____ las cintas.

1. Yo terminé el trabajo sin que tú me ayudases.

   Yo puedo terminar el trabajo sin que tú me _____.

2. Iré a la fiesta con tal que vengan José y María Vargas.

   Prometí ir a la fiesta con tal que _____ María y su hermano.

3. Antes de que vinieran, vimos cuatro programas.

   Antes de que _____, veremos cuatro programas.

4. Van a traer las cintas para que las oigas.

   Trajeron las cintas para que las _____.

5. Vinimos temprano en caso de que ustedes quisieran salir.

   Venimos temprano en caso de que ustedes _____ salir.

Conjunctions That *Sometimes* Take the Subjunctive

2 The following conjunctions are used with the indicative or the subjunctive, depending on the kind of clause they introduce:

aunque, although, even if	**así que**
cuando, when	**en cuanto** as soon as
después (de) que, after	**luego que**
hasta que, until	

a. **Aunque** is followed by the indicative if its clause states a fact, by the subjunctive if its clause states a supposition or possibility:

Aunque no **tienen** mucho dinero, viven bien.	Although they don't have much money, they live well. (It's a fact that they don't have much money.)
Aunque no **tengan** mucho dinero, viven bien.	Even though they may not have much money, they live well. (They don't *seem* to have much money.)

Note: The same principle applies to other tenses:

Aunque les **dijo** la verdad, nadie lo creyó.	Although he told them the truth, no one believed him.
Aunque les **dijera** la verdad, nadie lo creería.	Even if he told them the truth, no one would believe him.

b. The six other conjunctions in the list (**cuando, después (de) que, así que,** etc.) are used with the indicative if the clause refers to a regular or expected occurrence, with the subjunctive if the clause refers to an occurrence in the indefinite future:

Cuando papá **llega** a casa, nos sentamos a comer.	When dad gets home, we sit down to eat. (a routine occurrence)
Cuando papá **llegue** a casa, nos sentaremos a comer.	When dad gets home (we don't know when that will be), we will sit down to eat.

Todos nos callamos **así que** el profesor **entra.**	We all stop talking as soon as the teacher comes in. (a normal occurrence)
Todos nos callaremos **así que** el profesor **entre.**	We'll all stop talking as soon as the teacher comes in. (whenever that may be)

3 A useful clue: These conjunctions will most likely be followed by the subjunctive if the *other* clause is a command or in the future tense:

Cuando Ud. **llame** mañana, **cuénteme (discutiremos)** las noticias.	When you call me tomorrow, tell me (we will discuss) the news.

4 In the past tense, the indicative is used when referring to an event that actually occurred, the imperfect subjunctive when referring to an event that *was to occur* at an indefinite time:

Lo vimos **así que llegó.**	We saw him as soon as he arrived. (He did arrive.)
Dijo que lo veríamos **así que llegara.**	He said we would see him as soon as he arrived. (We didn't know when that would be.)

Practice B: Decide whether the indicative or the subjunctive is to be used; then underline the correct form.

1. Luego que (vienen/vengan), nos saludan.
2. En cuanto (vieron/vieran) el accidente, llamaron a la policía.
3. Me dijeron que te verían cuando (llegaste/llegaras).
4. Todo ocurre siempre después que (se van/se vayan).
5. Aunque (vieron/vieran) el programa, no lo comprendieron.
6. Hasta que (aprendes/aprendas) a conducir bien, no te permitiré usar el coche nuevo.
7. Así que te (veo/vea), te contaré las noticias.
8. Cierre Ud. la puerta cuando (sale/salga).
9. Esta mañana mamá nos dijo que prepararía la cena cuando (vino/viniera) a casa esta noche.
10. Cada vez que (ponemos/pongamos) la televisión, vemos unos programas horribles.

The Subjunctive with Indefinite Antecedents

5 An adjective clause describes a person or thing mentioned in the main clause; for example, "I met someone *who speaks Russian.*" In Spanish, the verb in the adjective clause may be in the indicative or in the subjunctive depending on whether the speaker is referring to a specific person or thing. Compare:

A	*B*
Encontré a un alumno que **sabe** manejar el proyector.	Busco un alumno que **sepa** manejar el proyector.
I found a student who knows how to operate the projector.	*I'm looking for a student who knows how to operate the projector.*
Conozco a alguien que **puede** ayudarnos.	¿Conoce Ud. a alguien que **pueda** ayudarnos?
I know someone who can help us.	*Do you know someone who can help us?*
Tengo algo que te **interesará.**	No tengo nada que te **interese.**
I have something that will interest you.	*I don't have anything that will interest you.*
En esta clase había alguien que **comprendió** el subjuntivo.	Ayer no había nadie en la clase que **comprendiera** el subjuntivo.
In this class there was someone who understood the subjunctive.	*Yesterday there was no one in class who understood the subjunctive.*

In column *A*, the persons or things described in the **que** clauses are known to the speaker or actually exist; in column *B*, they are indefinite, unknown, or do not exist. (The last two are often expressed in the main clause by negative pronouns such as **nada** and **nadie.**)

6 Note the absence of the personal **a** in the first sentence of column *B* (**Busco un alumno que**...). The personal **a** is not used before a noun denoting a person who is unknown to the speaker or may not exist. However, the personal **a** always precedes the words **alguien** and **nadie** when they are objects of the verb:

No conozco **a** nadie que sepa conducir.	I don't know anyone who knows how to drive.

Practice C: Complete the second sentence in each pair with the appropriate form of the underlined verb.

> EXAMPLES: No tengo nada que me <u>guste</u>.
> Tengo algo que me ____*gusta*____.
>
> Hay varias personas aquí que <u>saben</u> conducir.
> No hay nadie aquí que ____*sepa*____ conducir.

1. ¿Quiere Ud. ver una película que <u>trate</u> de la música española?

   Es una película que _____ de la vida de un músico famoso.

2. Tenemos un profesor de español que <u>es</u> una persona magnífica.

   Deseamos tener un profesor que _____ simpático, joven, y guapo.

3. ¿Conoces a alguien que <u>tenga</u> los últimos discos rock?

   Conoces a alguien que _____ esos discos, ¿verdad?

4. En aquel taller vive un artista que <u>hace</u> retratos muy finos.

   En nuestro pueblo no hay ningún artista que _____ retratos.

5. En ese restaurante me sirvieron una comida que me <u>gustó</u> mucho.

   Entre los platos que servían anoche no había ninguno que me _____ .

6. Quiero comprar una computadora que no <u>cueste</u> tanto dinero.

   Aquí tenemos una computadora que _____ sólo 500 dólares.

7. Cuando ella va de compras, algunas veces encuentra a un joven que <u>trabaja</u> en su oficina.

   Los fines de semana ella nunca encuentra a nadie que _____ en su oficina.

8. ¿Hay alguien aquí que <u>quiera</u> ayudarnos?

   Hay un hombre que _____ ayudarlos a Uds.

9. Anoche en la televisión vimos dos programas que <u>eran</u> sumamente violentos.

   Pero mi padre hubiera preferido ver uno que _____ menos violento.

10. ¿Necesitarás un abrigo que te <u>cubra</u> completamente?

    No, porque tengo uno que me _____ bastante.

The Subjunctive in *Si* Clauses

7 In English, an *if* clause in the present tense is often joined to a main clause in the future tense:

> If they leave now, they will get there on time.
> (*Or*: They will get there on time if they leave now.)

The same pattern occurs in Spanish:

> Si **salen** ahora, **llegarán** allí a tiempo.
> (*Or:* **Llegarán** allí a tiempo si **salen** ahora.)

Such sentences deal with cause and effect: If *X* happens, *Y* will result. For that reason, the main clause is also called the *result* clause.

8 The *if* clause and its "result" may be expressed in a tone of uncertainty or wishful thinking:

> If they left now, they would get there on time.
> (*Or:* They would get there on time if they left now.)

In Spanish, the verb in the **si** clause would be in the imperfect subjunctive, the verb in the result clause would be in the conditional:

> Si **salieran (saliesen)** ahora, **llegarían** allí a tiempo.
> (*Or:* **Llegarían** allí a tiempo si **salieran (saliesen)** ahora.)

The verb in the result clause may also be in the **-ra** form of the imperfect subjunctive (but not in the **-se** form):

...**llegaran** allí a tiempo.*

This is the only case in which the **-ra** and **-se** forms are not interchangeable.

Note: Not all **si** clauses are of the kind shown above. Compare these sentences:

a. Si María **estuviera** enferma, se lo **diría (dijera)** a sus padres.	If Mary were ill, she would tell her parents.
b. Si María **estaba** enferma, se lo **decía** a sus padres.	If Mary was ill, she would tell her parents.

In sentence *a*, the speaker only imagines or supposes what Mary would do if she were ill. In sentence *b*, the speaker describes *actual* occurrences: that's what Mary did if she was ill; therefore, the verbs are in the indicative.

9

Thus far, we have reviewed the following patterns:

(*a*) If *X* happens, *Y* will result.

Si Uds. **van** a la fiesta, **pasarán** un buen rato.	If you go to the party, you will have a good time.

(*b*) If *X* happened, *Y* would result.

Si Uds. **fueran (fuesen)** a la fiesta, **pasarían (pasaran)** un buen rato.	If you went to the party, you would have a good time.

We now review a third pattern, referring to the past:

(*c*) If *X* had happened, *Y* would have resulted.

Si Uds. **hubieran (hubiesen) ido** a la fiesta, **habrían (hubieran) pasado** un buen rato.	If you had gone to the party, you would have had a good time.

Here, the **si** clause is in the pluperfect subjunctive, the result clause is in the conditional perfect or in the **-ra** form of the pluperfect subjunctive.

Practice D: Complete the sentence with the appropriate form of the verb in parentheses.

1. (tener) Si yo _____ dinero, viajaría por todo el mundo.

2. (llegar) Si sales temprano, _____ a tiempo.

3. (ver) Si hubieran llegado a la hora indicada, _____ el espectáculo.

---

*This use of the imperfect subjunctive instead of the conditional in result clauses is rather "literary." In spoken Spanish, the conditional is much more common: "Si salieran ahora, **llegarían**..." (rather than **llegaran**).

4. (contestar) Si estabas en casa anoche, ¿por qué no _____ el teléfono?

5. (ser) Si ella _____ rica, yo me casaría con ella en seguida.

6. (ir) Si nosotros _____ al cine, nos habríamos encontrado con ellos.

7. (ir) Si tú _____ a la tienda, cómprame una docena de huevos.

8. (conocer) Si yo lo _____, lo hubiera saludado.

9. (poder) Nos veíamos todos los días; si yo no _____ ir a su casa, ella venía a la mía.

10. (saber) Si nosotros _____ la verdad, se la diríamos a Ud.

___ EJERCICIOS _____

A. Conteste en oraciones completas:

1. ¿Qué haría Ud. si ganara un millón de dólares en la lotería?

   _____

2. ¿Qué piensa Ud. hacer este fin de semana en caso de que llueva?

   _____

3. ¿Adónde le gustaría a Ud. ir después de que se gradúe?

   _____

4. ¿Conoce Ud. a alguien que sepa tocar la música rock?

   _____

5. ¿Tiene en su casa un ordenador que cueste más de mil dólares?

   _____

6. *a.* ¿Qué puede hacer un robot que no pueda hacer un hombre?

   _____

   b. ¿Qué puede hacer un hombre que no pueda hacer un robot?

   _____

7. Si Ud. se hubiera resfriado y tuviera que quedarse en casa todo el fin de semana, ¿cómo pasaría el tiempo?

   _____

8. ¿Hubiera sido descubierto el Nuevo Mundo si Cristóbal Colón no lo hubiese hecho?

   _____

9. Cuando llegue el año dos mil, ¿cuántos años tendrá Ud.?

   _____

10. ¿Qué le gustaría a Ud. hacer sin que sus padres lo supieran?

    _____

11. *a.* Para que su profesor de español le pueda dar una nota buena, ¿qué tendrá Ud. que hacer?

    _____

    b. Y si no le da una buena nota, ¿qué hará Ud.?

    _____

12. *a.* ¿Cómo se divertían sus abuelos antes de que se inventara la televisión?

_____

    b. ¿Y qué haría Ud. si no se hubiera inventado la televisión?

_____

13. ¿Tiene Ud. en casa algún aparato que pueda ayudarlo(-la) con sus tareas escolares? ¿Cuál es y cómo lo (la) ayuda?

_____

14. ¿Qué usaba el hombre para hacer sus cálculos antes de que se inventara la calculadora?

_____

15. Si no existiera la computadora (el ordenador), ¿de qué modo sería diferente su vida y la vida de su familia?

_____

B. Aquí están algunas *respuestas.* ¿Cuáles son las preguntas? Escriba una pregunta para cada respuesta. (Complete las respuestas que no sean oraciones.)

> EJEMPLO: hasta que nos cansemos
>   *¿Hasta cuándo piensan Uds. jugar al tenis?*
>   *Pensamos jugar hasta que nos cansemos.*

1. cuando la luna esté llena

_____

_____

2. Nos hubiéramos quedado en casa.

_____

3. luego que salieron

_____

_____

4. Seríamos mejores amigos.

_____

5. con tal que me traigas las cintas

_____

_____

6. Sí, hay muchas personas que saben manejar la computadora.

_____

7. Lo hago para que tú no tengas que trabajar.

_____

8. antes de que se inventara la cámara fotográfica

_____

_____

9. Lo haremos sin que lo sepan tus padres.

_____

10. sólo si me das un beso

_____

_____

11. No, no hay nada que pueda ayudarnos ahora.

_____

12. Sí, conozco a varias personas que son capaces de hacerlo.

_____

13. Eso ocurrió antes de que los astronautas llegaran a la luna.

_____

14. Yo haría un viaje al otro extremo del mundo.

_____

15. así que vuelvan de España

_____

_____

C. Complete la segunda oración de cada par, cambiando la forma del verbo subrayado _si es necesario._

EJEMPLO: Cuando <u>hablo</u> contigo, me siento muy feliz.

Cuando ____*hable*____ con ella, resolveremos el problema.

1. Luego que <u>empieza</u> a llover, todo el mundo abre el paraguas.

   Luego que _____ a nevar, habrá problemas con el tráfico.
2. Hasta que no* <u>aprendas</u> a conducir con cuidado, no podrás tener el coche.

   Hasta que no _____ a conducir, usa tu bicicleta.
3. Después que me <u>pagues</u> lo que me debes, te prestaré más dinero.

   Después que me _____ los cien dólares, seremos mejores amigos.
4. Así que <u>pongo</u> la televisión, mi hermano trata de cambiar el canal.

   Así que _____ la radio, mi hermano querrá oír otro programa.
5. Cuando <u>vuelvan</u> de la escuela, iremos al centro comercial.

   Cuando _____ de la escuela, se sientan a hacer sus tareas.

D. Complete la nueva oración, cambiando la forma del verbo subrayado del indicativo al subjuntivo o viceversa. Use la misma forma del verbo si no necesita cambiarla.

1. ¿Conoces a un mecánico que <u>pueda</u> arreglar nuestra computadora?

   Conozco a un buen mecánico que _____ hacer toda clase de reparaciones.
2. He visto en la televisión a un actor que <u>hace</u> muy bien su papel.

   ¿Hay un actor que _____ su papel tan bien como esa actriz?
3. Anoche no había ningún programa que me <u>interesara</u>.

   La semana pasada había un magnífico programa en la televisión que me

   _____ mucho.

*Do not translate **no**. The expression **hasta que no....** has an affirmative meaning in English ("Until you learn to drive,...").

4. Aquí no hay nadie que <u>hable</u> inglés.

¿Hay alguien aquí que _____ español?

5. Esta es una tienda en que se <u>vende</u> todo tipo de equipo fotográfico.

Buscamos una tienda en que se _____ las últimas cintas y los últimos discos populares.

E. Complete la segunda oración de cada par, usando el infinitivo subrayado según se indica en el ejemplo.

EJEMPLO: Antes de <u>venir</u> a casa, cómpranos una botella de vino.

Antes de que tú _____*vengas*_____ a casa, te prepararemos un bizcocho.

1. Para <u>ganar</u> mucho dinero, hay que trabajar largas horas.

Para que nosotros _____ un premio en la lotería, es necesario comprar un billete cada día.

2. Entraron sin <u>vernos</u>.

Entraron sin que ella los _____.

3. Después de <u>irse</u>, empezaron a discutir lo que pasó.

Después que ella _____, empezó a llover.

4. Se quedarán en casa hasta <u>terminar</u> su trabajo.

Se quedarán en casa hasta que yo _____ mi trabajo.

5. Saldrán bien en el examen con tal de <u>estudiar</u> bastante.

Saldrás bien en los exámenes con tal que tú _____ esta noche.

F. Complete la segunda oración de cada par, cambiando la forma del verbo subrayado según se indica en el ejemplo.

EJEMPLO: Si <u>vienes</u> con nosotros, verás una buena película.

Si _____*vinieras*_____ conmigo, verías algo muy bueno.

1. Si <u>hubiesen llegado</u> una hora antes, nos habrían visto.

Si _____ temprano, nos verían.

2. Si <u>quieres</u> ver un buen programa, pon el canal 4.

Si _____ ver ese programa, hubieras puesto el canal 2.

3. Si compras esa computadora, ¿<u>podrás</u> usarla?

Si compraras esta calculadora, ¿_____ hacer cálculos muy complicados?

4. Si <u>fueran</u> buenos amigos, nos ayudarían.

Si _____ buenos amigos, nos ayudarán.

5. Si haces tus ejercicios, <u>serás</u> muy fuerte.

Si hubieras hecho esos ejercicios, _____ más fuerte.

6. Si <u>escucháramos</u> estas cintas, aprenderíamos a hablar bien el español.

Si _____ estos discos, aprenderemos una lengua extranjera.

7. Si tú <u>hubieras conducido</u> mejor, no hubieras tenido el accidente.

Si tú _____ con cuidado, no tendrás ningún accidente.

8. Si te casas conmigo, seré la persona más feliz del mundo.

   Si te _____ con José, hubieras sido mucho más feliz.

9. Si yo fuera rico, no tendría que trabajar.

   Si yo hubiera sido rico, no _____ que trabajar tanto.

10. Si me regalas algo, seremos buenos amigos para siempre.

   Si me _____ un carro, seríamos mejores amigos.

G. Traduzca al español:

1. I'm looking for a personal computer that works ("functions") well.

   _____

2. In this store we have three kinds of computers that work very well.

   _____

3. In case you (*tú*) need a good tennis racquet, remember that you can buy it at the mall.

   _____

   _____

4. Last night I drove the car without my father's being with me.

   _____

5. When we leave school today, we'll go to the movies to see that new picture.

   _____

6. As soon as my friends arrived, the party livened up. (Use the verb *animarse*.)

   _____

7. Do you (*Uds.*) sell tapes that run for ("last") ninety minutes?

   _____

8. I can sell you this tape that runs for sixty minutes only.

   _____

9. If they saved more money, they would be able to buy that tape recorder.

   _____

10. If you (*tú*) had not wrecked your car, you would have been able to go out last night with us.

   _____

   _____

11. Is there any bank that can lend us money to buy the car?

   _____

12. There are several banks that will lend you the money if you need it.

   _____

13. In order for the machine to run ("function") properly, you have to keep it in good condition. (Use the expression *mantener en buen estado*.)

   _____

   _____

14. Until it stops raining, we'll have to use our umbrellas.

   _____

15. Even if I slept for ten hours, I would still be tired.

   _____

16. Before they arrived, we were having a good time.

   _____

17. There was no one in our school who was able to attend the conference.

   _____

18. Do you know a museum that exhibits the works of Pablo Picasso?

   _____

19. If we had not gone to the concert last night, we would have been very bored staying at home.

   _____

   _____

20. When you are ready, Johnny, we'll do our homework together.

   _____

La Isla de Pascua

A unos 3680 kilómetros (2300 millas) al oeste de la costa de Chile está la Isla de Pascua, llamada así porque fue descubierta el domingo de la Pascua Florida de 1722 por el explorador holandés Jacob Roggeveen. En esta isla triangular, formada de tres volcanes, viven unos 2000 habitantes, la mayor parte de los cuales son naturales de la isla. Algunos creen que los habitantes originales vinieron de Polinesia; otros creen que fueron una cultura preincaica.

Gran parte de la isla está cubierta de cenizas volcánicas, pero hay dos pequeñas playas de arena. Todos los habitantes viven en Hanga Roa, un pueblo con pocas calles donde la vida es muy sencilla. La mayoría de la gente viaja a caballo como si viviera en una época muy remota.

Lo más interesante de la isla son los *Moai*, unas 600 estatuas de piedra que se encuentran a lo largo de la costa. Estas estatuas están erigidas sobre pedestales llamados *ahus*. Cuando el antropólogo noruego Thor Heyerdahl llegó a la isla en 1947, encontró todas las estatuas volcadas, y él las restauró a sus *ahus*.

Las estatuas se tallaban en un volcán llamado Rano Raraku. Allí se encuentran todavía muchas estatuas inacabadas, en varias fases de desarrollo.

Según la leyenda, los *moai* andaban por sí mismos a colocarse en sus *ahus*. Según los arqueólogos, los *moai* eran transportados sobre tablas de madera tiradas por cuerdas hechas de fibras de árboles.

En el centro de la isla hay un sitio llamado Ahu Akivi, donde se encuentran siete enormes gigantes de piedra que miran hacia el mar. Las demás figuras miran hacia el interior.

CHAPTER **9** Nouns and Articles

Gender

Nouns in Spanish are either masculine or feminine. Gender is indicated in various ways:

Articles

1

a. The definite article used with masculine nouns is **el** (singular) or **los** (plural); with feminine nouns it is **la** (singular) or **las** (plural):

el libro   **la** mesa
los libros   **las** mesas

b. The indefinite article used with masculine nouns is **un** (singular) or **unos** (plural); with feminine nouns it is **una** (singular) or **unas** (plural):

un libro   **una** mesa
unos libros = some (a few) books

Natural Gender (Male and Female)

2

a. As one would expect, nouns denoting males are masculine, nouns denoting females are feminine:

el **hombre,** man   la **mujer,** woman
el **gallo,** rooster   la **gallina,** hen

b. Some nouns, especially those that denote a role or occupation, may be either masculine or feminine depending on whether the designated person is male or female. Only the article indicates the gender:

el ⎫
la ⎭ **artista,** artist

el ⎫
la ⎭ **joven,** youngster, (*m*) young man, (*f*) young woman

el ⎫
la ⎭ **atleta,** athlete

el ⎫
la ⎭ **modelo,** artist's or fashion model

el ⎫
la ⎭ **estudiante,** student

el ⎫
la ⎭ **testigo,** witness

el ⎫
la ⎭ **guía,** guide

Note, however:

el **policía,** policeman

la **mujer policía,** policewoman

el **presidente,** president, chairman

la **presidenta,** president, chairwoman

c. A related group are the following noun-pairs, which denote corresponding male and female roles:

el **marido,** husband
la **mujer,** wife

el **príncipe,** prince
la **princesa,** princess

el **conde,** count
la **condesa,** countess

el **rey,** king
la **reina,** queen

el **poeta** ⎫
la **poetisa** ⎭ poet

Gender Indicated by Noun Endings

3 Most nouns ending in **-o** are masculine, most nouns ending in **-a** are feminine:

el **cuaderno,** notebook

la **guerra,** war

4 Some masculine nouns end in **-a,** some feminine nouns end in **-o:**

el **día,** day
el **mapa,** map

la **mano,** hand
la **radio,** radio

a. Nouns ending in **-rama** are masculine:

el **crucigrama,** crossword puzzle
el **drama,** drama

el **programa,** program
el **telegrama,** telegram

b. Two common feminine nouns ending in **-o** are actually shortened forms of nouns that end in **-a:** la **foto** = **fotografía** (photograph); la **moto** = **motocicleta** (motorcycle).

5 Nouns ending in **-dad, -tad, -tud, -ión,** and **-umbre** are feminine:

la **ciudad,** city	la **explicación,** explanation
la **dificultad,** difficulty	la **muchedumbre,** crowd
la **actitud,** attitude	

Exceptions: el **avión,** airplane; el **camión,** truck.

Nouns That Have One Meaning When Masculine, Another Meaning When Feminine

6 Some nouns may be either masculine or feminine, depending on the meaning:

el **capital,** the capital (= money or assets)	la **capital,** the capital (city)
el **cura,** the priest	la **cura,** the cure
el **guía,** the (male) guide	la **guía,** the guidebook
el **orden,** the order (= arrangement)	la **orden,** the order (= command, rule)
el **policía,** the policeman	la **policía,** the police

Using the Article *EL* With Feminine Nouns That Begin With a Stressed *A-* or *HA-*

7 Many feminine nouns are pronounced with stress on the first syllable. If that syllable is stressed **a-** or **ha-,** the singular form of the noun takes the article **el** but remains feminine. The plural form takes the usual article, **las:**

el **agua,** the water	las **aguas,** the waters
el **hacha,** the axe	las **hachas,** the axes
el **águila,** the eagle	las **águilas,** the eagles

The masculine article is used because a phrase like "la agua" or "la hacha" would be too hard to pronounce as two distinct words.

Plural Forms of Nouns

8 Spanish nouns are made plural as follows:

a. Nouns that end in a vowel add **-s** to form the plural:

el libro   la calle

los libro**s**   las calle**s**

b. Nouns that end in a consonant (including **-y**) add **-es** to form the plural:

el papel   la pared   el rey

los papel**es**   las pared**es**   los rey**es**

c. Nouns that end in **-z** change **z** to **c** before adding **-es:**

el lápi**z**   la lu**z**

los lápi**ces**   las lu**ces**

d. If a noun ends in **-n** or **-s** and has an accent mark on the last syllable, the mark is omitted in the plural:

el inglés   la lección

los ingles**es**   las leccion**es**

e. If a noun of more than one syllable ends in **-n** and has no accent mark, it takes an accent mark over the stressed vowel in the plural:

el joven   la imagen

los j**ó**ven**es**   las im**á**gen**es**

f. Nouns that end in **-s** in the singular and are stressed on the next-to-last syllable remain the same in the plural:

el paraguas   el martes

los paraguas   los martes

Some Irregular Plurals

9 Some nouns stress a different syllable in the plural:

el car**á**cter, character   el r**é**gimen, regime

los **caracteres**   los **regímenes**

Using the Masculine Plural to Refer to "Mixed" Groups

10 When referring to groups consisting of both sexes, the masculine plural form is used:

Miguel, Elena y Bárbara son **los amigos** de Carmen.	Michael, Helen, and Barbara are Carmen's friends.

Note also:

los hermanos, the brothers *or* the brother(s) and sister(s)
los abuelos, the grandfathers *or* the grandparents
los padres, the fathers *or* the parents
los reyes, the kings *or* the king and queen
los señores López, Mr. and Mrs. López
los Mendoza, the Mendozas (= Mr. and Mrs. Mendoza *or* the entire Mendoza family)

Contractions

11 There are only two contractions in Spanish: **a + el = al** and **de + el = del.** The prepositions **a** and **de** do not combine with any other forms of the definite article:

Voy **al** campo.	I'm going to the country.
Venimos **del** parque.	We are coming from the park.

But:

Es el libro **de la** chica.	It is the girl's book.
Hablamos **de las** playas.	We are talking about the beaches.

The Neuter Article *Lo*

12 **Lo** is used as an article in the constructions **lo** + *adjective* and **lo** + *past participle* to form abstract noun phrases. The adjectives are in the masculine singular:

Lo bueno es que nos prestan su carro; **lo malo** es que tiene una llanta desinflada.	The good thing (What's good) is that they're lending us their car; the bad thing (what's bad) is that it has a flat tire.
Lo curioso de esa dama es que nunca sonríe.	What is curious (The curious thing) about that lady is that she never smiles.
Lea Ud. **lo escrito.**	Read what is written.
Lo hecho vale más que **lo dicho.**	What is done is worth more than what is said. (Actions speak louder than words.)

Some Special Uses of the Articles

13 *Before titles.* The definite article is used before titles such as **señor (Sr.), señorita (Srta.), señora (Sra.),** and **doctor (Dr.)** when the person's name is mentioned in conversation:

El Sr. Jones es nuestro profesor.	Mr. Jones is our teacher.
La Srta. Molina es alta.	Miss Molina is tall.
El Dr. Sánchez lo verá ahora.	Dr. Sánchez will see you now.

When the person is addressed directly, however, the article is omitted:

¿Dónde estaba Ud. ayer, **Sr.** Jones?	Where were you yesterday, Mr. Jones?
¿Cómo está Ud., **Srta.** Molina?	How are you, Miss Molina?
Dr. Sánchez, lo llaman al teléfono.	Dr. Sánchez, you're wanted on the telephone.

14 *With parts of the body and articles of clothing.* When referring to parts of the body or articles of clothing, the definite article is used instead of the possessive adjectives (**mi, tu, su,** etc.):

Quítese **el** sombrero.	Take off your hat.
Los chicos se lavaron **la** cara y **las** manos.	The children washed their faces and hands.
¿Qué lleva en **la** cabeza?	What is he wearing on his head?

Note that the article of clothing or part of the body remains in the singular even when its possessor is more than one person (**Los chicos** se lavaron **la cara**...)—unless the part referred to normally comes in two's (...y **las manos**). Similarly:

Las muchachas se ponen **el abrigo** y **los guantes.**	The girls put on their coats and gloves.

15 *With the names of the seasons*

Mi estación favorita es **la** primavera.	My favorite season is spring.
El invierno es la estación para esquiar.	Winter is the season for skiing.

16 *With days of the week, meaning "on"*

¿Qué haces **el** sábado?	What are you doing on Saturday?

In this sentence, **el sábado** refers to a particular Saturday, not to Saturdays in general. If *on* is meant to imply *every*, Spanish uses the plural:

Los domingos vamos a la iglesia.	On Sunday we go to church.

Note: If the verb **ser** is used to tell what day it is, the article is omitted as in English: **Hoy es jueves. Mañana será viernes.** However, if **ser** is used to tell on what day something is scheduled, the article *is* used:

"¿Cuándo es el examen?" "Es **el** lunes."	"When is the exam?" "It's on Monday."
El concierto será **el** viernes.	The concert will be (held) on Friday.

17 *Before nouns used in a general sense*

Los niños miran demasiado la televisión.	Children watch television too much.
El dinero es un buen remedio contra **la pobreza.**	Money is a good remedy for poverty.

18 Before the names of languages, except after **hablar, de,** and **en:**

El francés es una lengua muy bella.	French is a very beautiful language.

But:

¿Habla Ud. **inglés?**	Do you speak English?
Nuestra clase **de español** es la mejor de todas.	Our Spanish class is the best of all.
El artículo está escrito **en ruso.**	The article is written in Russian.

Note:

a. The article *is* used when any word other than the subject pronoun comes between **hablar** and the name of the language:

Habla bien **el** español.	He speaks Spanish well.

b. The article is often omitted after the verbs **aprender, comprender, escribir, estudiar, leer,** and **saber:**

Estudiamos español (*or* **el** español).
Aprendo inglés (*or* **el** inglés).

Omitting the Indefinite Article after *Ser*

19 When a form of the verb **ser** is used to identify its subject by occupation, religion, or nationality, the article **un(-a)** is omitted:*

---

*This rule is not always observed in spoken Spanish.

Ese señor **es arquitecto.**	That gentleman is *an* architect.
¿**Es** usted **profesora**?	Are you *a* teacher?
Ella **es cristiana.**	She is *a* Christian.
Es norteamericano.	He is *an* American.

The article *is* used, however, if the noun of occupation, religion, or nationality is modified:

Es **un** arquitecto **rico.**	He is a rich architect.
¿Es Ud. **una** profesora **de español?**	Are you a Spanish teacher?
Es **un** norteamericano **famoso.**	He is a famous American.

Six Spanish Words That Are Not Used with the Indefinite Article

20 Compare the Spanish words in dark type with their English equivalents in italics:

cien pesos	*a (one) hundred* pesos
cierta persona	*a certain* person
mil dólares	*a (one) thousand* dollars
otro hombre	*another* man
¡Qué película!	*What a* movie!
tal actor	*such an* actor

EJERCICIOS

A. Cambie el plural al singular o viceversa.

1. las almas _____
2. el borrador _____
3. los días _____
4. las amistades _____
5. la vez _____
6. los exámenes _____
7. el rumor _____
8. los secuaces _____
9. el águila _____
10. el alemán _____
11. los ladrones _____
12. el bufón _____
13. la bendición _____

14. el dólar _____
15. los cortaplumas _____
16. el árbol _____
17. los relojes _____
18. la raíz _____
19. el crucigrama _____
20. el zapato _____
21. los caracteres _____
22. el haba _____
23. la pata _____
24. los portugueses _____
25. la ley _____

B. Cambie la forma masculina a la femenina o viceversa.

1. la reina _____
2. la mujer _____
3. la vaca _____
4. el señor _____
5. el padre _____
6. la poetisa _____
7. el doctor _____
8. la abogada _____
9. la mujer policía _____
10. el príncipe _____

11. el jefe _____
12. la hembra _____
13. la inglesa _____
14. la nuera _____
15. el emperador _____
16. el presidente _____
17. el actor _____
18. el duque _____
19. el modelo _____
20. la violinista _____

C. Traduzca al español:

1. *a.* You see only the ugly side (what's ugly) in people.

   _____

   b. But I sometimes see the beautiful side (what's beautiful).

   _____

2. *a.* Where is Dr. Ramírez? _____
   b. He is not here, Mr. Rivera, but Mrs. Ramírez is home.

   _____

3. "Did she put on her gloves?" "No, but she took off her jacket."

   _____

4. Winter is not a pleasant season but spring is very beautiful.

   _____

5. "I'll see them on Wednesday." "But they're coming on Thursday!"

   _____

6. *a.* I always have my guitar lesson on Monday.

   _____

   b. And my sister takes her piano lesson on Saturday.

   _____

7. *a.* Teachers are weird people. _____
   b. Young people are hardworking. _____
8. The speech was made in German, but the rest of the program was in English.

   _____

9. He's a wonderful artist, and she's a distinguished pianist.

   _____

10. "Is she a lawyer?" "No, she's an engineer."

    _____

11. *a.* Please don't send me such a picture.

_____

   b. What I need is another record and a certain tape.

_____

12. *a.* A certain rock star is staying at this hotel.

_____

   b. And a certain actress is here too.

_____

13. *a.* When does your Spanish club meet?

_____

   b. It meets after our English class.

_____

14. *a.* They say that television is not very educational.

_____

   b. Anyway, radio is more exciting these days.

_____

15. *a.* You prefer the artistic to the useful, don't you?

_____

   b. No, I think the same as (*que*) you.

_____

16. *a.* I saw you at the concert last night, Mrs. Green.

_____

   b. And I saw you too, Mr. White.

_____

17. *a.* How many uncles and aunts do you have?

_____

   b. And how many children (= sons and daughters) do they have?

_____

18. *a.* Mr. and Mrs. Sandoval are coming tonight to see us.

_____

   b. They will come with the Guerreros.

_____

19. *a.* Is she putting on her hat outside?

_____

   b. Yes, and she's putting on her coat too.

_____

20. *a.* The next president will be a Democrat.

_____

   b. But the next governor will be a Republican.

_____

Zipaquirá

Una de las maravillas de la América Latina es la enorme catedral de Zipaquirá, situada a unos 56 kilómetros (35 millas) de Bogotá, Colombia. Turistas de todo el continente vienen a este lugar para rezar ante un altar hecho de sal, dentro de muros hechos de sal. Este sitio fue originalmente una mina de sal explotada por los indios chibchas, quienes se servían de este tesoro para dominar a las tribus viecinas. Se dice que esta mina podría dar sal al mundo entero por cien años.

La idea de construir una catedral dentro de la mina fue de unos mineros. En 1950 se inició el proyecto, que tardó cuatro años en terminar.

La catedral está apoyada sobre 14 enormes columnas de sal, cada una de las cuales mide once metros cuadrados (120 pies cuadrados) en la base; la cumbre de la "nave" tiene 23 metros (77 pies) de alto. En cualquier momento dado 10.000 fieles pueden rezar en esta "catedral".

El recorrido desde la entrada hasta la puerta de la catedral es de 480 metros (1575 pies). Hasta 1975 se permitía la entrada en auto. Se entraba por la parte de abajo y se salía por un túnel. Esto se prohibió debido a que las vibraciones, los gases y el peso de los autos estaban afectando la estructura. Hoy sólo se puede visitar el lugar a pie.

CHAPTER 10

Adjectives and Adverbs

Agreement of Adjectives

Spanish adjectives are said to "agree with" their nouns in gender and number; that is, the form of an adjective is determined by the form of the noun it modifies.

Adjectives with Four Forms

1 Most Spanish adjectives have four possible endings, depending on whether they are masculine or feminine, singular or plural. They may be grouped as follows:

A. *Adjectives that end in* **-o** *in the masculine singular*

Adjectives in this group have the endings **-o, -a, -os, -as:**

El edificio alt**o** es modern**o**.	The tall building is modern.
Los edificios alt**os** son modern**os**.	The tall buildings are modern.
La mujer hermos**a** es viej**a**.	The beautiful woman is old.
Las mujeres hermos**as** son viej**as**.	The beautiful women are old.

B. *Adjectives with masculine singular endings* **-dor, -ón, -án, -ín**

Adjectives in this group have the following endings:

EXAMPLE

-dor, -dora, -dores, -doras	**hablador, habladora**, etc.
	talkative
-ón, -ona, -ones, -onas	**preguntón, preguntona**, etc.
	inquisitive
-án, -ana, -anes, -anas	**holgazán, holgazana**, etc.
	lazy
-ín, -ina, -ines, -inas	**chiquitín, chiquitina**, etc.
	tiny

Luisa es muy encanta**dora** y sus hermanos son encanta**dores** también.

Louise is very charming and her
brother(s) and sister(s) are charming too.

Pepe es muy holgaz**án** y su hermana
María es bonach**ona.** Los dos son
chiquit**ines** y burl**ones.**

Joe is very lazy and his sister Mary is
good-natured. They are both tiny
and fond of teasing.

Note that accent marks occur only in the masculine singular: holgaz**á**n, holgazana, etc.; chiqui-
t**í**n, chiquitina, etc.

C. *Adjectives of nationality*

Some adjectives of nationality belong in groups A and B, above: **italiano (-a, -os, -as);
alemán, alemana,** etc. Also familiar are the forms **español, española, españoles, españolas.**

Other adjectives in this group have the endings **-és, -esa, -eses, -esas:**

José es **cubano** y su primo Enrique
es **portugués;** no es **español.**
Ana es **cubana** y su prima **María** es
portuguesa; no es **española.**

Joseph is Cuban and his cousin Henry
is Portuguese; he is not Spanish.
Anne is Cuban and her cousin Mary
is Portuguese; she is not Spanish.

In this group, as in group B, note that accent marks occur only in the masculine singular:
franc**é**s, francesa, etc.; ingl**é**s, inglesa, etc.; portugu**é**s, portuguesa, etc.

Adjectives With Two Forms

2 Adjectives other than those of groups A to C, above, have only two forms, singular and
plural. The masculine and feminine forms are the same:

El jugador **popular** es **inteligente.**
Los jugadores **populares** son **inte-
ligentes.**
La mujer **pobre** está **triste.**
Las mujeres **pobres** están **tristes.**

The popular player is intelligent.
The popular players are intelligent.

The poor woman is sad.
The poor women are sad.

Position of Adjectives

3 *Limiting* adjectives (*another* house, *some* boys, *this* book, *many* toys, *five* cows) answer
the questions *which one? how much? how many?* In both Spanish and English, the limiting
adjective precedes the noun: **otra** casa, **algunos** chicos, etc.

Descriptive adjectives (a *small* room, the *pretty* flowers, *French* cooking, *interesting* stories)
answer the question *what kind?* In Spanish, the word order is most often the opposite of English:
un cuarto **pequeño,** las flores **bonitas,** etc.

Mis dos abuelos tienen **muchos** amigos **ricos.**	My two grandparents have many rich friends.
Tantas personas **inteligentes** tienen **poco** sentido **común.**	So many intelligent people have little common sense.

In general: descriptive adjectives (including adjectives of nationality) follow their nouns. Adjectives of quantity and number and demonstrative and possessive adjectives precede their nouns as in English.

The Two Positions of Descriptive Adjectives

4 *a.* A descriptive adjective generally *precedes* the noun it modifies if the adjective describes an inherent, unchanging, or well-known characteristic of the person or thing the noun refers to:

La **blanca** nieve estaba rayada de huellas.	The white snow was streaked with footprints. (Snow is characteristically white.)
Alberto le pidió su autógrafo a la **famosa** actriz.	Albert asked the famous actress for her autograph. (Her fame is taken for granted.)

b. The adjective *follows* the noun if it is used to distinguish the person or thing the noun refers to from other persons or things of the same kind:

Dicen que esa dama fue una vez una actriz **famosa.**	They say that lady was once a famous actress. (Not just an actress but a *famous* actress.)
Los edificios **altos** están en el centro.	The *tall* buildings are downtown.
But:	
Los turistas siempre admiran los **altos** edificios de Nueva York.	Tourists are always admiring the tall buildings of New York. (New York is known for its tall buildings.)

Adjectives with Meanings That Depend on Whether They Precede or Follow Their Nouns

5 An adjective may have one meaning when it precedes the noun, another meaning when it follows the noun. For example:

ADJECTIVE	BEFORE THE NOUN	AFTER THE NOUN
antiguo	old (= former)	old (in years)
cierto	a certain	sure, definite
gran, grande	great	large, big
medio	half	average
mismo	same	-self (himself, herself, itself, etc.)
nuevo	new (= another, additional)	new (= brand new)
pobre	poor (= unfortunate)	poor (= without money)
propio	own	proper, suitable
único	only	unique, special
viejo	old (= long-time)	old (= elderly)

Adjectives That Have "Short" Forms

6

a. The adjectives **bueno, malo, primero,** and **tercero** may precede or follow their nouns. If they precede a masculine singular noun, their **-o** ending is dropped:

un hombre **bueno**	*or* un **buen** hombre	a good man
un lugar **malo**	*or* un **mal** lugar	a bad place
el párrafo **primero**	*or* el **primer** párrafo	the first paragraph
el edificio **tercero**	*or* el **tercer** edificio	the third building

b. **Alguno** and **ninguno** generally precede the nouns they modify. They lose their **-o** ending before a masculine singular noun. When the **-o** is dropped, an accent mark is added to the **u:**

> **algún** señor   some gentleman   **ningún** actor   no actor

c. **Gran** means *great* and precedes a singular noun of either gender. Its plural form is **grandes:**

El Sr. López es un **gran** hombre. Su esposa es una **gran** mujer. Son **grandes** personas.	Mr. López is a great man. His wife is a great woman. They are great people.

Grande(s) means *large* or *big* when it follows the noun:

un hombre (una mujer) **grande**	a large man (woman)
Viven en casas **grandes.**	They live in big houses.

d. **San, santo, santa.** Note how the title of *saint* is expressed in Spanish:

San Pablo	Saint Paul	**Santa** Ana	Saint Anne
San José	Saint Joseph	**Santa** Teresa	Saint Theresa

The masculine form is **San,** the feminine form, **Santa.** Two exceptions:

Santo Tomás   Saint Thomas
Santo Domingo   Saint Dominic

Adverbs Ending in *-mente*

7 Many English adverbs are formed by adding the suffix *-ly* to an adjective: *cleverly, immediately, rapidly, slowly*. The Spanish equivalent of *-ly* is the suffix **-mente,** which is added to the feminine form of the adjective if there is one:

La mujer triste habló **tristemente** de su desgracia.	The sad woman spoke sadly of her misfortune.
Los hombres perfectos hacen todo **perfectamente.**	Perfect men do everything perfectly.
El trabajo fácil se hace **fácilmente.**	Easy work is done easily.

If the adjective has an accent mark, the accent is retained when **-mente** is added: fácilmente, rápidamente, cortésmente.

Note: Spanish has many adverbs that do *not* end in **-mente,** for example, **bien,** well; **mal,** badly; **despacio,** slowly; **de prisa,** fast; **apenas,** scarcely *or* hardly.

8 If a verb is modified by a series of two or more adverbs ending in **-mente,** the suffix is dropped from all but the last:

Mi hermano hace su trabajo **rápida, alegre, fácil** y **correctamente.**	My brother does his work rapidly, cheerfully, easily, and correctly.

Adverbial Phrases

9 The meaning of an English adverb can often be expressed in Spanish in three ways; for example:

Our teacher treats us *patiently*

= Nuestra profesora nos trata **pacientemente.**
                        con paciencia.
                        de un modo
                        de una manera } **paciente.**

We should speak to him *very politely*

= Debemos hablarle **muy cortésmente.**
$\qquad\qquad$ **con mucha cortesía.**
$\qquad\qquad$ **de un modo** ⎫
$\qquad\qquad$ **de una manera** ⎬ **muy cortés.**

The Spanish adverbial equivalent is obtained by either adding the suffix **-mente** to the feminine form of an adjective or forming a phrase of the type **con** + *noun* or **de un modo (de una manera)** + *adjective*.

Further examples:

atentamente = con atención = de un modo atento = de una manera atenta
muy cariñosamente = con mucho cariño = de un modo muy cariñoso = de una manera muy cariñosa

Note that (*a*) "very" becomes "much" (**mucho, -a**) when a *-ly* adverb is translated as a phrase beginning with **con;** (*b*) the gender of the adjective following **de un (una)...** depends on whether the adjective modifies **modo** or **manera.**

__ *EJERCICIOS* _____

A. Use las palabras para formar dos tipos de oración según se indica en el ejemplo.

$\qquad$ EJEMPLO: hombres/rico/tanto/riquezas
$\qquad\qquad\qquad$ *a. Los hombres son ricos y tienen tantas riquezas.*
$\qquad\qquad\qquad$ *b. Los hombres ricos tienen tantas riquezas.*

1. mujer/elegante/poco/defectos

$\quad$ *a.* _____

$\quad$ *b.* _____

2. ese/iglesias/antiguo/mucho/estatuas/famoso

$\quad$ *a.* _____

$\quad$ *b.* _____

3. aquel/jardín/grande/mucho/flores/bonito

$\quad$ *a.* _____

$\quad$ *b.* _____

4. perros/cariñoso/mucho/amigos/bondadoso

$\quad$ *a.* _____

$\quad$ *b.* _____

5. muchachas/simpático/tanto/amigas/leal

$\quad$ *a.* _____

$\quad$ *b.* _____

6. nuestro/ciudad/famoso/poco/monumentos/interesante

   a. _____

   b. _____

7. mi/trajes/viejo/demasiado/manchas/permanente

   a. _____

   b. _____

8. este/señora/alemán/mucho/casa/bonito

   a. _____

   b. _____

9. ese/programas/interesante/tanto/actores/famoso

   a. _____

   b. _____

10. mi/amigos/español/alguno/parientes/francés

   a. _____

   b. _____

B. Complete la oración con la forma apropiada del adjetivo entre paréntesis, colocándolo en el blanco correcto: antes o después del sustantivo.

1. (cierto) _____ persona _____ viene a vernos esta noche.

2. (grande) Babe Ruth fue un _____ jugador _____ de béisbol.

3. (inteligente) Las _____ personas _____ saben aprovecharse de lo que aprendieron en la escuela.

4. (pobre) Aunque tenga mucho dinero, ese _____ hombre _____ no tiene ningunos amigos.

5. (único) Estos son los _____ libros _____ que tengo.

6. (mismo) "Rosa sacó la nota más alta de la clase." "¿Cómo lo sabes?" "La _____ profesora _____ me lo dijo."

7. (rojo) La _____ sangre _____ que corre por nuestras venas lleva sustento a todas las partes del cuerpo.

8. (viejo) El Sr. Rojas es un _____ amigo _____ mío.

9. (propio) Mis _____ padres _____ no quieren prestarme dinero.

10. (verde) Las _____ hojas _____ de esos árboles son bonitas.

C. Escriba la oración de nuevo, usando la palabra entre paréntesis en lugar de la palabra subrayada.

   EJEMPLO: (muchacho) Algunas chicas traviesas vienen a la fiesta.
            Algún muchacho travieso viene a la fiesta.

1. (señora) Ese buen señor español es mi único amigo.

   _____

2. (hermana) Mis propios <u>hermanos</u> son malos estudiantes.

_____

3. (hombres) Las mismas <u>personas</u> simpáticas son muy ricas.

_____

4. (viajero) La <u>turista</u> extranjera es una mujer sumamente inteligente y encantadora.

_____

5. (caballero) Algunos <u>hombres</u> portugueses son buenos comerciantes.

_____

6. (Tomás) Santa <u>Isabel</u> fue una gran mujer caritativa.

_____

7. (alumnas) Pocos <u>alumnos</u> son estúpidos y holgazanes.

_____

8. (libros) Hay muchas <u>novelas</u> nuevas en la biblioteca grande.

_____

9. (dramas) Esa <u>película</u> es cómica y muy interesante.

_____

10. (atleta, _m_) ¿Has visto a los fuertes <u>jugadores</u> ingleses?

_____

11. (tentativa) Los primeros <u>esfuerzos</u> son los más difíciles y vigorosos.

_____

12. (compañera) Mis viejos <u>compañeros</u> están muy cansados y tristes.

_____

13. (Enrique y Ana) <u>Juanita</u> es la chica más popular de la escuela pero es muy habladora y burlona.

_____

_____

14. (individuo) Ninguna <u>persona</u> es perfecta ni totalmente amable.

_____

15. (políticos) El gran <u>gobernador</u> es muy joven y feliz.

_____

D. Debajo de cada expresión adverbial escriba dos expresiones equivalentes según se indica en el ejemplo.

> EJEMPLO: Tú haces esto <u>muy fácilmente</u>.
> _de un modo (una manera) muy fácil_
> _con mucha facilidad_

1. Esas personas luchan <u>con fuerza</u>.

_____

_____

2. Aquel chico habla <u>de un modo muy inocente</u>.

   _____

   _____

3. El caracol se mueve <u>muy lentamente</u>.

   _____

   _____

4. Tienes que hacer eso <u>con mucho cuidado</u>.

   _____

   _____

5. La profesora lo explica todo <u>claramente</u>.

   _____

   _____

6. Los jets vuelan <u>con mucha rapidez</u>.

   _____

   _____

7. La madre trata al bebé <u>muy cariñosamente</u>.

   _____

   _____

8. Esos hombres se portan <u>de una manera peligrosa</u>.

   _____

   _____

9. Esa pareja vieja anda <u>con mucha lentitud</u>.

   _____

   _____

10. El pobre viejo ha contado su historia <u>de un modo muy triste</u>.

    _____

    _____

E. Traduzca al español:

1. Some people ("persons") say that flying saucers really* exist; others say they are optical illusions. (optical = *óptico, -a*)

   _____

   _____

2. Is there a great possibility of a nuclear war in the near future?

   _____

3. Our former president was a great politician.

   _____

*Use the *-mente* form, not an adverbial phrase.

4. Last night he played his guitar magnificently.

_____

5. Some computers are terribly expensive.

_____

6. The astronauts traveled to the moon at an incredibly high speed.

_____

7. Many intelligent people are highly (*muy*) addicted to the new electronic games.

_____

_____

8. I'm taking an interesting course in human relations at a nearby university. (to take a course = *seguir un curso*)

_____

_____

9. You shouldn't mix too many ingredients at a low temperature.

_____

10. The firefighters worked silently and quickly at (*en*) their dangerous task.

_____

11. The average citizen has some money in the bank and supports the present government.

_____

12. He is the only student in this class who can work independently.

_____

13. The old system seems to be better than the present system.

_____

14. The ideal place for the Olympics (Olympic Games) would be our own city.

_____

15. That old lady is suffering from a severe illness.

_____

16. This famous pianist is German, but her grandparents were French.

_____

17. I myself have the same tastes as (*que*) my rich friends.

_____

18. The new student in our class has some unique qualities.

_____

19. No teacher in this school has as many talents as our Spanish teacher.

_____

20. The average American citizen has at least a half-cup of coffee every morning.

_____

_____

CHAPTER **11**

Expressing Possession; Possessive Adjectives and Pronouns

1 **¿De quién?** means *whose?* It becomes **¿de quiénes?** if the possessor is assumed to be more than one person. The preposition **de** is used in both the question and the answer:

—**¿De quién** es el tocadiscos? "Whose record player is it?"
—Es **de Roberto.** "It is Robert's."

—**¿De quién** son las plumas? "Whose pens are they?"
—Son **del profesor.** "They are the teacher's." ("They belong to the teacher.")

—**¿De quiénes** es ese coche? "Whose car is that?"
—Es **de los Mendoza.** "It belongs to the Mendozas."

—¿Es **de Cristina** esa pulsera? "Is that bracelet Christine's?"
—No, es **de su hermana.** "No, it's her sister's."

2 To translate *whose?*, change it to *of whom?* and phrase the question as it would be expressed in Spanish. For example, *Whose bicycle did you use?* becomes "Of whom is the bicycle that you used?"—In Spanish, **¿De quién(es) es la bicicleta que usaste?** Similarly:

Whose books does he have? = "Of whom are the books that he has?"
¿De quién(es) son los libros que tiene?

3 *Whose* as a relative pronoun is **cuyo, -a:**

Ella es la muchacha **cuyo** padre visita la escuela hoy.
She is the girl whose father is visiting the school today.

¿Es Ud. el señor **cuyas** hijas tocan en la banda?
Are you the gentlemen whose daughters play in the band?

Note that **cuyo, -a** agrees in gender and number with the noun that directly follows it.

Expressing Possession with *De*

4 In Spanish, *Philip's house* becomes literally "the house of Philip" (**la casa de Felipe**); *the boys' father* becomes "the father of the boys" (**el padre de los muchachos**):

Mi casa y **la casa de Felipe** están en la misma cuadra.

My house and Philip's house are in the same block.

To avoid repetition, the noun preceding **de** can be dropped and its article used as a pronoun:

Mi casa y **la de Felipe** están en . . .

My house and Philip's are in . . .

Similarly:

Sus amigos y **los de mi tío** son ricos.

His friends and my uncle's are rich.

In this example, **los de mi tío = los amigos de mi tío.**

Possessive Adjectives

5 *a.* The following three adjectives are the same for both genders. The plural form ends in **-s:**

mi, mis	my
tu, tus	your (*fam. sing.*)
su, sus	your, his, her, its, their

mi amigo(-a)   **mis** amigos(-as)

b. The adjectives **nuestro** and **vuestro** have four possible endings, depending on whether the noun that follows is masculine or feminine, singular or plural:

nuestro, -a, -os, -as	our
vuestro, -a, -os, -as	your (*fam. pl.; used only in Spain*)

nuestro(-a) amigo(-a)   **nuestros(-as)** amigos(-as)

6 **Su(s)** has several possible meanings. The intended meaning is often indicated by the subject of the sentence:

Elena tiene **sus** guantes.   Helen has her gloves.
Ellos charlan con **su** profesor.   They are chatting with their teacher.

Replacing *Su(s)* with More Specific Expressions

7 The intended meaning of **su(s)** may sometimes be unclear:

El ayudante de la Srta. Cruz presentó **su** informe.	Miss Cruz's assistant submitted (your? his? her? their?) report.

In such cases, a more specific expression can be used instead:

. . . presentó **el** informe **de ella.**	. . . submitted *her* report.

To avoid confusion, **su(s)** can be replaced by one of the expressions shown in the following example:

$$\textbf{su } \text{libro} = \textbf{el } \text{libro} \begin{cases} \textbf{de Ud(s).} & \text{your book} \\ \textbf{de él} & \text{his book} \\ \textbf{de ella} & \text{her book} \\ \textbf{de ellos(-as)} & \text{their book} \end{cases}$$

Similarly, **sus** revistas = **las** revistas **de Ud., de Uds., de él, de ella, de ellos,** or **de ellas**—depending on which meaning of **sus** is the one intended.

Such substitutions are especially needed when more than one meaning of **su(s)** has to be expressed in the same sentence:

Tengo **los** libros **de Ud.** y **la** grabadora **de ellos.**	I have *your* books and *their* tape recorder.

Using the Definite Article in Place of the Possessive Adjective

8 When referring to articles of clothing or parts of the body, the definite article often replaces the possessive adjective:

Mi madre se ha puesto **los** guantes.	My mother has put on *her* gloves.
Juanito se rompió **el** brazo jugando al fútbol.	Johnny broke *his* arm playing soccer.
¿Qué tienes en **la** mano?	What do you have in *your* hand?

Possessive Pronouns

9 The possessive *adjective* is always followed by the noun it modifies: "*my* house is larger than *your* house." To avoid repetition, the adjective and its noun can be replaced by a possessive *pronoun:* "my house is larger than *yours.*"

Here are the Spanish possessive pronouns:

el mío, la mía, los míos, las mías, mine
el tuyo, la tuya, los tuyos, las tuyas, yours (*fam. sing.*)
el suyo, la suya, los suyos, las suyas, yours, his, hers, theirs
el nuestro, la nuestra, los nuestros, las nuestras, ours
el vuestro, la vuestra, los vuestros, las vuestras, yours (*fam. pl.*)

The possessive pronoun agrees in gender and number with the noun it refers to, *not* with the possessor:

Estos son mis **libros;** María, ¿dónde están **los tuyos?**

These are my books; Mary, where are yours?

10 As we saw, the noun determines the form of the pronoun:

mis **cuadernos** = **los míos**
su **escuela** = **la suya**

nuestra **familia** = **la nuestra**
sus **amigos** = **los suyos**

Tu **casa** es nueva, **la mía** es vieja.

Your house is new, mine is old.

Mi **casa** es grande, **la tuya** es pequeña.

My house is large, yours is small.

Sus **amigos** y **los nuestros** llegaron hace poco.

His friends and ours arrived a short time ago.

Nuestros **padres** y **los suyos** son amigos.

Our parents and his are friends.

Replacing the Forms of *El Suyo* with More Specific Expressions

11 The intended meaning of a form of **el suyo** may sometimes be unclear:

Yo tengo mis entradas; ¿tiene Ud. **las suyas?**

I have my tickets; do you have yours (his, hers, theirs)?

For greater clarity, the **el suyo** form can be replaced by one of the following expressions:

$$
\begin{array}{l}
\textbf{el}\ \text{suyo} = \textbf{el} \\
\textbf{la}\ \text{suya} = \textbf{la} \\
\textbf{los}\ \text{suyos} = \textbf{los} \\
\textbf{las}\ \text{suyas} = \textbf{las}
\end{array}
\left\{
\begin{array}{l}
\textbf{de Ud.} \\
\textbf{de Uds.} \\
\textbf{de él} \\
\textbf{de ella} \\
\textbf{de ellos} \\
\textbf{de ellas}
\end{array}
\right.
\begin{array}{l}
\text{yours} \\
\text{his} \\
\text{hers} \\
\text{theirs}
\end{array}
$$

Omitting the Article When the Possessive Pronoun Follows *Ser*

12 If a possessive pronoun follows a form of the verb **ser,** the definite article is generally omitted:

—¿De quién son estos papeles?	"Whose papers are these?"
—**Son míos.** No **son tuyos.**	"They are mine. They are not yours."
—**¿Son nuestros** estos libros?	"Are these books ours?"
—No, **son suyos (son de él).**	"No, they are his."

Other Forms of the Possessive Adjective

13 The forms **mío, tuyo, suyo,** etc., are used as adjectives when they follow the noun instead of replacing it:

José es **un amigo nuestro.**	Joseph is a friend of ours.
Somos **alumnos suyos.**	We are students of his (hers, yours, theirs).

The meanings of Spanish possessives used in this way are expressed in English by *of* + a possessive: *of mine, of yours,* etc. For greater clarity, the forms of **suyo** can be replaced by more specific expressions, as we saw earlier:

Ella es una prima **suya** (una prima **de él**).	She is a cousin of his.

EJERCICIOS

A. Use un pronombre posesivo en lugar de las palabras subrayadas y escríbalo en el blanco a la derecha.

EJEMPLO: <u>Mis diamantes</u> valen mucho dinero.   *Los míos*

1. <u>Su habitación</u> no es muy grande.   _____

2. ¿Quieres visitar <u>nuestra ciudad</u>?   _____

3. Aquí tengo <u>tus cintas</u>.   _____

4. No voy a ver a <u>tus parientes</u>.   _____

5. <u>Mis padres</u> están de vacaciones.   _____

6. He traído <u>sus discos</u> a la fiesta.   _____

7. <u>Nuestros profesores</u> son muy severos.   _____

8. No me gustan <u>sus vecinos</u>.   _____

9. Me gustaría aprender <u>tu idioma</u>.   _____

10. ¿Tienes <u>mi tocadiscos</u>?   _____

B. *El suyo, la suya, etc.* El significado sobrentendido (*implied*) de la forma subrayada se indica entre paréntesis. Exprésolo más claramente usando una expresión específica. Escríbala en el blanco a la derecha.

EJEMPLO: Esta mañana he visto <u>los suyos</u>. (his)   *los de él*

1. Nos gustaría ver <u>la suya</u>. (theirs)   _____

2. No tengo <u>el suyo</u>. (hers)   _____

3. Si Ud. los quiere, voy a traer <u>los suyos</u>. (yours)   _____

4. <u>Las suyas</u> son muy bonitas. (his)   _____

5. Si Uds. lo buscan, <u>el suyo</u> está en la mesa. (yours).   _____

C. Conteste la pregunta de dos maneras según se indica en el ejemplo.

EJEMPLO: ¿Qué bicicleta vas a usar? (mi primo)
  (*a*) *Voy a usar la bicicleta de mi primo.*
  (*b*)   . . . *la de mi primo.*

1. ¿Qué problema tenemos que solucionar? (los jugadores)

   (*a*) _____

              (*b*) _____

2. ¿Qué cintas quieres tocar? (José)

   (*a*) _____

              (*b*) _____

3. ¿De qué país es ella? (mis amigas)

   (*a*) _____

              (*b*) _____

4. ¿Qué discos tienen ellos? (María)

(*a*) _____

(*b*) _____

5. ¿Qué carrera quiere Ud. escoger? (el profesor)

(*a*) _____

(*b*) _____

D. Conteste la pregunta según se indica en el ejemplo.

EJEMPLO: ¿De quién es el libro que quieres leer? (la profesora)
El libro que quiero leer es de la profesora.

1. ¿De quién son los discos que vamos a usar? (Ana)

_____

2. ¿De quién es el coche que quieres tener? (mi tía)

_____

3. ¿De quiénes es la casa que veo desde aquí? (los Rivera)

_____

4. ¿De quién son estas bolsas grandes? (esa señora)

_____

5. ¿De quién es el juguete que rompió el niño? (el bebé)

_____

E. Aquí están algunas *respuestas*. ¿Cuáles son las preguntas? Escriba una pregunta para cada respuesta, usando una expresión que pueda ser "representada" por el pronombre posesivo.

EJEMPLO: No, no quiero usar la tuya.   *¿Quieres usar mi pluma?*

1. Sí, voy a visitar la suya. _____

2. No, no quisiera comprar el suyo. _____

3. Sí, ellos van a traer los míos. _____

4. Sí, queremos usar la nuestra. _____

5. No, prefiero el tuyo. _____

F. En la primera columna, escriba una forma de *suyo* que se pueda usar en lugar de la expresión subrayada. En la segunda columna, escriba la forma posesiva más específica.

EJEMPLO: Tengo unos libros de María.   *suyos*   *de ella*

1. Necesito un poco del dinero de mi padre. _____ _____

2. Encontré unos objetos de esa mujer. _____ _____

3. Quiero llevar una camisa de mi hermano. _____ _____

4. Tengo unas plumas de los profesores. _____ _____

5. Ella quiere prestarme un reloj de su madre. _____ _____

G. Traduzca al español. Las palabras con asterisco (*) deben traducirse usando la forma posesiva más específica. (Ejemplo: his* pencils and hers* = *los lápices de él y los de ella.*)

1. Their president and ours are meeting in Washington tonight.

_____

2. My customs and his* are quite different from yours.*

_____

3. Several friends of ours are coming to our house later.

_____

4. Johnny, your computer is more expensive than mine.

_____

5. "Whose skates are those?" "They are hers. They are not mine."

_____

6. "Mrs. Gómez, is this calculator yours?" "No, it is Michael's. It used to be his brother's."

_____

_____

7. The party is taking place at my house, not at theirs.*

_____

8. Several records of mine are very old and valuable.

_____

9. "Whose house is that? Is it theirs*?" "No, it's mine."

_____

10. Because of the heat they took off their shoes.

_____

11. Close your umbrella; it is no longer raining (it's not raining anymore).

_____

12. Gentlemen, I would like to work in your* company, not in theirs.*

_____

13. His family is going to visit ours next week.

_____

14. I want to see her* photos and his.*

_____

15. I know their address but I don't know yours. Where do you (*vosotros*) live?

_____

16. Whose money did the thieves steal, Miss Mendoza, your mother's or yours?

_____

17. Is he the boy whose records we have?

_____

18. Their team and my school's are playing tonight.

    _____

19. Listen, Pancho, a friend of yours has my tape recorder. Will you lend[+] me yours?

    _____

20. He raised his hand to answer the teacher's question.

    _____

+When the question *Will you (do something)?* means "Will (Would) you do me the favor of . . . ?," it is generally expressed in Spanish by using a form of **querer:**

   Hace frío afuera; **¿quieres cerrar la ventana?**   It's cold outside; would you close the window?

Machu Picchu

La ciudad perdida de los incas, descubierta en 1911 por el senador norteamericano Hiram Bingham, se considera el sitio arqueológico más famoso y espectacular del hemisferio occidental. Hay varias teorías acerca de Machu Picchu. Algunos creen que fue una fortaleza construida por los incas para protegerse contra sus enemigos. Otros creen que fue un santuario de un grupo de mujeres escogidas del Dios Sol. Lo más probable es que fuera el refugio final del último rey inca y su comitiva (retinue) al huir de los españoles hacia la seguridad de la selva.

Para visitar este sitio hay que tomar el tren en Cuzco muy temprano por la mañana. El tren tarda tres horas y media en recorrer los 112 kilómetros (70 millas), pero el viaje ofrece grandes contrastes panorámicos. El tren llega al pie de la montaña, y para llegar a la cumbre hay que tomar un microbús en el que caben unas 20 personas. La subida a la montaña es muy pintoresca e imponente, pero lo más espectacular ocurre cuando el microbús llega a la entrada de Machu Picchu y se ve un complejo arquitectónico sin igual.

El pico más alto se llama Huayna Picchu. Vale la pena subir la espeluznante escalera de piedras, porque desde allí se puede ver todo Machu Picchu. Allí también está situado el famoso Templo de la Luna.

Los mejores momentos para los visitantes son las horas entre el amanecer y las 10:30 de la mañana y entre las 3 y 6 de la tarde. Durante estas horas hay sólo los turistas que se alojan en el único hotel del sitio, y se puede gozar del paisaje sin la molestia de las muchedumbres que pululan por todas partes.

Cuando Hiram Bingham descubrió este lugar, estaba sumergido bajo una selva densa. Con el tiempo se han desmontado árboles y escombros, se han restaurado muchos edificios, hasta los techos de paja de algunos de éstos; y las corrientes de agua se han puesto en movimiento otra vez.

CHAPTER 12 Comparisons

Expressing Equalities

1 tan . . . como, *as . . . as*

This expression occurs in the patterns **tan** + *adjective* + **como** and **tan** + *adverb* + **como:**

> Mis discos son **tan** caros **como** los tuyos.

> My records are as expensive as yours.

> Martín no habla **tan** claramente **como** tú.

> Martin doesn't speak as clearly as you do.

2 tanto(-a) . . . como, *as much . . . as;* tantos(-as) . . . como, *as many . . . as*

These expressions have the form **tanto(-a)** + *noun* + **como.** The form of **tanto(-a)** agrees in gender and number with the noun that follows it:

> Recibí **tanto** dinero **como** mi hermano.

> I received as much money as my brother.

> Tengo **tantas** cintas **como** ella.

> I have as many tapes as she (has).

3 tanto como, *as much as*

In this expression, **tanto** is an adverb and does not change:

> ¿Trabajaste **tanto como** yo?

> Did you work as much (as hard) as I did?

Practice A: Form sentences as shown in the examples.

> EXAMPLE: Mi música es buena. La música rock es buena también.
> *Mi música es tan buena como la música rock.*

1. Nuestro coche es rápido. Su coche es rápido también.

2. José corre despacio. María corre despacio también.

_____

3. Las casas de nuestro barrio son caras. Las casas del otro barrio son caras también.

_____

4. Marta canta bien. Su hermana también canta bien.

_____

EXAMPLE: Yo bebo mucho café. Tomás bebe mucho café también.
Yo bebo tanto café como Tomás.

5. Yo bebí mucha agua. Ella bebió mucha agua también.

_____

6. Nuestros amigos ganaron mucho dinero. Nosotros ganamos mucho dinero también.

_____

7. Ellas tienen mucha hambre. Yo tengo mucha hambre también.

_____

EXAMPLE: Tengo muchos discos. Ella también tiene muchos discos.
Tengo tantos discos como ella.

8. Mi amigo compró muchas revistas. Yo también compré muchas revistas.

_____

9. ¿Vendieron ellos muchos billetes? ¿Vendiste tú muchos billetes también?

_____

10. Anoche vimos muchos programas. Nuestros amigos vieron muchos programas también.

_____

EXAMPLE: Pepe trabaja mucho. Ricardo trabaja mucho también.
Pepe trabaja tanto como Ricardo.

11. María me ayuda mucho. Dorotea me ayuda mucho también.

_____

12. Susana come mucho. Sus hermanos comen mucho también.

_____

EXAMPLE: José y Marta están cansados y necesitan descanso.
José está tan cansado como Marta y necesita tanto descanso como ella.

13. Teresa y Carlos están ocupados y necesitan ayuda.

_____

14. Esteban y Sarita están enfermos y necesitan medicina.

_____

15. Pablo y los otros niños están aburridos y quieren juguetes nuevos.

_____

Expressing Inequalities

4 **Más . . . que,** *more . . . than;* **menos . . . que,** *less . . . than*

a. Used with adjectives or adverbs:

Mi perro es **más** inteligente **que** su gato.	My dog is more intelligent than your cat.
Su gato es **menos** inteligente **que** mi perro.	Your cat is less intelligent than my dog.
Ana es **más** bonita **que** María.	Ann is prettier than Mary.
María es **menos** bonita **que** Ana.	Mary is less pretty than Ann.
Tú hablas **más** rápidamente **que** yo.	You talk faster than I do.
Tomás habla **menos** claramente **que** Juana.	Thomas speaks less clearly than Joan.

b. Used with nouns:

Ayer trabajé **más** horas **que** Ud. y gané **más** dinero. Ud. trabajó **menos** horas que yo y ganó **menos*** dinero.	Yesterday I worked more hours than you did and I earned more money. You worked fewer hours than I did and earned less money.

Irregular Comparative Forms

5 The Spanish equivalent of an English adjective of comparison consists of **más** or **menos** + an adjective. Thus, *smaller* becomes "more small" (**más pequeño**), *taller* becomes "more tall" (**más alto**), *smarter* becomes "more smart" (**más inteligente**), etc. The following Spanish adjectives are exceptions:

[†]**mayor, -es,** older, oldest; greater, larger
[†]**menor, -es,** younger, youngest; smaller, lesser, least
mejor, -es, better, best
peor, -es, worse, worst

*When followed by a noun, **menos** may mean either *less* or *fewer.* Recall that *less* refers to an amount or quantity whereas *fewer* refers to things that can be counted:

menos leche (dinero, helado)	*less* milk (money, ice cream)
menos hombres (libros, calorías, impuestos)	*fewer* men (books, calories, taxes)

†The meanings of these adjectives may also be expressed by the regular comparative forms **más viejo(-a, -os, -as), más joven (jóvenes), más grande(-es),** and **más pequeño(-a, -os, -as).**

a. These adjectives have only two forms, singular and plural:

Ella es **menor que** tú.　　　　　　She is younger than you (are).

Ellos son **mayores que** yo.　　　　They are older than I.

Este jugador es **mejor** que ése.　　This player is better than that one.

Las niñas son malas pero estas chi-　The children (f.) are naughty but these
quitas son **peores que** las otras.　　　little girls are worse than the oth-
　　　　　　　　　　　　　　　　　　　ers.

b. As adverbs, **mejor** and **peor** do not change:

Estos cantantes cantan **mejor que** los　These singers sing better than the oth-
otros.　　　　　　　　　　　　　　　ers.

Nosotros hablamos **peor que** él.　　We speak worse than he does.

Practice B: Express a similar idea by starting the sentence with the words in italics and using the opposite term of comparison.

EXAMPLE:　Mi hermano es más diligente que *yo.*
　　　　　Yo soy menos diligente que mi hermano.

1. La profesora es más inteligente que *los alumnos.*

_____

2. Usted tiene menos dinero que *yo.*

_____

3. Tú comes más despacio que *tu hermana.*

_____

4. Nuestra casa es menos cara que *la casa de Alberto.*

_____

5. María es más hermosa que *Diana.*

_____

6. Roberto es menor que *usted.*

_____

7. En esta clase los chicos son peores que *las chicas.*

_____

8. Mi abuelo es mayor que *mi abuela.*

_____

9. Nuestros jugadores son mejores que *los jugadores de tu escuela.*

_____

10. Mi padre juega al tenis mejor que *nosotras.*

_____

Expressing "Than" in Spanish

6 If a noun or pronoun follows, *than* becomes **que:**

Tengo más cintas **que** tú.   I have more tapes than you (have).

7 If a number follows, *than* becomes **de:**

Tengo más **de*** diez cintas.   I have more than ten tapes.

8 If a clause follows in which a different verb is used, *than* is expressed in two ways:

a. **del que, de la que, de los que, de las que**

Tengo más cintas **de las que** nece-   I have more tapes than I need.
sito.

The pronoun **las** refers to **las cintas.** The expression **de las que** means "than those that." The pronoun agrees in gender and number with the preceding noun. Note that the two verbs, **Tengo** and **necesito,** have the same noun as object: **Tengo cintas; las (cintas) que necesito.** Similarly:

Mi padre me dio menos dinero **del**   My father gave me less money than I
que le pedí.   asked for.

b. **de lo que**

Tengo más cintas **de lo que** crees (te   I have more tapes than you think
imaginas).   (imagine).

The neuter pronoun is used because it refers to a thought or belief. The expression **de lo que crees** means "than what you think (I have)." As in English, the object of **crees** is an unexpressed clause such as **que tengo.**

The same principle applies when the key term of the comparison is an adjective:

Carolina era más bonita **de lo que**   Caroline was prettier than they had
habían esperado.   expected.

Here, too, **lo** is used because there is no noun for it to "stand for."

*If **más de** + *a number* is used negatively, **de** changes to **que.** The expression **no . . . más que** is usually translated as *only:*

No tengo **más que** tres libros.   I have only three books.

9 Here are further examples. Note the ways in which *than* is expressed when it follows an adjective or an adverb:

Su trabajo es más fácil **que** el nuestro.	Her work is easier than ours.
Ella trabaja más lentamente **que** nosotros.	She works more slowly than we (do).
Su trabajo es más fácil **de lo que** creíamos.	Her work is easier than we thought.
Ella trabaja más lentamente **de lo que** quisiéramos.	She works more slowly than we would like.

Practice C: Complete the sentence with the appropriate Spanish equivalent of *than* (*que, de, de lo que, del que, de la que, de los que, de las que*).

1. Mi tocadiscos nuevo es mejor _____ yo esperaba.

2. Ayer compré más _____ veinte artículos en la tienda.

3. Aquel cine es peor _____ éste.

4. La semana pasada gané menos dinero _____ mi amigo Enrique.

5. El profesor de español asignó más ejercicios _____ podíamos hacer.

6. Este anillo vale menos _____ se cree.

7. Hoy tengo más trabajo _____ ayer.

8. Estoy más cansado _____ tú te imaginas.

9. Mi padre trajo a casa menos flores _____ mi madre le había pedido.

10. Esta tarde hemos visto más _____ tres programas de televisión.

The Superlative Degree

10 There are three degrees of comparison:

POSITIVE

Juan es **alto**.	John is *tall*.

COMPARATIVE

María es **más alta** que Juan.	Mary is *taller* than John.

SUPERLATIVE

Enrique es **el más alto**.	Henry is *the tallest*.

The superlative degree is expressed in Spanish by using the definite article with **más** or **menos**:

$$\left.\begin{array}{l} \textbf{el} \\ \textbf{la} \\ \textbf{los} \\ \textbf{las} \end{array}\right\} \textbf{más (menos)} + \text{adjective}$$

Article and adjective agree in gender and number with the noun they modify:

la chica **más alta***	the tallest girl
el regalo **menos caro**	the least expensive gift
los alumnos **más inteligentes**	the smartest students

11 The word order in the Spanish superlative is usually the reverse of English: *the largest house* becomes "the house most large" (**la casa más grande**), *the most interesting stories* becomes "the stories most interesting" (**los cuentos más interesantes**). To avoid repetition, the noun may be omitted:

—¿Quién es **el jugador más fuerte** del equipo?	"Who is the strongest player on the team?"
—Paco es **el más fuerte.** Teresa es **la menos fuerte.**	"Frank is the strongest. Theresa is the least strong."

12 The superlative degree is also used with adverbs:

De todos sus profesores, ¿quién explica las lecciones **más claramente?**	Of all your teachers, who explains the lessons most clearly?
Carlitos es el que se queja **más ruidosamente** y el que menos hace.	Charlie is the one who complains loudest and does the least.

13 After a superlative, the word *in* is generally expressed by **de** in Spanish:

el banco más grande **de** la ciudad	the largest bank in the city

Using the Irregular Comparatives in the Superlative Degree

14 The irregular adjectives of comparison discussed on pages 109–110 are also used as superlatives. They usually precede the noun they modify if it is expressed:

---

*Note how such phrases are translated into English when only two persons or things are being compared. Of two girls, **la chica más alta** would be "the *taller* girl" (not the tallest); of two gifts, **el regalo menos caro** would be "the *less* expensive gift" (not the least expensive). Similarly, **el alumno más inteligente** is either the *smarter* student of two or the *smartest* student among three or more.

Mi madre es **la mejor cocinera** del mundo.	My mother is the best cook in the world.
Ellos son **los peores jugadores** del equipo.	They are the worst players in the team.
¿Quiénes son **los menores*** de la familia?	Who are the youngest in the family?

Practice D: Form a sentence using the superlative degree of the adjective.

EXAMPLE: mi padre/viejo/la familia
Mi padre es el mayor (el más viejo) de la familia.

1. esa familia/rica/ciudad _____
2. ¿Qué mes/corto/año? _____
3. ese edificio/grande/calle _____
4. esta cinta/mala/colección _____
5. Roberto/bueno/equipo _____
6. mis abuelos/religiosos/familia _____
7. Conchita/joven/clase _____

Practice E: Change the sentence as shown in the example.

EXAMPLE: Ellos eran soldados muy valientes en el ejército.
Ellos eran los soldados más valientes del ejército.

1. El tenis es un deporte muy popular en ese centro turístico.

_____

2. El español es una asignatura muy importante en nuestra escuela.

_____

3. La Srta. Brown fue una profesora muy buena en el colegio.

_____

4. Martin fue un mal actor en el club dramático.

_____

5. Mi prima era una bailarina muy distinguida en esa compañía.

_____

6. El arroz con pollo es un plato muy delicioso en ese restaurante.

_____

7. Las casas son muy viejas en ese barrio.

_____

---

*The superlative meanings of **menor(-es)** and **mayor(-es)** may also be expressed by the regular forms **el (la) más joven, los (las) más jóvenes, el (la) más viejo(-a), los (las) más viejos(-as):**

Mi padre es **el más viejo** de la familia.	My father is the oldest in the family.
Lola y Roberto son **los más jóvenes** de la clase.	Lola and Robert are the youngest in the class.

The Absolute Superlative

15 The absolute superlative is a form of the adjective that ends in **-ísimo(-s)** or **-ísima(-s).** The suffix means *very, extremely, exceedingly.* It is attached directly to the positive form of the adjective. If the adjective ends in a vowel, drop the vowel before adding the suffix:

Esos edificios son **grandísimos.**   Those buildings are very (exceedingly) large.

Vivo en una casa **pequeñísima.**   I live in a very small house.

Esta lección es **facilísima.**   This lesson is extremely easy.

a. Spelling Changes. If the adjective ends in **c, g,** or **z,** make the following changes before adding the **-ísimo** suffix:

c to **qu**   **g** to **gu**   **z** to **c**

Los desiertos son se**qu**ísimos.   The deserts are exceedingly dry.

Esa fruta es amar**gu**ísima.   That fruit is very bitter.

Mis alumnos son feli**c**ísimos.   My students are extremely happy.

b. Very much is always expressed as **muchísimo.** Do not use **muy:**

Eso me gusta **muchísimo.**   I like that very much.

Practice F: Replace the underlined expression with the absolute superlative form of the adjective.

1. Hoy me siento <u>muy triste</u>.   _____

2. Chica, tienes la cara <u>muy pálida</u>.   _____

3. Estas reglas son <u>muy útiles</u>.   _____

4. Esos niños son <u>sumamente delgados</u>.   _____

5. Para los aburridos, los días parecen <u>muy largos</u>.   _____

6. Mi abuela tiene el pelo <u>muy blanco</u>.   _____

7. En nuestro zoo hay unos animales <u>extremadamente feroces</u>.   _____

__ EJERCICIOS _____

A. Conteste en oraciones completas:

1. ¿Es su madre menor que Ud.?

   _____

2. ¿Quién es el alumno* más inteligente de su escuela?

   _____

*If a noun has a masculine and a feminine form, the masculine form may be used in a general sense to designate a person of either sex. Thus, you may answer by referring to "*la alumna* más inteligente de . . ." if you think a *girl* deserves the compliment.

3. ¿Tiene Ud. más dinero del que necesita?

_____

4. En su opinión, ¿cuál es el animal más feroz del mundo? ¿Por qué?

_____

_____

5. ¿Quiénes hablan mejor el inglés, los neoyorquinos, los californianos o los floridanos?

_____

6. ¿Qué país es más grande que los Estados Unidos?

_____

7. Todos los muchachos mencionados a continuación son de la misma estatura (*height*). Si Ramón pesa 200 libras, Felipe pesa 180 libras y Paco pesa 175 libras, ¿quién es el menos gordo? Si Esteban pesa 105 libras, Pepe pesa 85 libras y Susana pesa 91 libras, ¿quién es el más flaco?

_____

8. De todos los deportes, ¿cuál le gusta más a Ud.? ¿Y cuál le gusta menos?

_____

9. ¿Cuál es la estación más bonita del año? ¿Por qué lo cree Ud.?

_____

_____

10. En su opinión, ¿quién fue el peor alcalde de su pueblo o ciudad?

_____

B. Complete las oraciones según los datos citados.

EJEMPLO: Juan tiene 20 años. Ana tiene 17 años.

Juan es ____*mayor que*____ Ana. Ana es ____*menor que*____ Juan.

1. Alfredo come cinco veces al día. Paula no come más que dos veces al día.

Alfredo come _____ Paula. Paula come _____ Alfredo.
2. David estudia una hora cada noche. Paco estudia media hora.

Paco estudia _____ David. David estudia _____ Paco.
3. Mi tía maneja el carro a 70 millas por hora. Mi tío sólo maneja a 45 millas por hora.

Mi tía maneja _____ mi tío. Mi tío maneja _____ mi tía.
4. Lola pesa 98 libras. Francisca pesa 98 libras también.

Lola pesa _____ Francisca. Francisca pesa _____ Lola.
5. *a.* Martín gana $400.000* al año, Julio gana $450.000 y Norma gana $550.000.

Norma es _____ los tres. Martín y Julio no son _____ como Norma.
   b. Pedro gana $4000 al año, Isabel gana $3500 y Alberto gana $3000.

Pedro gana _____ Isabel y Alberto. Alberto es _____ los tres.

*Note that Spanish uses a dot rather than a comma to set off thousands.

6. Yo compré más de seis discos. Mi amigo compró menos de cuatro discos.

   Yo compré _____ mi amigo. Mi amigo compró _____ yo.

7. Carlos mide cinco pies y ocho pulgadas. Efraín mide cinco pies y nueve pulgadas.

   Efraín es _____ Carlos. Carlos _____ Efraín.

8. Ayer Isabel corrió por dos horas. Marta corrió por una hora y media.

   Isabel corrió _____ Marta. Marta corrió _____ Isabel.

9. Anoche en la fiesta Jorge bebió seis botellas de soda. Manolo bebió ocho botellas.

   Jorge bebió _____ Manolo. Manolo bebió _____ Jorge.

10. Mi cuarto mide 250 pies cuadrados (square feet). El cuarto de Pancho mide 320 pies cuadrados. El cuarto de Quique mide 145 pies cuadrados.

    El cuarto de Quique es _____ de los tres cuartos.

    El cuarto de Pancho es _____ de los tres cuartos.

C. Conteste la pregunta añadiendo un sustantivo apropiado según se indica en el ejemplo.

> EJEMPLO: ¿Es José el más fuerte del grupo?
> *Sí, José es el chico (el muchacho, el jugador, el atleta) más fuerte del grupo.*

1. ¿Es el fútbol el más divertido de todos?

   _____

2. ¿Es el de Colón el más interesante de San Juan? (Use *monumento*.)

   _____

3. ¿Es ella la más popular de la escuela?

   _____

4. ¿Son ellos los mejores del equipo?

   _____

5. ¿Son ellas las más hermosas de la fiesta?

   _____

6. ¿Quién es el mayor de su familia?

   _____

7. ¿Quiénes eran los peores de la ciudad?

   _____

8. ¿Soy yo la más alta de nuestro club?

   _____

9. ¿Es Ud. el menos agradable de su familia?

   _____

10. ¿Son ellos los más corteses de esta clase?

    _____

D. Cambie las palabras subrayadas por una frase equivalente que tenga la forma *más (menos) . . . -mente.* Escriba la frase en el blanco a la derecha.

EJEMPLO: José escucha con más atención que
su hermano.

más atentamente

1. Tú conduces de un modo más peligroso que tu padre.

2. Allí viven con más seguridad que aquí.

3. Ella hace el trabajo con menos facilidad que yo.

4. Este camarero sirve las comidas con más amabilidad que el otro.

5. Nuestro profesor explica las lecciones de una manera más clara que antes.

6. En ese banco tratan a los clientes con menos cortesía que en mi banco.

7. Carlos canta con más tristeza que tú.

8. Mi madre prepara las comidas con más cuidado que mi padre.

9. Nuestros abuelos nos tratan con más paciencia que nuestros padres.

10. Las chicas del equipo corren con más rapidez que los chicos.

E. Traduzca al español:

1. Who are the best candidates in the party?

2. Johnny used to be the weakest boy in the class, but now he is the strongest.

3. My father's new car can run (*andar*) faster than you think.

4. We danced more than six hours last night at the discotheque.

5. Yesterday's show (*espectáculo*) was very* enjoyable—even more enjoyable than tonight's (*el de esta noche*).

6. She has more clothes than she needs.

*Use the *-ísimo* suffix instead of *muy*.

7. These roads are not as dangerous as those.

_____

8. This year our basketball team did not win as many games (*partidos*) as our soccer team.

_____

9. The youngest members of the government aren't always the worst.

_____

10. Our school's computers are larger than you think.

_____

11. At night you must drive more slowly than seems necessary.

_____

12. Do you play tennis as well as your cousin, or does he play better than you do?

_____

_____

13. Last night's basketball game was worse than we expected.

_____

14. The bookshop sent me more books than I had ordered.

_____

15. Today's guitar lesson was exceedingly long.

_____

CHAPTER **13**

Expressing "To Be" in Spanish

Review the idioms with **hacer** and **tener** on pages 271–272.

This chapter deals with various ways of translating *to be* into Spanish. Sometimes a verb other than **ser** or **estar** must be used. For example, in Spanish *I am hungry* becomes "I have hunger," which is expressed with a form of **tener.** We shall consider certain kinds of expressions in Spanish that have nothing in common except that their meanings are expressed in English by using the verb *to be.*

The Uses of *Estar* and *Ser*

1 Both **estar** and **ser** mean *to be* but they cannot be used interchangeably. The following are uses of **estar:**

a. *Location.* The verb **estar** answers the question *Where?*

¿Dónde **están** sus padres?	Where are your parents?
Mañana **estaremos** en Madrid.	Tomorrow we shall be in Madrid.
Londres **está** en Inglaterra.	London is in England.

b. *State of health, mood, and other reversible states*

Ayer **estuve enfermo** pero hoy **estoy bien.**	Yesterday I was sick but today I am well.
Mi madre **estará cansada** después de preparar la comida.	My mother will be tired after preparing dinner.
La botella **está vacía; estaba llena** antes.	The bottle is empty; it was full before.
Ahora los alumnos **están tristes,** pero después del examen **estarán alegres.**	Now the pupils are sad, but after the exam they will be happy.

c. With past participles used as adjectives

La ventana **estaba abierta*** hace cinco minutos. Ahora **está cerrada.**

The window was open five minutes ago. Now it is closed.

Esos libros **están** bien **escritos.**

These books are well written.

Mi reloj **está roto.**

My watch is broken.

d. As a helping verb in the progressive tenses (see chapter 6)

—¿Qué **están haciendo** ellos?

"What are they doing?"

—**Están mirando** la televisión.

"They are watching television."

2 The verb **ser** is used as follows:

a. To identify objects

"¿Qué **es** esto?" "**Es** una computadora."

"What is this?" "It is a computer."

b. To identify persons by nationality, religion, occupation, or relation

Sandra **es**
- norteamericana.
- católica.
- abogada.
- la hermana de Pablo.

Sandra is
- an American.
- (a) Catholic.
- a lawyer.
- Paul's sister.

c. With adjectives denoting a trait or characteristic

—¿Cómo **es** Margarita?

"How is Margaret?" (Describe her.)

—**Es** alta, delgada, y muy bonita.

"She is tall, slender, and very pretty."

Estas maletas **son** pesadas.†

These suitcases are heavy.

d. To indicate place of origin

—¿De dónde **es** su padre?

"Where is your father from?"

—**Es** de California.

"He is from California."

*Either **estar** or **ser** can be used with the past participle as adjective, but note the difference in meaning:

La puerta **estaba cerrada** cuando llegué.   The door was closed when I arrived.
La puerta **fue cerrada** por el portero.   The door was closed by the doorman.

The first sentence describes the state in which the door was found when someone got there. The second sentence is an example of the passive voice (see chapter 14) and describes what was done to the door by someone.

†The use of **ser** means the suitcases are heavy *when empty*. (They are "characteristically" heavy.) If they are heavy at a given moment because too much has been packed into them (a "reversible" state), use **estar:** "Estas maletas **están** pesadas."

e. To tell what something is made of

—¿De qué **es** su falda?	"What is her skirt made of?"
—**Es** de lana.	"It's made of wool (It is woolen)."

f. To tell the date, the season, what day it is, what time it is

—¿Cuál **es** la fecha?	"What is the date?"
—**Es** el 10 de octubre.	"It is October 10."
Es el otoño (la primavera).	It is autumn (spring).
"¿Qué día **es?**" "**Es** jueves."	"What day is it?" "It's Thursday."
"¿Qué hora **es?**" "**Son** las dos."	"What time is it?" "It's two o'clock."

g. With impersonal expressions

Es posible (necesario).	It is possible (necessary).
Era tarde.	It was late.

h. In the sense of "to take place"

La fiesta **será** en mi casa.	The party will be at my house.
¿Dónde **fue** el accidente?	Where was the accident? (Where did it occur?)

3   If **estar** is used instead of **ser** before some adjectives (see §2c), the verb has the sense of *to look, appear (to be):*

Es bonita.	She is pretty.
¡Qué bonita **está!**	How pretty she looks!
Mario **es** joven.	Mario is young.
Mario **está** más joven sin los bigotes.	Mario looks younger without his mustache.

Note how the meaning of an adjective can vary, depending on whether **ser** or **estar** is used:

ADJECTIVE	MEANING WITH Ser	MEANING WITH Estar
aburrido, -a	boring	bored
cansado, -a	tiresome	tired
cómodo, -a	comfortable (objects)	comfortable (people)
distraído, -a	absentminded	confused, distracted
inquieto, -a	restless (by nature)	worried, upset
listo, -a	clever, smart	ready
maduro, -a	mature	ripe
rico, -a	rich, wealthy	tasty, delicious

ADJECTIVE	MEANING WITH Ser	MEANING WITH Estar
soltero, -a*	(m) a bachelor; (f) an unmarried woman	unmarried, single
verde†	green	unripe
vivo, -a	lively	alive

4 *To be happy* is **ser feliz, estar contento(-a),** or **estar alegre.** The word **alegre** is closer in meaning to *merry, in high spirits.*

5 When **ser** or **estar** is followed by an adjective, the adjective agrees in gender and number with the subject of the verb: "**Ella** es **hermosa**"; "**Mis padres** están **ocupados.**"

Weather

6 The weather is described by using the third person singular form of the verb **hacer:**

¿Qué tiempo **hace** hoy?	How is the weather today?
Hace frío, pero ayer **hizo** fresco y viento.	It is cold, but yesterday it was cool and windy.
Creo que mañana **hará** mucho sol.	I think it will be very sunny tomorrow.

To Be Warm, Cold, Hungry, Thirsty, Sleepy

7 When *to be* means *to feel* and the subject is a person or an animal, *to be warm, cold,* etc., is expressed by using the verb **tener:**

Tenemos frío.	We are cold.
Tienen mucho calor.	They are hot (= very warm).
¿Tienes mucha hambre?	Are you very hungry?
Ella se acostó temprano porque **tenía mucho sueño.**	She went to bed early because she was very sleepy.
Si no bebemos ahora, **tendremos mucha sed** más tarde.	If we don't drink now, we will be very thirsty later.

***Es soltero,** *he is a bachelor,* describes a man who has never married. **Está soltero,** *he is unmarried* (*single*), describes his current marital status as a circumstance that might change.

†"Las hojas **son** verdes" describes the characteristic color of the leaves. "Las hojas **están** verdes todavía" tells us they haven't yet turned brown (as in early fall).

Note: If the subject is not a person or animal, *to be warm* = **estar caliente,** *to be cold* = **estar frío(-a):**

El agua **está fría.**	The water is cold.
La sopa **está muy caliente.**	The soup is hot.

There Is, There Are, There Was, There Were, There Will Be

8 **Hay,** *there is, there are,** is a form of the verb **haber.** The third person singular forms of **haber** are used in various tenses:

¿**Hay** un teléfono cerca de aquí?	Is there a telephone near here?
Había veinte policías en el sitio del accidente.	There were twenty police officers at the site of the accident.
Mañana **habrá** mucho que hacer.	Tomorrow there will be a lot to do.

"To Be" As a Helping Verb That Vanishes in Translation

9 When the English progressive tenses (*to be . . .-ing*) are translated into Spanish by using a simple tense (that is, by a verb form that is a single word), the helping verb *to be* disappears:

Lee una revista.	He is reading a magazine.
¿Con quién **hablabas?**	Whom were you speaking with?

However, *to be* as helping verb in the progressive tenses becomes **estar** in the corresponding forms of the Spanish progressive: ¿**Qué estabas haciendo allí?** *What were you doing there?* See chapter 6.

___ EJERCICIOS ___

A. Complete cada oración con una forma de *ser, estar, tener, hacer,* o *haber.* Si el sentido de la oración no indica el tiempo del verbo, escoja cualquier tiempo apropiado.

EJEMPLO: Me gusta nadar en el lago cuando ___*hace*___ calor pero ayer el agua ___*estaba*___ muy fría.

*When this expression is used to "point to" someone or something, the Spanish equivalent is **allí está(n).** Note the difference in meaning:

Hay un libro en la mesa.	There is a book on the table.
Allí está el libro que perdiste.	There is the book that you lost.

1. Hoy _____ frío afuera. Por eso, yo no _____ contento.

2. _____ imposible comer las manzanas porque _____ verdes.

3. El aire de nuestra ciudad _____ muy contaminado hoy día.

4. Mi tanque _____ vacío. ¿ _____ una estación de gasolina cerca de aquí?

5. Esta noche mi padre no _____ de buen humor porque _____ sueño.

6. Isabel, ¿ _____ tú lista para salir ahora?

7. El mes pasado mis padres _____ muy inquietos porque no _____ suficiente dinero para pagar todos los gastos. (Do not use *tener*.)

8. ¿Qué tiempo _____ ayer en la ciudad cuando nosotros _____ en el campo?

9. Mi abuelo no _____ muy viejo; de todos modos, _____ joven para su edad, ¿no es verdad?

10. ¿Qué _____ Uds. haciendo?

11. Ayer _____ domingo y muchas tiendas _____ cerradas.

12. Nosotras _____ muy contentas porque mañana _____ de vacaciones.

13. ¿Cómo _____ su profesora de español? Me dicen que ella _____ simpática y hermosa.

14. "¿Qué _____ aquel objeto?" "Debe de _____ un Objeto Volador No Identificado (OVNI)". "¿Cómo lo sabes?" "No puedo identificarlo".

15. "¿ _____ de España ese doctor?" "No; él _____ de Portugal y sus padres _____ de Inglaterra."

16. ¿Qué hora _____ cuando llegaron sus abuelos?

17. La conferencia _____ en Chicago el año pasado. Entre los conferencistas _____ algunos sabios eminentes. Los discursos _____ aburridos. _____ difícil mantenerse despierto. Por lo visto, el público _____ aburrido o _____ sueño.

18. Ayer _____ un horrible accidente de tráfico en la esquina. No sé si los ocupantes del coche _____ muertos o vivos.

19. Nosotros _____ cansados de ver los mismos programas de televisión cada semana.

20. Mamá, tú _____ una excelente cocinera. Esta noche la comida _____ muy rica, y yo _____ mucha hambre.

21. En el almacén la madre se dio cuenta de que sus dos hijos _____ perdidos. Pero pronto _____ encontrados por uno de los empleados.

22. Paula, tú debes _____ en casa antes de medianoche. Si no, yo

_____ enfadada e inquieta.

23. Mis tíos, que _____ de México, y que ahora _____ en el Canadá,

nos escriben que allí ellos _____ mucho frío.

24. Dicen que mañana _____ muchas personas en la reunión y que todos

_____ muy interesados en el programa.

25. "Creo que los alumnos _____ aburridos." "Ud. _____ razón,

ellos necesitan un descanso porque ya han estudiado mucho y empiezan a

_____ sueño."

B. Aquí están unas *respuestas*. ¿Cuáles son las preguntas? Escriba una pregunta para cada respuesta.

1. Somos de Alemania. _____

2. Es de plata. _____

3. Están en la cancha de tenis. _____

4. Hay rosbif y papas fritas. _____

5. No, ella es soltera. _____

6. Sí, y también tiene sueño. _____

7. Él estaba escribiendo a máquina su informe semestral. _____

_____

8. Es la una y media. _____

9. Será en nuestra casa. _____

10. Soy arquitecto. _____

11. Es muy cómodo y práctico. _____

12. Está en el sótano de mi casa. _____

13. Creo que hará frio. _____

14. Es un nuevo tipo de raqueta. _____

15. Fue abierta por Julio. _____

16. No es posible porque está roto. _____

17. La bandera es roja, blanca y azul. _____

18. Quiero ser dentista. _____

19. Me acuesto. _____

20. Ellos están muy bien, gracias. _____

C. Escriba una oración con las expresiones dadas, usando el verbo *ser* o *estar*. (Cambie la forma del adjetivo si no concuerda con el sujeto del verbo.)

EJEMPLO: mañana/las tiendas/cerrado

Mañana las tiendas estarán cerradas.

1. en este momento/los alumnos/triste

   _____

2. anoche/el televisor/roto

   _____

3. el año próximo/las cosas/diferente

   _____

4. la profesora/siempre/simpático

   _____

5. hoy día/los jóvenes/más maduro

   _____

6. dentro de tres días/la fruta/maduro

   _____

7. en estos días/tales leyes/necesario

   _____

8. esta noche/la fiesta/en mi casa

   _____

9. ayer por la tarde/el Presidente/en Nueva York

   _____

10. el mes que viene/las hojas/verde*

   _____

D. Traduzca al español:

1. *a.* They say it is cold today, but I am warm.

   _____

   b. How was the weather yesterday? Was it windy?

   _____

2. *a.* Where are your relatives from?

   _____

   b. Some of them are from Spain; others are from the United States.

   _____

3. Our teacher (*f.*) was angry yesterday because we weren't attentive.

   _____

4. *a.* How many computers are there in your school?

   _____

   b. There are only six, but next year there will be thirty.

   _____

5. *a.* Are you comfortable, Miss Jones?

   _____

   b. Yes, thank you. This chair is very comfortable.

   _____

*See the second footnote on page 123.

6. The colors of her dress are very bright ("lively").

_____

7. *a.* Where was the concert last night?

_____

   b. It was at the stadium. Next month it will be at our school.

_____

   c. Will you be there?

_____

8. In certain places the water is polluted. You have to be careful.

_____

9. Although my grandmother is old, she looks young for her age (*para su edad*).

_____

10. *a.* What is your uncle?

_____

   b. He used to be a policeman, but now he's a fireman.

_____

11. Can you be here tomorrow at ten o'clock? There will be some interesting guests.

_____

_____

12. How many students were there at the basketball game on Saturday?

_____

13. Although she seems to be lazy, she is very hard-working.

_____

14. *a.* It was one thirty in the morning and we were very sleepy.

_____

   b. Where were you (*vosotros*) at that time?

_____

15. *a.* Is your sister married?

_____

   b. No, she is single, and she says she is quite happy.

_____

16. *a.* Is the television set broken?

_____

   b. Yes, it was broken by my brother yesterday afternoon.

_____

17. *a.* (*Use a simple tense.*) What are they doing now?

_____

   b. They are playing baseball.

_____

c. Yesterday they were running for three hours.

_____

d. Tomorrow they will be preparing ("themselves") for the sports competitions.

_____

18. *a.* The water in the bathtub (*la bañera*) is cold.

_____

b. The waters of the Arctic (*del Ártico*) are cold.

_____

19. *a.* The child is very clever. She learns everything quickly.

_____

b. Yes, she will soon be ready to (*para*) go to kindergarten.*

_____

20. The show (*espectáculo*) was lots of fun.

_____

*commonly called *el kindergarten* in Spanish

Altamira: Arte Rupestre

Como otros países del mundo, España no carece de maravillas naturales. Cerca del pueblo de Santillana del Mar, y no muy lejos del Mar Cantábrico, se encuentran las famosas Cuevas de Altamira, que hasta hace algunos años fueron una gran atracción turística. Descubiertas en el año 1869, cuando un perro cayó en una de las cuevas, no despertaron ningún interés hasta 1875, cuando se iniciaron unas exploraciones.

Al entrar en las cuevas hay que pasar por unos pasillos muy estrechos en donde se ven estalagmitas y estalactitas, comunes en toda cueva que se visite. Al final de un caminito se entra en una cueva que tiene un techo muy bajo. Si el visitante no mira hacia arriba, no se da cuenta de lo maravilloso de la cueva: en el techo hay pinturas de animales—toros, bisontes, ciervos, caballos—todos dibujados en colores. Los animales parecen estar dormidos.

Se cree que estos animales fueron pintados sobre las rocas de las cuevas hace unos veinte mil años por los cazadores prehistóricos que vivían en los contornos. Algunos historiadores creen que los cazadores amaban a los animales que pintaban. Otros creen que los pintaban a fin de poder dominarlos. Pero no se ha explicado con exactitud cómo los cazadores podían pintar los animales en el techo.

Por desgracia hoy día las visitas a las cuevas se limitan sólo a ciertos grupos que deben obtener permiso para visitarlas. Esto se debe al peligro que existe actualmente dentro de las cuevas.

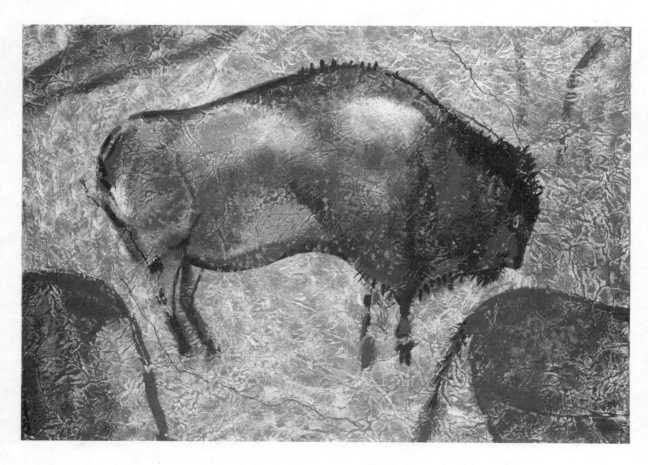

CHAPTER 14
The Passive Voice

In the active voice, the subject of the verb performs the action: *John wrote the letters.* In the passive voice, the subject of the verb receives the action: *The letters were written by John.*

1 The passive voice in Spanish consists of a form of **ser** + a past participle: "Las cartas **fueron escritas** por Juan." In this example, **Juan** is called the agent or doer. Note that **escritas** agrees in number and gender with the subject (**Las cartas**). Some further examples:

ACTIVE VOICE	PASSIVE VOICE
Los alumnos leen los libros.	Los libros **son leídos** por los alumnos.
The students read the books.	The books are read by the students.
El padre castigó a los hijos.	Los hijos **fueron castigados** por el padre.
The father punished the children.	The children were punished by the father.
Los turistas visitarán la ciudad.	La ciudad **será visitada** por los turistas.
The tourists will visit the city.	The city will be visited by the tourists.

2 The passive voice can be used in any tense:

La casa **es** destruida por el viento.	The house is destroyed by the wind.
fue	was
será	will be
sería	would be
ha sido	has been
había sido	had been
habría sido	would have been

3 Do not confuse the passive voice with a similar construction, **estar** + *past participle,* in which the participle is used as a descriptive adjective. Note the difference in meaning:

a. La tienda **fue abierta.**   The store was opened.
b. La tienda **estaba abierta.**   The store was open.

Sentence *a* is in the passive voice and tells us that something *was done to* the store—it was opened by someone—although the agent, or doer, is not mentioned. Sentence *b* merely describes the store: it was open. (See also the footnote on page 121.)

4 If the agent is mentioned, *by* = **por:**

Fue saludada **por** sus parientes.	She was greeted by her relatives.

If the passive verb expresses a thought or feeling, *by* = **de:** *

Era amada **de** todos sus amigos.	She was loved by all her friends.
Nuestro profesor es admirado **de** sus alumnos.	Our teacher is admired by his pupils.

The Passive *Se*

5 The active voice is preferred to the passive, which is generally avoided, if possible, by using an "active" construction with passive meaning:

Aquí **se habla** español.	Spanish is spoken here.

The reflexive pronoun **se** + a third-person verb form can replace the passive voice if the subject is a thing[†] and no agent is mentioned. The verb is singular or plural, depending on whether its subject is singular or plural:

En esa tienda . . .	In that store . . .
. . . **se vende** leche.	. . . milk is sold.
. . . **se venden** sombreros.	. . . hats are sold.
Se mostraron varios cuadros.	Several pictures were shown.

When **se** is passive, the noun subject most often *follows* the verb.

6 If the subject is a person, the passive voice can be avoided by using **se** with the singular form of the verb. In this construction, the passive subject becomes the object of the active verb:

Los ladrones fueron detenidos ⟶ **Se detuvo** a los ladrones.
  The thieves were arrested.
        Fueron detenidos ⟶ **Se les detuvo.**
  They were arrested.

---

*This is no longer true in most Hispanic countries, where **por** is used in almost all cases.

[†]If the subject is a *person*, then **se** may have its usual reflexive meaning:

La niña **se vio** en el espejo.	The child saw herself in the mirror.
But:	
La película **se vio** en la televisión.	The film was seen on television.

El cantante será oído $\longrightarrow$ **Se oirá** al cantante.
   The singer will be heard.
         Será oído $\longrightarrow$ **Se le oirá.**
   He will be heard.

María no ha sido invitada $\longrightarrow$ **No se ha invitado** a María.
   Mary has not been invited.
      No ha sido invitada $\longrightarrow$ **No se la ha invitado.**
   She has not been invited.

Note:

a. The **se** construction cannot be used as an alternative to the passive voice if the agent is mentioned.

b. In the **se** construction, the noun object can be replaced by a direct object pronoun, except that **lo** becomes **le** ("se **le** oirá") and **los** becomes **les** ("se **les** detuvo").

c. Some verbs cannot be used in the passive voice if the passive subject is a person. For example, *I was given the books* cannot be translated word for word into Spanish since "yo fui dado" would mean that "yo," the passive subject, was the thing that was given! For the same reason, *they will be paid* cannot be expressed as "serán pagados" unless *they* refers to bills, debts, or cash. When the English equivalents of verbs like **dar** and **pagar** are used passively with "personal" subjects (*we were given, I was paid, they are asked, he is answered,* etc.), they must be rephrased for translation with the passive **se** or some other "active" construction:

I was given the books = The books were given to me.
                  Se me dieron los libros.
            Or, preferably:
                  Me dieron los libros.

We will be paid tomorrow = They will pay us tomorrow.
                  Se nos pagará mañana.
               Or, preferably:
                  Nos pagarán mañana.

The Indefinite *Se*

7 **Se** is used with the third person singular form of the verb to express an indefinite subject:

Se dice que ella es rica.	It is said (People say, They say) that she is rich.
Se creía que eran tontos.	People believed (It was believed, They believed) that they were foolish.

No se hablará en esta clase.	There will be no talking in this class.
Para subir al autobús, **se necesita** tener el importe exacto.	To get on the bus, you need (one needs) to have the exact amount.
Se puede jugar al tenis aquí.	You (One) can play tennis here. (Tennis can be played here.)

The indefinite **se** has several possible translations: *they, people, you (= people), one.* The last two examples, above, can be seen as further instances of the passive **se** explained in §5, the only difference being that the subject is an infinitive phrase instead of a noun. Note the similarity:

Se necesita dinero.	Money is needed.
Se necesita tener dinero.	You need (One needs) to have money. ("To-have-money is needed.")

EJERCICIOS

A. Cambie la oración de la voz activa a la voz pasiva o viceversa.

EJEMPLOS: Mi madre preparó la comida anoche.
Anoche la comida fue preparada por mi madre.

¿Cuándo fueron arrestados los criminales por la policía?
¿Cuándo arrestó la policía a los criminales?

1. ¿Cuántos alumnos serán castigados por el director?

_____

2. Mi abuelo construyó nuestra casa hace treinta años.

_____

3. Tres candidatos fueron elegidos por los ciudadanos.

_____

4. La nueva compañía empleará a mil trabajadores.

_____

5. Mi amigo José es admirado por todos sus compañeros de clase.

_____

B. Repita la oración, usando un pronombre en lugar de las palabras subrayadas.

EJEMPLO: Se respeta mucho a nuestro profesor de español.
Se le respeta mucho.

1. Se invitó a la fiesta a todos nuestros parientes.

_____

2. Se visitará a mi tía en noviembre.

_____

3. No se quiere mucho a ese chico.

_____

4. Se saludará <u>al Presidente</u> cuando llegue a la ciudad.

_____

5. Siempre se ayudaba <u>a los pobres de ese país</u>.

_____

C. Cambie la oración de la voz pasiva a la construcción reflexiva (con *se*) o viceversa.

> EJEMPLOS: Se ve a muchas personas en la feria.
> *Muchas personas son vistas en la feria.*
>
> Los niños fueron llevados al cine.
> *Se llevó a los niños al cine.*

1. No se vio claramente al actor.

_____

2. Mucha gente fue alabada durante el discurso.

_____

3. ¿Por qué no se detuvo al asesino?

_____

4. Esos cantantes siempre son aplaudidos.

_____

5. Se regañó a los chicos traviesos.

_____

D. Aquí están algunas *respuestas*. ¿Cuáles son las preguntas? Escriba una pregunta para cada respuesta.

> EJEMPLO: Se venden en esa tienda.
> *¿Dónde se venden artículos para la casa?*

1. Se oyeron en la calle.

_____

2. Se compran en una farmacia.

_____

3. Se enseñará mañana.

_____

4. Se habla portugués.

_____

5. Se puede ver en la televisión.

_____

6. Se entra por aquella puerta.

_____

7. No, eso se prohíbe en la escuela.

_____

8. Se juega en una cancha.

_____

9. Se corta con un cuchillo.

_____

10. Se publicó el mes pasado.

_____

E. Conteste con oraciones completas:

1. ¿En qué sitio se puede bailar toda la noche?

_____

2. ¿Dónde se sirven buenas comidas en su barrio?

_____

3. ¿Por quién fue construida su casa?

_____

4. ¿Dónde se pueden comprar los mejores discos de música rock en su ciudad (pueblo)?

_____

5. ¿Cómo se sacan buenas notas en la escuela?

_____

6. En su opinión, ¿a quiénes se debe admirar?

_____

7. Además del inglés, ¿qué idiomas se hablan en los Estados Unidos?

_____

8. ¿Por quién fue inventada la luz eléctrica?

_____

9. ¿Qué se pudo ver en la televisión el domingo pasado por la tarde?

_____

10. ¿Dónde se jugarán los próximos Juegos Olímpicos?

_____

11. ¿Cómo se podía cruzar el Océano Atlántico en el siglo XIX?

_____

12. ¿Qué cambios importantes se han hecho en su escuela durante el año pasado?

_____

13. ¿Cómo se podrá evitar otra guerra mundial?

_____

14. En el siglo XIV, ¿qué se creía con respecto a la forma de la Tierra?

_____

15. ¿Qué se sabe acerca de los OVNIs (objetos voladores no identificados)?

_____

F. Traduzca al español, usando la forma _se_ donde sea posible. El asterisco (*) significa que se debe traducir la oración de dos maneras.

1. _a._ What do people say about video games?

_____

    b. They say the games are popular with (*entre*) the youngsters.

_____

2. In what year and by whom was the telephone invented?

_____

3. When my grandfather was a child, you could buy a meal for a dollar. What can you buy for a dollar nowadays?

_____

_____

4. *How many automobiles were sold in the United States last year?

_____

_____

5. *a.* The principal of our school is respected by all the students.

_____

    b. Yesterday he was given an award.

_____

6. *a.* When will the results of the election be known? (Use the plural form *elecciones*.)

_____

    b. They were known last night but they haven't yet been announced.

_____

7. *a.* Some serious errors were made on our Spanish exam.

_____

    b. Will they be made again?

_____

8. *a.* *Our school was built fifteen years ago.

_____

_____

    b. The old building had been destroyed by a fire.

_____

9. *a.* Smoking is not permitted in the front section of the plane.

_____

    b. It is also prohibited in many public buildings.

_____

10. *a.* I have been told that you need tickets to see the exhibit.

_____

    b. You don't need to buy tickets, they are free. They can be obtained at the box office.

_____

_____

11. *a.* *At what time is dinner served at your house?

_____

_____

   b. *It will be served tonight at seven o'clock.

   _____

12. *a.* How many people were hurt in the train accident?

   _____

   b. And how many children were rescued?

   _____

13. *a.* His book will be published next month by a large publishing house.

   _____

   b. *When was his last book written?

   _____

14. There was a lot of drinking, singing, and dancing at last night's party. ("One drank, sang, and . . . a lot . . . ")

   _____

   _____

15. *a.* How many houses were destroyed by the flood?

   _____

   b. I don't know, but our house was saved by the firefighters.

   _____

CHAPTER 15 Pronouns

Subject Pronouns

yo, I
tú, you (*fam.*)
usted (Ud.), you (*formal*)
él, he; **ella,** she

nosotros(-as), we
vosotros(-as), you (*fam.*)
ustedes (Uds.), you
ellos, ellas, they

1 Since the verb ending usually indicates the subject, these pronouns are often omitted. They are expressed chiefly for clarity, emphasis, or courtesy:

Ella tocaba la radio mientras **yo** leía.   She played the radio while I read.
Nosotras lo haremos, no ellos.   *We* will do it, not they.
¿Desea **usted** ver el menú?   Do you wish to see the menu?

2 *It* as subject pronoun is generally not expressed in Spanish:

"¿Qué es?" "Es una estrella."   "What is it?" "It is a star."

3 *You* as subject can be expressed in four ways:

a. **Tú,** the familiar form, is used when speaking to family members, close friends, classmates, children, and animals. Its plural, **vosotros(-as),** is used only in Spain. In Spanish America, the plural of **tú** is **ustedes.**

b. **Usted** is the formal or "polite" form. Its plural is **ustedes.**

Prepositional Pronouns

para **mí,** for me
sin **ti,** without you (*fam.*)
con **usted (Ud.),** with you
detrás de **él,** behind him (*or* it, *m*)
delante de **ella,** in front of her (*or* it, *f*)

cerca de **nosotros(-as),** near us
para **vosotros(-as),** for you (*Spain only*)
con **ustedes (Uds.),** with you
sin **ellos (ellas),** without them

conmigo, with me   **contigo,** with you (*fam.*)
consigo, with you, him, her, them

Hablábamos **de ella.**   We were talking (We talked) about her (about it, *f*).

Hablan **de sí.**   They are talking about themselves.

4 The prepositional pronouns are the same as the subject pronouns except for **mí, ti,** and **sí.**

5 The form **consigo** is used only when the object of the preposition and the subject of the preceding verb are the same person:

Ella trajo su paraguas **consigo.**   She brought her umbrella with her. (She brought along her umbrella.)

But:
Marta vino **con ella.**   Martha came with her.

6 *It* as object of a preposition is either **él** or **ella,** depending on the gender of the noun it stands for:

Era **un edificio** bajo, y cerca de **él** estaban unos árboles altos.   It was a low building, and near it stood some tall trees.

"¿Dónde está **la casa?**" "Nos acercamos a **ella.**"   "Where is the house?" "We are approaching it."

The Personal A

Before we review the Spanish object pronouns, which are discussed in pages 142–147, we must first review the use of a preposition called the personal **a.**

7 The direct object of a verb may be a thing—"I see *the house*"—or a person—"I see *Philip* (I visit *my friends*)." In Spanish, if the direct object is a noun denoting persons, it is preceded by **a:** "Veo **a** Felipe (Visito **a** mis amigos)."

The direct object answers the question *what?* (**¿qué?**) or *whom?* (**¿a quién, -es?**):

¿Qué ven ellos?   **¿A quién** ven ellos?
What do they see?   Whom do they see?

Ellos ven el edificio.   Ellos ven **al** cartero.
They see the building.   They see the mailman.

¿Qué no comprendió?   **¿A quiénes** no comprendió?
What didn't he understand?   Whom didn't he understand?

No comprendió la regla.   No comprendió **a** sus profesores.
He did not understand the rule.   He did not understand his teachers.

Note that the personal **a** conforms to the rule **a** + **el** = **al:** "Ellos ven **al** cartero."

Personal *A* and Prepositional *A*

8 The indirect object answers the question *to whom?*. Note the following Spanish and English equivalents:

DIRECT OBJECT	INDIRECT OBJECT
¿A quién vieron?	**¿A quién** escriben?
Whom did they see?	To whom are they writing?
Vieron a su abuelo.	Escriben **a su abuelo.**
They saw their grandfather.	They are writing to their grandfather.

The preposition in the first column is the personal **a,** which cannot be translated into English, whereas the preposition in the second column means *to.* For convenience, we shall call the second kind the prepositional **a** (although both kinds are, of course, prepositions).

In the examples above, it does not seem to matter whether **a** is personal or prepositional, that is, whether the noun is the direct or the indirect object of the verb ("Vieron **a su abuelo**"; "Escriben **a su abuelo.**"). In either case, if the noun denotes persons, it is preceded by **a.** The difference becomes important, however, if the noun is replaced by a pronoun:

Vieron a su abuelo.   Escriben a su abuelo.

Lo vieron.   **Le** escriben.
They saw *him.*   They are writing *to him.*

This difference is discussed more fully in the section on object pronouns.

Practice A: Complete the Spanish sentence, using the personal *a* if it is required.

1. *a.* Do you admire our president?

   ¿Admira Ud. _____?
   b. Do they admire the works of art?

   ¿Admiran _____?
   c. Does Michael admire his uncle?

   ¿Admira Miguel _____?
2. *a.* Did she see the monuments?

   ¿Vio ella _____?

  b. Did they see their relatives?

   ¿Vieron ellos _____?
  c. Did you see the paintings?

   ¿Viste _____?
3. *a.* I greeted my friends.

   Saludé _____ .
  b. Whom did you greet?

   ¿ _____ saludó Ud.?
  c. We greeted the mayor.

   Saludamos _____ .
4. *a.* I'm going to visit my grandparents.

   Voy a visitar _____ .
  b. We are going to visit the country.

   Vamos a visitar _____ .
  c. They are going to visit the school.

   Van a visitar _____ .
5. *a.* Do you believe the story?   ¿Crees _____?

  b. Does he believe Mary?   ¿Cree _____?

  c. Whom do they believe?   ¿ _____ creen ellos?

  Practice B: Write a question that can be answered by the given sentence. Start each question with *Qué, A quién,* or *A quiénes.*

 1. Vi a mi tío.   ¿ _____?

 2. Escribimos las cartas.   ¿ _____?

 3. Oímos a nuestros padres.   ¿ _____?

 4. Visitamos esa ciudad.   ¿ _____?

 5. Llamo a mi amiga.   ¿ _____?

 6. Hablé a mi tío.   ¿ _____?

 7. Enviamos los discos a José y a María. ¿ _____?

 8. Compraron unas cintas.   ¿ _____?

 9. Lavé el coche.   ¿ _____?

10. Invitaremos a todos nuestros amigos. ¿ _____?

Object Pronouns

9   The object pronouns include the reflexive pronouns. Some object pronouns are direct ("we saw *him*"), some are indirect ("we gave *him* the book"). The pronouns **me, te, nos,** and **os** may be either direct or indirect:

DIRECT	INDIRECT	REFLEXIVE
Me llamó.	**Me** mandó una carta.	**Me** lavé.
He called me.	He sent me a letter.	I washed myself.
Te vi ayer.	**Te** vendió el carro.	**Te** compraste un vestido.
I saw you yesterday.	He sold you the car.	You bought yourself a dress.
Nos saludaron.	**Nos** darán el dinero.	**Nos** vestimos ahora.
They greeted us.	They will give us the money.	We are dressing ourselves (getting dressed) now.
No **os** conocen.	**Os** devolverá los libros.	¿A qué hora **os** levantáis?
They don't know you.	He will return the books to you.	At what time do you get up?

Os, the familiar plural, is used only in Spain. Elsewhere, the plural of **te** is **los** or **les** (see below).

10 Here are the other object pronouns. The *you* among their meanings is the polite form of address corresponding to **usted(-es):**

DIRECT

***lo** { you, *m.* / him / it, *m.* **la** { you, *f.* / her / it, *f.* **los** { you, *pl.* / them **las** { you, *f. pl.* / them

INDIRECT

le { (to) you / (to) him / (to) her / (to) it   **les** { (to) you, *pl.* / (to) them

REFLEXIVE[†]

se   yourself (-selves), himself, herself, itself, themselves

In the following examples, each object pronoun is given only one meaning in English for the sake of simplicity:

DIRECT	INDIRECT	REFLEXIVE
Lo oigo.	**Le** presto dinero.	
I hear him.	I lend him money.	
Ella **lo** lava.	Ella **le** mandó una tarjeta.	Ella **se** lava.
She washes him.	She sent him a postcard.	She washes herself.

*In Spain, **le** is used instead of **lo,** except when **lo** = *it*.

†Reflexive pronouns can be either direct or indirect objects without changing their form.

DIRECT	INDIRECT	REFLEXIVE
La vi ayer. I saw her yesterday.	**Le** hablé. I spoke to her.	
Los visitaré. I will visit them.	**Les** escribiré. I will write to them.	**Se** comprarán unos discos. They will buy themselves some records.
Las invité a la fiesta. I invited them (f.) to the party.	**Les** mostré el cuadro. I showed them the picture.	
Lo cocino bien. I cook it well.	**Le** añado sal. I add salt to it.	**Se** llama puchero. It is called ("calls itself") stew.

11 The indirect object pronoun replaces (or stands for) a phrase beginning with **a:**

Envío unas fotos **a mis padres.**   I'm sending my parents some photos.

Les envío unas fotos.   I'm sending them some photos.

Clarifying Phrases

12 Since the object pronouns shown in §10 have several possible meanings, the intended meaning can be more clearly expressed, if necessary, by adding a phrase such as **a Ud(s).**, **a él, a ella, a ellos,** or **a ellas:**

Las invité **a Uds. (a ellas)** a la fiesta.   I invited you (them, *f*) to the party.
Le presté dinero **a él (a ella).**   I lent him (her) money. (I lent money to him [her].)

¿Puede Ud. repetir en inglés el men-   Can you repeat Paul's message in En-
saje de Pablo? No **lo** entiendo **a Ud.**   glish? I don't understand you (him).
(a él).

In the last example, no clarifying phrase is necessary if **lo** = *it:*

¿. . . el mensaje de Pablo? No **lo** en-   . . . Paul's message? I don't understand
tiendo.   it.

The Redundant Object Pronoun

13 Normally, the object of a verb may be either a noun or the pronoun that is substituted for it:

Hablo **a María.**   I speak to Mary.
Le hablo.   I speak to her.

¿Mandaste los discos **a tus amigos?**	Did you send the records to your friends?
¿Les mandaste los discos?	Did you send them the records?

In Spanish, however, it is very common to express both the noun object and its pronoun substitute in the same sentence:

Le hablo **a María.**	I speak to Mary.
¿Les mandaste los discos **a tus amigos?**	Did you send the records to your friends?

This is done especially with the indirect objects **le** and **les.** In sentences like the above, the pronoun is called redundant because it adds nothing to the meaning of the sentence. The redundant pronoun cannot be translated into English.

Double Object Pronouns

14 A verb may have two pronouns as its object:

Si no pueden venir, **nos lo** dirán.	If they can't come, they will tell us so.
"¿Dónde obtuviste los libros?" "Marcos **me los** dio."	"Where did you get the books?" "Mark gave them to me."
Si no necesita su bicicleta, **¿te la** prestará?	If he doesn't need his bicycle, will he lend it to you?

When two object pronouns are used together, the *in*direct object—usually a person—comes first.

15 If both object pronouns begin with the letter *l*, the first, or indirect object, changes to **se:**

Yo **le** mostré las fotos + Yo **las** mostré a Susana
I showed her the photos   I showed them to Susan

= Yo ~~le~~ **las** . . .

se las mostré.   I showed them to her

Similarly:

Yo **les** describí el accidente.   I described the accident to them.

Yo **se** lo describí.   I described it to them.

16 *a.* Since **se** has several possible meanings, the intended meaning can be more clearly indicated by adding a clarifying phrase like those shown in §12:

Yo **se** lo describí **a ellos (a Uds.).**	I described it to them (to you).

"¿Le* mandaron los cuadros a Luis?"
"No **se** los mandaron **a él, se** los mandaron **a Ud.** ¿No los recibió Ud.?"

"Did they send the pictures to Louis?"
"They did not send them to him, they sent them to you. Didn't you receive them?"

b. **Se** is often used redundantly:

Los mandaron a Luis.
But more commonly:
Se los mandaron a Luis.   }   They sent them to Louis.

Position of Object Pronouns

17As we saw in the preceding examples, object pronouns precede the conjugated verb form:

"¿Recibiste las fotos?" "Sí, ellos **me las** dieron ayer."

"Did you receive the photos?" "Yes, they gave them to me yesterday."

Other positions:

As Object of an Infinitive

The pronoun is attached to the infinitive:

Después de saludar**me,** salió de la sala.

After greeting me, he left the room.

If the infinitive follows a conjugated verb form, the pronoun is either attached to the infinitive or placed directly before the other verb:

No puedo llamar**te** mañana.
No **te** puedo llamar mañana.   }   I can't call you tomorrow.

¿Quiere Ud. prestár**melo?**
¿Me lo quiere Ud. prestar?   }   Will you lend it to me?

When a double object pronoun is attached to the infinitive, an accent mark is placed on the vowel of the infinitive ending (. . . prest**á**rmelo).

As Object of a Present Participle (*Gerundio*)

The pronoun is either attached to the present participle or placed directly before the helping verb (usually a form of **estar**):

*Notice the redundant object pronoun.

Estamos mandándo**lo.**
Lo estamos mandando.   }   We are sending it.

¿Estás prometiéndo**noslo?**
¿Nos lo estás prometiendo?   }   Are you promising it to us?

If pronouns are attached to the *gerundio,* an accent mark is placed on the vowel that is stressed when the word is pronounced *without* attached pronouns: prometi**e**ndo—prometi**é**ndoselo.*

The participle can also be used without a helping verb:

Entregándo**selo,** se fue en seguida.   Handing it to her, he left at once.

As Object of a Command

AFFIRMATIVE	NEGATIVE
Escríba**le** una carta.	No **le** escriba una carta.
Write him (her) a letter.	Do not write him (her) a letter.
Escríba**sela.**	No **se la** escriba.
Write it to him (her).	Do not write it to him (her).

(*a*) The object pronouns are attached to the verb in an affirmative command, precede the verb in a negative command. When a single or double object pronoun is attached to the verb, an accent mark is placed over the vowel that is normally stressed in pronunciation: escriba—escr*í*bale, escr*í*basela.†

(*b*) For greater clarity, a phrase like those shown in §12 can be added:

Escríba**le a ella.**   Write to *her.*
No **se** lo mande **a ellos.**   Don't send it to *them.*

__ EJERCICIOS _____

A. Repita la oración usando un pronombre en lugar de las palabras subrayadas. Algunas oraciones deben cambiarse de dos maneras.

EJEMPLOS: ¿Leyeron Uds. la novela?   No puedo recordar su nombre.
           La leyeron Uds.?   (*a*) *No puedo recordarlo.*
                                  (*b*) *No lo puedo recordar.*

1. ¿Cuándo enviarás las cintas? _____

2. ¿Quiere Ud. leer este libro? (*a*) _____

    (*b*) _____

*If you prefer to count syllables, use this rule: If one pronoun is attached, the accent mark falls on the *third* syllable from the last (pro-me-**tién**-do-lo); if two pronouns are attached, the accent mark falls on the *fourth* syllable from the last (pro-me-**tién**-do-nos-lo).

†No accent appears if the word formed by the verb and its attached pronoun consists of only two syllables: **dime,** *tell me;* **ponlo aquí,** *put it here.*

3. Estamos cantando <u>la nueva canción</u>. (*a*) _____

   (*b*) _____

4. Compre Ud. <u>este coche</u>. _____

5. No coman Uds. <u>esa fruta</u>. _____

6. ¿Por qué no miran Uds. <u>la televisión</u>? _____

7. ¿Cuándo construyeron <u>esos edificios</u>? _____

8. No pudimos ver <u>la película</u>. (*a*) _____

   (*b*) _____

9. ¿Estaban Uds. tomando <u>el desayuno</u> con sus amigos? (*a*) _____

   _____ (*b*) _____

10. ¿Harás <u>los ejercicios</u> con nosotras más tarde?

   _____

B. Siga como en el ejercicio A, usando *dos* pronombres.

> EJEMPLOS: Denles Uds. <u>el paquete</u> a ellos.   ¿Vas a traernos <u>los discos</u>?
> *Dénselo Uds. a ellos.*   (*a*) *¿Vas a traérnoslos?*
>   (*b*) *¿Nos los vas a traer?*

1. No quiero mostrarte <u>las fotos</u>. (*a*) _____

   (*b*) _____

2. La madre estaba leyendo <u>el cuento</u> a su hija. (*a*) _____

   _____ (*b*) _____

3. ¿Cuándo me enviarás <u>la carta</u>? _____

4. Yo le ofrecí <u>diez dólares</u> a ella. _____

5. El comerciante logró venderles <u>la ropa</u>. (*a*) _____

   _____ (*b*) _____

6. No le preste Ud. <u>el dinero</u> a él. _____

7. ¿Cuándo les diste <u>las cintas</u>? _____

8. Cuéntenos Ud. <u>su historia</u>. _____

9. No le hemos dicho <u>la verdad</u>. _____

10. Os van a explicar <u>la lección</u>. (*a*) _____

(*b*) _____

C. Conteste cada pregunta usando uno o dos pronombres.

> EJEMPLOS: ¿Quiénes te mandarán el dinero?
> *Mis abuelos me lo mandarán.*
>
> ¿Quién va a pagar la cuenta?
> (*a*) *Papá va a pagarla.*   (*b*) *Papá la va a pagar.*

1. ¿Quién no puede oír la música?

   (a) _____ (b) _____

2. ¿Quiénes estaban preparando la comida?

   (a) _____ (b) _____

3. ¿Quién te prometió el puesto?

   _____

4. ¿Quién le sirvió la comida a su padre anoche?

   _____

5. ¿Quiénes no querían ver esa película en el Canal 11?

   (a) _____ (b) _____

6. ¿Quién nos mandó estas revistas?

   _____

7. ¿Quiénes hicieron el trabajo ayer?

   _____

8. ¿Quién está leyendo el periódico ahora?

   (a) _____ (b) _____

9. ¿Quiénes deben hablar al profesor?

   (a) _____ (b) _____

10. ¿Quién me escribió la tarjeta postal de España?

    _____

D. Aquí están algunas *respuestas*. ¿Cuáles son las preguntas? Escriba una pregunta para cada respuesta.

> EJEMPLO: Me levantaré a las siete.
>> *¿A qué hora te levantarás (se levantará Ud.) mañana?*

1. Se acostó a las once. _____

2. Nos fuimos porque era tarde. _____

3. Se escondieron detrás del muro. _____

4. Me sentaré en esta silla. _____

5. Me vestí rápidamente porque tenía prisa. _____

E. Conteste cada pregunta usando pronombres en lugar de sustantivos según se indica en los ejemplos.

> EJEMPLOS: ¿Quién le dará a Ud. los libros?
>> *Mi profesor me los dará.*
>
>> ¿Va Ud. a pedirle el menú a la camarera?
>> *a. Sí, voy a pedírselo.*
>> *b. Sí, se lo voy a pedir.*

1. ¿Se quejará Ud. si su profesor les da a Uds. un examen largo?

   _____

2. ¿Les enseña el español bien a Uds. su profesor de español?

_____

3. ¿Les ha mostrado su disco nuevo a sus padres?

_____

4. ¿Vio Ud. el programa en el Canal 2 anoche?

_____

5. ¿Quiere Ud. prestarle a su profesor mil dólares?

   a. _____

   b. _____

6. ¿Quién le prestaría a Ud. cien dólares?

_____

7. ¿Dónde puede Ud. oír la música *rock?*

   a. _____

   b. _____

8. ¿Está Ud. sirviéndoles el almuerzo ahora a sus amigos?

   a. _____

   b. _____

9. ¿Me regalará Ud. todos sus discos si se los pido?

_____

10. ¿Cuándo se quita Ud. los zapatos?

_____

F. Conteste la pregunta usando una de las formas *conmigo, contigo, consigo.* Atención: Una de las preguntas se debe contestar sin usar ninguna de esas formas.

1. ¿Qué llevas contigo ahora?

_____

2. Si va a llover, ¿qué hace Isabel?

_____

3. ¿Irán sus amigos con Lupita? (No repita "Lupita" en la respuesta.)

_____

4. Si Ud. no quiere volver a casa para comer, ¿lleva su almuerzo consigo?

_____

5. ¿Qué debo hacer para ayudarte si necesitas más refrescos para la fiesta?

_____

G. Conteste la pregunta usando un pronombre (u *otro* pronombre) en lugar de las palabras subrayadas.

> EJEMPLO: ¿Pondrás las flores en este florero?
> *Sí, pondré las flores en él.*

1. ¿Van Uds. con los muchachos?

   _____

2. ¿Hablas de tu profesor de inglés?

   _____

3. ¿Vas a comprar una cinta para tu grabadora?

   _____

4. ¿Vienen Uds. con Juan y Dorotea?

   _____

5. ¿Son estos libros para tu padre?

   _____

6. ¿Quiénes van a la fiesta con Uds.?

   _____

7. ¿Qué hay de comer para nosotros?

   _____

8. ¿Cuánto pides por el tocadiscos?

   _____

9. ¿Vienes sin tu hermana?

   _____

10. ¿Qué hay delante de la pared?

    _____

H. Traduzca al español:

1. *a.* We went downtown to see the basketball game.

   _____

   b. We didn't see it because it rained.

   _____

2. *a.* Last night we visited our grandparents.

   _____

   b. When we saw them, we gave them birthday presents.

   _____

   c. As soon as we gave them to them, they thanked us.

   _____

3. *a.* I wanted to buy the computer.

   _____

   b. I couldn't buy it because it cost too much.

   _____

4. *a.* Do you have the tapes? I need them.

   _____

   b. If you don't have them now, send them to me as soon as possible.

   _____

5. Take off your hat, Johnny. Take it off at once.

_____

6. *a.* This morning I met my friend at the bus stop. (Use *encontrar.*)

_____

   b. When I met him, I spoke to him about our homework.

_____

   c. Since he didn't have change for the bus, I lent it to him.

_____

7. *a.* Did you (*Ud.*) send Robert the stamps?

_____

   b. He asked you for them last week.

_____

   c. He needed them for his collection.

_____

8. *a.* Michael, did your father promise you the calculator?

_____

   b. Yes, he promised it to me last week.

_____

9. What did you (*tú*) find out about her? Was it very interesting?

_____

10. *a.* She wanted to bring you the records, Mr. Pérez.

_____

    b. She couldn't bring them to you because she had lent them to her brother.

_____

    c. When will she be able to bring them to me?

_____

11. *a.* Mr. Mendoza, what did they tell you about that building?

_____

    b. It is tall and they built it last year.

_____

12. *a.* Are you (*Uds.*) going to the concert tonight?

_____

    b. We're going to it tomorrow evening.

_____

13. *a.* Have they shown her the blouse?

_____

    b. Yes, they have shown it to her, but she hasn't bought it yet.

_____

14. *a.* Will you (*tú*) go with me to the mall this afternoon?

_____

    b. Yes, I will go with you, but call me first.

_____

15. *a.* Don't stay in school today after three o'clock.

_____

    b. I'll call you at home.

_____

16. *a.* How much did they offer us for the car?

_____

    b. The offered us a thousand dollars, but we didn't accept it.

_____

17. *a.* Will she bring us the records later?

_____

    b. No, she can't bring them to us because she doesn't have them all.

_____

18. *a.* Who will win the next election? (Use the plural: *elecciones*.)

_____

    b. The most popular candidate will win it ("them").

_____

19. *a.* I see the stage but I can't see the actors very well.

_____

    b. Can you (*Ud.*) see them?

_____

    c. I can see them with my opera glasses.

_____

    d. May I ("Can I") lend them to you?

_____

20. I bought a new pair of shoes and put them on this morning.

_____

21. *a.* What are you (*tú*) bringing for me?

_____

    b. This package is not for you. I'm not bringing you anything.

_____

22. This lesson is very difficult but we have to learn it.

_____

23. *a.* Do we have the photocopies yet?

_____

    b. No, John is sending them to us. (*Do not use the progressive tense.*)

_____

24. *a.* The children's stories were very interesting.

_____

b. Their mother was reading them to them. (*Use the past progressive and translate in two ways.*)

_____

_____

25. "Did she lend it to *him?*" "No, she lent it to *them.*"

_____

Semana Santa en Sevilla

Un espectáculo muy emocionante tiene lugar todos los años en la ciudad andaluza de Sevilla. Durante ocho días, desde el Domingo de Ramos hasta el Domingo de Resurrección (la Pascua Florida), se celebra en Sevilla una fiesta religiosa sin igual en cualquier otra parte del mundo. Los preparativos para estos eventos se hacen muchos meses de antemano. Durante esta semana todos los sevillanos se visten del modo más elegante posible.

Cada parroquia tiene su *cofradía* (brotherhood). Durante el año, los miembros de una cofradía se reúnen para obtener fondos para su iglesia y sobre todo para planear las procesiones para la Semana Santa. Estas procesiones van por las calles de la ciudad y acompañan los célebres *pasos* (floats) que representan escenas de la pasión y muerte de Jesús. Los miembros de las cofradías que se pasean se llaman *nazarenos* y se visten como penitentes de la Edad Media, llevando *capirotes** sobre la cabeza. Los pasos son muy pesados (desde media tonelada hasta varias toneladas) y son llevados por más de veinte miembros de las cofradías llamados *costaleros* (sackmen).

Desde los balcones las mujeres cantan *saetas*, que son canciones religiosas extáticas. El punto culminante del desfile ocurre en la famosa calle estrecha llamada *Sierpes* (snakes). Los costaleros pasan por esta calle con mucho cuidado para no hacer daño a los pasos. Al salir de la calle de Sierpes, el desfile pasa por el Ayuntamiento rumbo a la Catedral donde reciben las bendiciones. Luego vuelven con los pasos a sus propias parroquias. La ruta que cada paso tiene que seguir es fijada de antemano y la marcha a la Catedral tarda unas doce horas.

Miles de espectadores se reúnen por las calles para ver pasar los pasos. En esta época del año no sólo ocurre esta celebración religiosa sino que también se celebran, antes y después de la Semana Santa, ferias, carnavales, corridas de toros y paseos a caballo. Durante varias semanas Sevilla es sin duda la ciudad más animada y concurrida de España.

*Un capirote es un gorro puntiagudo de un metro de alto que cubre la cabeza y se extiende sobre los hombros. Hay dos agujeritos para los ojos.

CHAPTER 16 The Infinitive

The Spanish infinitive ends in **-ar, -er,** or **-ir.** The English infinitive is usually combined with *to,* as in *to have, to speak, to walk.* It occurs without *to* after verbs like *can* and *let.* The Spanish and English infinitives are often direct translations of each other:

Me gusta **bailar.**	I like *to dance.*
Puede **cantar.**	She can *sing.*
Me deja **conducir.**	He lets me *drive.*

Uses of the Infinitive

1 IN IMPERSONAL EXPRESSIONS

Es un placer **estar** aquí.	It is a pleasure to be here.
¿Es posible **hablar** con la directora?	Is it possible to speak with the principal?

2 AS OBJECT OF CERTAIN VERBS

a. The following verbs are followed directly by the infinitive:*

deber, should, ought to; to be supposed to
decidir, to decide
desear, to wish, want
esperar, to hope
lograr, to manage (to), succeed in
pensar, to intend

poder, to be able, can
preferir, to prefer
prometer, to promise
querer, to want
saber, to know how (to)
soler, to be accustomed (to), "usually," (*imperfect*) used to

La clase **debe empezar** a la una.	The class is supposed to begin at one o'clock.
Lograron llegar a tiempo.	They managed to arrive on time.

*For some verbs in this list, the infinitive is replaced by a **que** clause if the subject changes:

Él quiere **leer.**	He wants *to read.*
But:	
Él quiere **que ellos lean.**	He wants *them to read.*

In such cases, the verb in the **que** clause is in the subjunctive form. See page 50.

¿Qué **piensan hacer?**	What do they intend to do?
Queremos partir mañana.	We want to leave tomorrow.
Sabemos nadar.	We know how to swim.
Marta **suele levantarse** temprano.	Martha usually gets up (is accustomed to getting up) early.

b. The verbs **oír** and **ver** belong in this group. Note how they are used:

Oí llegar al profesor.	I heard the teacher arrive.
Los vimos jugar en la televisión.	We saw them play (playing) on television.

3 AS OBJECT OF A PREPOSITION

A verb that follows a preposition must be in the infinitive form:

después de comer	after eating
sin escuchar	without listening
Estamos aquí **para aprender.**	We are here to learn.
Le agradecimos **por ayudar** a los niños.	We thanked him (her) for helping the children.
Están contentos **de verte.**	They are glad to see you.
Estoy cansado **de estudiar.**	I am tired of studying.
Fue el primero **en llegar.**	He was the first to arrive.

4 IN PHRASES OF THE FORM **al** + infinitive

Al + infinitive can be expressed in English by on (upon) . . . -ing or when . . . + verb:

Al salir del cuarto, no te olvides de cerrar la puerta.	On leaving (When you leave) the room, don't forget to close the door.
Al oír el timbre, se sentaron y abrieron sus libros.	On hearing (When they heard) the bell, they sat down and opened their books.

5 AFTER VERBS USED WITH PREPOSITIONS

Some verbs are used with a preposition when they precede an infinitive:

Verbs followed by *A*

a. *Verbs of motion:* **ir a,** to go (be going) to; **venir a,** to come (be coming) to; **salir a,** to go out to; **apresurarse a,** to hurry to

Vino a ayudarme.	He came to help me.
Los niños **salen a jugar.**	The children go out to play.
Se apresuraron a contarle la buena noticia.	They hurried to tell her the good news.

b. *Verbs that mean "to begin":* **comenzar a, empezar a, principiar a, ponerse a, echarse a**

Se echaron a correr.	They began to run.

c. *Other verbs:* **Aprender a,** to learn to; **enseñar a,** to teach to; **acostumbrarse a,** to get used to; **atreverse a,** to dare to; **decidirse a,** to decide, make up one's mind, to; **invitar a,** to invite to; **negarse a,** to refuse to; **volver a,** to . . . again

No puedo **acostumbrarme a trabajar** de noche.	I can't get used to working at night.
Se decidió a buscar empleo.	He decided (made up his mind) to look for a job.
Volví a ver esa película.	I saw that film again.
Lo **invitan a asistir** a la reunión.	They are inviting him to attend the meeting.
Se niega a contestar.	He refuses to answer.

Verbs followed by *DE*

acabar de, to have just

Acabo de llegar.	I have just arrived.
Acababan de salir.	They had just left.

acordarse de, to remember to

Acuérdate de escribir a tus padres.	Remember to write to your parents.

tratar de, to try to

Trataba de estudiar.	She was trying to study.

cesar de, dejar de, to stop

¡Dejen de hacer tanto ruido!	Stop making so much noise!

olvidarse de, to forget to

Me olvidé de traer mis libros.	I forget to bring my books.

alegrarse de, to be glad to

      Se alegraron de vernos.   They were glad to see us.

Verbs followed by *EN*

consentir en ⎫
convenir en ⎬ to agree to

      Convinieron en ayudar a los   They agreed to help the students.
      alumnos.

insistir en, to insist on

      Insiste en viajar con ellos.   He insists on traveling with them.

tardar en, to take long to, to take (*time interval*) to

      Tardaron tres horas **en llegar** aquí.   It took them (They took) three hours
                    to get here.

Verbs followed by *CON*

amenazar con, to threaten to

      El jefe **amenazó con despedir** a los   The boss threatened to fire those who
      que siempre llegaban tarde.   always came late.

contar con, to count on

      Cuento con quedarme una se-   I'm counting on staying for a week.
      mana.

soñar con, to dream of

      Sueño con viajar a Sudamérica.   I dream of traveling to South America.

5 As Verbal Noun

When the infinitive serves as a noun, it is generally preceded by the article **el.** It is often equivalent to the English gerund, which ends in *-ing:*

      El patinar sobre el hielo es mi   Skating on ice (Ice-skating) is my
      pasatiempo favorito.   favorite hobby.
      El fumar es peligroso para la salud.   Smoking is dangerous for your health.

Tener que ⎫
Haber que ⎬ + Infinitive

6 When either of these two expressions is used, the infinitive or the other verb may have a direct object. Note the difference in meaning:

Tengo que hacer algo.	I have to do something.
Tengo algo **que hacer.**	I have something to do.
Tenía que aprender dos canciones.	He had to learn two songs.
Tenía dos canciones **que aprender.**	He had two songs to learn.
Había que escribir unas cartas.	It was necessary to write some letters.
Había unas cartas **que escribir.**	There were some letters to write.
No hay que hacer nada.	One must not do anything.
No hay nada que hacer.	There is nothing to do.

___ EJERCICIOS _____

A. Complete la oración:

1. He left without saying anything.

   Partió sin _____ nada.
2. Instead of watching television, you should do your homework.

   En vez de _____ la televisión, debes _____ tus tareas.
3. They were glad to stay home.

   Estaban contentos _____ en casa.
4. We came here to study.

   Vinimos aquí _____.
5. Do you hear the birds singing?

   ¿Oyes _____ los pájaros?

B. Complete la oración con una preposición o con la palabra *que*. Si la oración ya está completa, no escriba nada en el blanco.

1. No estoy seguro _____ tener el dinero.

2. ¿Qué prefieren Uds. _____ hacer esta noche?

3. Tardaron ocho horas _____ llegar a casa.

4. _____ evitar el tráfico, hemos decidido _____ dejar el carro en el garaje y tomar el tren.

5. ¿Dónde aprendiste _____ patinar así?

6. Cuento _____ verte muy pronto.

7. ¿Tienes algo _____ darnos?

8. No era necesario _____ venir esta noche.

9. ¿Te gusta _____ mirar la televisión?

10. Siempre tratamos _____ ayudar a nuestros amigos.

11. ¿Qué van Uds. _____ hacer más tarde?

12. Ella no sabe _____ esquiar muy bien.

13. Esta tarde habrá cosas _____ arreglar.

14. ¿A qué hora comenzaste _____ comer?

15. No se acordaron _____ mandar los paquetes.

16. _____ ver la noticia, empecé _____ llorar.

17. ¿Por qué insistes _____ molestarme tanto?

18. Anoche vimos _____ jugar al equipo de nuestra escuela.

19. Los López nos han invitado _____ comer en su casa esta noche.

20. Nos alegramos _____ verlos a Uds.

21. La niña corrió _____ saludar a su padre cuando éste llegó a casa.

22. ¿Qué piensan Uds. _____ hacer ahora?

23. Tendremos _____ partir en cinco minutos.

24. ¿Quién acababa _____ entrar en la habitación?

25. Es imposible _____ comprender lo que dice el profesor hoy.

C. Conteste en oraciones completas:

1. ¿Qué prefiere Ud. hacer los domingos?

_____

2. ¿Cuánto tiempo tardan Uds. en llegar a la escuela?

_____

3. ¿Se alegra su profesor* de dar exámenes difíciles?

_____

4. ¿A qué hora se puso Ud. a hacer esta tarea?

_____

5. ¿Sueña Ud. con ganar el premio gordo en la lotería?

_____

6. ¿Ha visto Ud. bailar al director* de su escuela?

_____

7. ¿Me invitará Ud. a comer en su casa esta noche?

_____

8. ¿Qué suele hacer su padre todas las noches después de la comida?

_____

*See the footnote on page 31.

9. ¿Siempre insiste Ud. en tomar café con el desayuno?

_____

10. ¿Le gustaría a Ud. enseñar a alguien a jugar al tenis?

_____

11. ¿Se acuerdan sus padres siempre de darle a Ud. un regalo de cumpleaños?

_____

12. ¿Se atrevería Ud. a subir una montaña escarpada?

_____

13. ¿Ha oído Ud. cantar a su profesor de español?

_____

14. ¿Adónde va Ud. después de salir de la escuela?

_____

15. ¿Qué piensa Ud. hacer después de graduarse?

_____

D. Traduzca al español:

1. I can't drive without wearing my glasses.

_____

2. The students hurry to get to class before the bell rings.

_____

3. It started to rain at five o'clock but it stopped raining at seven thirty.

_____

4. Will you (*Uds.*) remember to tell your parents that they are supposed to attend the meeting?

_____

_____

5. *a.* Yesterday we visited the zoo again. (Do not use *otra vez.*)

_____

   b. We saw the elephants eating. We didn't go to see the lions but we heard them roar. (To roar = *rugir*)

_____

_____

6. Smoking is a bad habit. Chewing gum (Gum-chewing) is another. (to chew gum = *mascar chicle*)

_____

7. Instead of wasting time, why don't you (*Uds.*) start doing your homework? (to waste time = *perder tiempo*)

_____

8. After finishing my homework, I'll go out to visit my friends.

_____

9. "Please* sit down." "I prefer to stand, thank you."

_____

10. I got used to getting up early.

_____

11. We left the museum without seeing the exhibit.

_____

12. We waited until we saw ("until seeing") the people leave.

_____

13. *a.* I have to give them a report of the meeting.

_____

  b. I have nothing to tell them since I didn't manage to get there in time.

_____

14. Tomorrow there will be a lot to do in class.

_____

15. My relatives have just returned from their trip to Spain.

_____

16. *a.* The teacher threatened to flunk most of (*la mayoría de*) the class.

_____

  b. It won't take her long to change her mind.

_____

17. Are you (*tú*) counting on visiting them before you leave ("before leaving") the city?

_____

18. Last night I dreamt of winning the grand prize in the lottery.

_____

19. *a.* Why did they decide to move? (to move = *mudarse de casa*)

_____

  b. They made up their minds to move because the landlord had just raised the rent.

_____

20. They will agree to come to the party if we promise to bring the photos.

_____

*Do not use *por favor*.

Pamplona: El Encierro de los Toros

Las Fiestas de San Fermín evocan una imagen de procesiones, desfiles, conciertos y corridas de toros. Pero lo que más se destaca son los toros que corren por las calles—y las personas que los acompañan.

De ordinario Pamplona, ciudad situada en el norte de España y capital de la provincia de Navarra, es muy tranquila, donde no ocurre nada especial. Sin embargo, todo este aspecto cambia durante las Fiestas de San Fermín, que duran del siete al catorce de julio.

Poco antes de la medianoche se dejan sueltos los toros, que corren a un corral donde pasan la noche. A las seis de la mañana siguiente las bandas empiezan a tocar por toda la ciudad despertando a todos los pamploneses. Las calles están llenas de más de 25.000 personas de todas las edades. A las siete explota un cohete, indicando que las puertas del corral se han abierto. En ese momento los toros se precipitan hacia la calle acompañados de personas aventureras que arriesgan la vida, aunque tienen que seguir ciertas reglas. Los toros no tardan más que dos minutos en llegar a la Plaza de Toros, y su llegada es anunciada por otro cohete. Poco después de la llegada de los toros, empieza un espectáculo bastante emocionante. Se abre otra puerta y sale al ruedo una novilla (heifer) que corre a toda velocidad derribando a los jóvenes que se han atrevido a quedarse en el ruedo para luchar con ella. La banda toca, la gente grita y aplaude, varios jóvenes quedan heridos y algunos son llevados al hospital.

A eso de las ocho la ciudad empieza a descansar por unas horas, esperando la corrida de toros que tiene lugar a las cinco de la tarde.

Todo lo sobredicho es repetido por ocho días. La ciudad de Pamplona está en continua excitación y animación. Se dice que algunas personas permanecen borrachas durante los ocho días de las fiestas y otras no duermen del todo. Después de las fiestas, la ciudad vuelve a la normalidad de antes.

CHAPTER 17 Commands

Affirmative

1 Note the affirmative command forms of some common verbs:

	USTED	USTEDES	TÚ	VOSOTROS	
tomar	*tome*	*tomen*	*toma*	*tomad*	take
leer	*lea*	*lean*	*lee*	*leed*	read
escribir	*escriba*	*escriban*	*escribe*	*escribid*	write
pensar	*piense*	*piensen*	*piensa*	*pensad*	think
volver	*vuelva*	*vuelvan*	*vuelve*	*volved*	return
dormir	*duerma*	*duerman*	*duerme*	*dormid*	sleep
pedir	*pida*	*pidan*	*pide*	*pedid*	ask (for)
traer	*traiga*	*traigan*	*trae*	*traed*	bring
saber	*sepa*	*sepan*	*sabe*	*sabed*	know

a. The forms of the polite commands are the same as the **usted(-es)** forms of the present subjunctive (see pages 246–247): **hable Ud.,** *speak;* **oigan Uds.,** *listen.*

b. With some exceptions (see §3), the forms of the affirmative **tú** commands are the same as the third person singular of the present tense: **habla,** *speak;* **oye,** *listen.*

c. The forms of the affirmative **vosotros** commands (used only in Spain) are obtained from the infinitive by changing the **-r** ending to **-d,** as in **hablad,** *speak;* **oíd,** *listen.*

Negative

2 All negative command forms are forms of the present subjunctive:

	USTED	USTEDES	TÚ	VOSOTROS	
hablar	*no hable*	*no hablen*	*no hables*	*no habléis*	don't speak
poner	*no ponga*	*no pongan*	*no pongas*	*no pongáis*	don't put
oír	*no oiga*	*no oigan*	*no oigas*	*no oigáis*	don't listen
mentir	*no mienta*	*no mientan*	*no mientas*	*no mintáis*	don't lie
cerrar	*no cierre*	*no cierren*	*no cierres*	*no cerréis*	don't close

Irregular *Tú* Commands

3 The following verbs have irregular affirmative **tú** command forms. Note, however, that the *negative* command forms are regular; that is, they are forms of the present subjunctive:

decir:	*di,* tell, say	*But:*	**no digas,** don't tell (say)
hacer:	*haz,* do, make		**no hagas,** don't do (make)
ir:	*ve,* go		**no vayas,** don't go
poner:	*pon,* put		**no pongas,** don't put
salir:	*sal,* leave, go out		**no salgas,** don't leave (go out)
ser:	*sé,* be		**no seas,** don't be
tener:	*ten,* have		**no tengas,** don't have
venir:	*ven,* come		**no vengas,** don't come

Position of Object Pronouns As Objects of Commands

4 Object pronouns are attached to the verb in affirmative commands but directly precede the verb in negative commands:

Usted

Tráiga**me** el paquete.
Bring me the package.

Tráiga**melo.**
Bring it to me.

No **me** traiga el paquete.
Don't bring me the package.

No **me lo** traiga.
Don't bring it to me.

Ustedes

Dígan**le** la verdad.
Tell her the truth.

Dígan**sela.**
Tell it to her.

No **le** digan la verdad.
Don't tell her the truth.

No **se la** digan.
Don't tell it to her.

Tú

Pon**lo** aquí.
Put it here.

Pón**melo** allí.
Put it there for me.

No **lo** pongas aquí.
Don't put it here.

No **me lo** pongas allí.
Don't put it there for me.

Vosotros

Escribid**le** la carta.	Escribíd**sela.**
Write him the letter.	Write it to him.
No **le** escribáis la carta.	No **se la** escribáis.
Don't write him the letter.	Don't write it to him.

5 An affirmative command and its attached pronouns form one word.

a. If the word has only two syllables, it has no accent mark: "**Hazme** un favor," "**Ponlos** aquí," "**Dime** la verdad."
Exception: **Déme** Ud. el libro.
Give me the book.

b. If the word has more than two syllables, an accent mark is placed on the vowel that is normally stressed in pronunciation without attached pronouns—that is, in the third or fourth syllable from the end:

pónmelo   dígame   díselo   contéstensela

Exceptions: The affirmative **vosotros** command forms (**hablad, comed, escribid,** etc.). The accent marks are placed as follows:
If *one* pronoun is attached, add *no* accent marks: **habladme, escribidnos.**
If *two* pronouns are attached, add an accent mark to the third syllable from the end: escribídmelo, entregádselo.

Reflexive Verbs

6 A "reflexive verb" is a verb that has a reflexive pronoun as its object. The position of reflexive pronouns as objects of commands is the same as that of all other object pronouns: they are attached to the verb in affirmative commands and directly precede the verb in negative commands:

levantarse, to get up, stand up, rise

	GET UP	DON'T GET UP
USTED	levánte**se**	no **se** levante
USTEDES	levánten**se**	no **se** levanten
TÚ	levánta**te**	no **te** levantes
VOSOTROS	levanta**os**	no **os** levantéis

ponerse, to put on (a garment)

	PUT ON	DON'T PUT ON
USTED	pónga**se**	no **se** ponga
USTEDES	póngan**se**	no **se** pongan
TÚ	pon**te**	no **te** pongas
VOSOTROS	pone**os**	no **os** pongáis

dormirse, to fall asleep, go to sleep

	Go To Sleep	Don't Go To Sleep
Usted	duérma**se**	no **se** duerma
Ustedes	duérman**se**	no **se** duerman
Tú	duérme**te**	no **te** duermas
Vosotros	dormí**os**	no **os** durmáis

7 The affirmative form of the **vosotros** command—**levantad, poned, dormid,** etc.—loses its **-d** ending when the reflexive pronoun **os** is attached. An accent mark is added to the **i** preceding **os** in **-ir** verbs:

levanta**os**   pone**os**   dormí**os**

Exception: (irse) **¡idos!** go away!

Let Us (Let's)

8 *a.* *Let us* or *let's* can be expressed in Spanish by using the **nosotros** form of the present subjunctive:

   Salgamos.   Let's leave.

b. When the verb is used reflexively in the affirmative, its **-s** ending is dropped before **nos** is attached:

   Sentémo**nos.**   Let's sit down.

c. If **se** is added as part of a double object, only one **s** is required:

   Digámo**selo.**   Let's tell him (her, them) so.

d. When pronouns are attached, an accent mark is placed on the vowel that is stressed when the verb is pronounced without "attachments":

dig**a**mos   dig**á**moslo   dig**á**moselo

Note that the accent is added in the third or fourth syllable from the end.

e. Object pronouns directly precede the verb in the negative("let's not"): **no nos sentemos, no se lo digamos,** etc.

9 Further examples:

Tomemos este camino.	**Tomémoslo.**	**No lo tomemos.**
Let's take this road.	Let's take it.	Let's not take it.
Devolvamos la carta a José.	**Devolvámosela.**	**No se la devolvamos.**
Let's return the letter to Joseph.	Let's return it to him.	Let's not return it to him.
Lavemos el coche.	**Lavémonos.**	**No nos lavemos.**
Let's wash the car.	Let's wash ourselves.	Let's not wash ourselves.
Pongamos los guantes en la mesa.	**Pongámonos** los guantes.	**No nos pongamos** los guantes.
Let's put the gloves on the table.	Let's put on our gloves.	Let's not put on our gloves.
	Pongámonoslos.	**No nos los pongamos.**
	Let's put them on.	Let's not put them on.

Vamos a + Infinitive

10 *Let's* can also be expressed in Spanish by using **vamos a** + an infinitive. This expression can mean *let's* only when it is used in the affirmative:

   Vamos a comer.   Let's eat.

The negative meaning—*let's not*—is expressed with the **nosotros** form of the subjunctive:

   No comamos.   Let's not eat.

Exception—**Vamos,** *let's go,* and its reflexive form:

   Vamos a casa.   Let's go home.
   Vámonos.   Let's leave.

But here again, the negative sense requires the subjunctive:

   No vayamos a casa.   Let's not go home.
   No nos vayamos.   Let's not leave.

Let Him, Let Her, Let Them

11 *Let him (her, them)* is expressed in Spanish by **que** + the present subjunctive. The subject, if expressed, usually follows the verb:

Que entren ahora.	Let them come in now.
Que se acueste el niño.	Let the child go to bed.
Que se lo diga Ana.	Let Ann tell it to them.

Object pronouns directly precede the verb ("Que **se lo** diga . . .").

Note: It is common in spoken Spanish to use the form **que** + *subjunctive* as an alternate way of expressing *direct* commands, but it is not as forceful:

Do the work.	**Haz** el trabajo.	*Or:*	**Que hagas** el trabajo.
Come here.	**Venid** acá.		**Que vengáis** acá.
Bring the records.	**Traiga Ud.** los discos.		**Que traiga Ud.** los discos.
Send us the money.	**Mándenos Ud.** el dinero.		**Que nos mande Ud.** el dinero.
Tell it to me.	**Dímelo** tú.		**Que me lo digas** tú.
Don't speak to us.	**No nos hablen Uds.**		**Que no nos hablen Uds.**
Don't put it on.	**No te lo pongas.**		**Que no te lo pongas.**

— EJERCICIOS

A. Cambie el mandato a la forma afirmativa.

    EJEMPLO: No salgas ahora.   *Sal ahora.*

1. No hagas eso, chico. _____

2. No vengas antes de las ocho. _____

3. No digas la verdad. _____

4. No pienses en eso. _____

5. No vayas a casa ahora. _____

B. Cambie el mandato a la forma negativa.

    EJEMPLO: Di la verdad.   *No digas la verdad.*

1. Da el dinero a Juan. _____

2. Vuelve a casa después de las once. _____

3. Escribe esa carta. _____

4. Toma ese vino. _____

5. Sé un buen niño. _____

C. Cambie el mandato a la forma afirmativa.

    EJEMPLO: No te acuestes tarde.   *Acuéstate tarde.*

1. No lo pongas allí. _____

2. No me mandes esos libros. _____

3. No se lo digas ahora. _____

4. No te levantes ahora. _____

5. No nos las prometas. _____

D. Cambie el mandato a la forma negativa.

EJEMPLO: Hazlo por mí. _____*No lo hagas por mí.*_____

1. Duérmete en seguida. _____

2. Vete en este momento. _____

3. Tráeselo antes de mañana. _____

4. Háblame de ella. _____

5. Métete en otros asuntos. _____

E. Cambie el mandato al plural (*vosotros*), escribiendo las formas afirmativa y negativa según se indica en los ejemplos.

EJEMPLOS: Trae los paquetes.
Traed los paquetes.   *No traigáis los paquetes.*

Escríbeme una tarjeta.
Escribidme una tarjeta.   *No me escribáis una tarjeta.*

1. Dinos la verdad. _____   _____

2. Ten paciencia. _____   _____

3. Vuelve temprano. _____   _____

4. Acuéstate ahora. _____   _____

5. Mándanoslo mañana. _____   _____

F. Repita la oración, cambiando el mandato del tratamiento de *tú* al de *usted* o viceversa.

EJEMPLOS: Toma una copa de vino, Miguel.
Tome una copa de vino, señorita.

Venga Ud. a mi casa.
Ven a mi casa.

1. Siéntate aquí, niño. _____, señorita.

2. Aprenda esta lección, señor. _____, chico.

3. Diviértase allí, señor Gómez. _____, Juanito.

4. Devuélveme el dinero, Mario. _____, señora.

5. Vaya Ud. al museo, señora. _____, mi hija.

6. Oye la música, Rosita. _____, señor profesor.

7. Hazlo por mí, mamá. _____, señor doctor.

8. Póngala en la mesa, señor. _____, Rosario.

9. Dime la verdad, hijo mío. _____, Sr. López.

10. Mándemelos Ud. esta noche. _____, María.

G. Exprese el mismo significado de otro modo, luego cámbielo a la forma negativa según se indica en el ejemplo.

EJEMPLO: Vamos a sentarnos.

Sentémonos.   *No nos sentemos.*

1. Vamos a bailar el tango.   _____   _____
2. Vamos a verlo más tarde.   _____   _____
3. Vamos a aprenderla.   _____   _____
4. Vamos a hacer eso.   _____   _____
5. Vamos a levantarnos.   _____   _____

H. Complete la oración según se indica en el ejemplo.

EJEMPLO: Me niego a salir ahora. ____*Que salgan*____ ellos.

1. Me niego a ir al centro.   _____ tu hermana.
2. Me niego a asistir a la conferencia.   _____ tus amigos.
3. Me niego a entrar en el cuarto.   _____ Felipe.
4. Me niego a correr de prisa.   _____ ellos.
5. Me niego a venir con ellos.   _____ sus padres.

I. Complete la oración según se indica en el ejemplo, usando un pronombre en lugar de la expresión subrayada.

EJEMPLO: No quiero hacer el trabajo.   ____*Que lo haga*____ ella.

1. No quiero tener el carro.   _____ ellos.
2. No quiero poner la televisión.   _____ José.
3. No quiero traer los discos.   _____ Ana.
4. No quiero empezar esta tarea.   _____ tus hermanos.
5. No quiero decir la respuesta.   _____ Roberto.

J. Exprese el mismo mandato usando la forma *que* + *subjuntivo.*

EJEMPLO: Dame el libro.   *Que me des el libro.*

1. Tráenos el dinero.   _____
2. Ven temprano esta noche.   _____
3. Toma este vaso de agua.   _____
4. Salid a las ocho.   _____
5. Hazme este favor.   _____

K. Las oraciones de la izquierda son respuestas negativas a los mandatos que Ud. escribirá en la columna de la derecha. Escriba un mandato apropiado para cada respuesta.

EJEMPLOS: No quiero ir. _____*Vaya*_____ Ud. _____*al museo hoy*_____.

No queremos hablar. _____*Hablen*_____ Uds. _____*de su viaje*_____.

1. No quiero salir. _____ tú _____.

2. No queremos venir. _____ vosotros _____.

3. No quiero correr. _____ Ud. _____.

4. No queremos cantar. _____ Uds. _____.

5. No quiero volver. _____ tú _____.

L. Siga como en el ejercicio *K*, usando sustantivos apropiados en lugar de los pronombres subrayados.

EJEMPLOS: No quiero escribir<u>lo</u>. _____*Escriba*_____ Ud. _____*el artículo*_____.

No queremos decír<u>sela</u>. _____*Decidle*_____ vosotros _____*la verdad*_____.

1. No quiero beber<u>la</u>. _____ tú _____.

2. No queremos leer<u>la</u>. _____ Uds. _____.

3. No queremos estudiar<u>las</u>. _____ vosotros _____.

4. No quiero hacer<u>los</u>. _____ tú _____.

5. No quiero ponér<u>melo</u>. _____ Ud. _____.

M. Traduzca al español. Los pronombres entre paréntesis indican a quién se dirige el mandato.

1. *a.* Leave this room right now, gentlemen.

_____

b. Do not leave the office yet, Johnny.

_____

2. *a.* Dad, don't get up too early tomorrow morning.

_____

b. Get up at seven a.m., David. _____

3. (*Traduzca de dos modos.*) Let's stay home tonight.

a. _____ *b.* _____

4. *a.* Don't go to the party tonight, Jane.

_____

b. Let your cousin go. _____

5. Sit down here, my friends.

a. (Uds.) _____ *b.* (vosotros) _____

6. Don't sit on the sofa.

a. (*Uds.*) _____ *b.* (vosotros) _____

7. *a.* Don't sell your car, Mr. Rivera.

_____

    b. Let someone else drive it. _____

8. *a.* Don't be a nuisance, Johnny. _____

    b. Be a good boy, Steven. _____

9. Have patience with your younger brother, Caroline.

    _____

10. Don't be in a hurry, Peter. _____

11. Come home early tonight, children.

    a. (*Uds.*) _____

    b. (*vosotros*) _____

12. Don't come after midnight.

    a. (*Uds.*) _____ *b.* (vosotros) _____

13. *a.* Tell us your secret, Paul. _____

    b. Don't tell it to them, Robert. _____

14. (*Uds.*) Read this article for tomorrow; don't read it now.

    _____

15. Be at school before eight a.m.

    a. (*Uds.*) _____ *b.* (*vosotros*) _____

16. Don't arrive too late.

    a. (*Uds.*) _____ *b.* (*vosotros*) _____

17. (*vosotros*) *a.* Children, put on your shoes later.

    _____

    b. Don't put them on now. _____

18. *a.* Let's go; it's late already. _____

    b. Let's not go home yet. _____

19. Know this lesson for tomorrow.

    a. (*tú*) _____ *b.* (*Ud.*) _____

20. Do not forget the important details.

    a. (*tú*) _____ *b.* (*Ud.*) _____

México: El Pueblo y Sus Costumbres

México es nuestro vecino hispánico más cercano. Tiene una frontera de unos 3200 kilómetros (2000 millas) que comparte con cuatro estados: Texas, Nuevo México, Arizona y California.

En las ciudades de México la gente vive y se viste más o menos como nosotros. Se notan diferencias sobre todo en el campo. Se ven, por ejemplo, en el modo de vestir. El campesino lleva un traje blanco parecido a un pijama, sombrero de ala ancha y huaraches, que son una forma de sandalias; la mujer lleva un rebozo, que es un chal (shawl). La manera en que la mujer lleva su rebozo refleja su lugar de origen dentro del país.

En cuanto a la familia, aunque ha habido cambios en años recientes, se podría decir que el hombre es aún la figura principal. Los lazos familiares son muy fuertes, y todos los miembros de la familia toman parte en las celebraciones, tales como bautizos, bodas y cumpleaños. Este espíritu de familia se destaca por todas partes.

A muchos mexicanos les ponen el nombre de un santo, y el día de su santo asume más importancia que su cumpleaños.

En algunos pueblos de México existe la costumbre llamada *el paseo* (o *la retreta*, como se llama en otros países hispanoamericanos). Es un acto social que tiene lugar en una plaza pública los domingos por la tarde, generalmente durante un concierto al aire libre. Mientras toca la banda, grupos de muchachas se pasean cogidas del brazo (arm in arm) alrededor del quiosco de música (bandstand) mientras los grupos de muchachos se pasean en dirección contraria en un círculo exterior. Cuando un grupo se encuentra con otro, durante una pausa en el concierto, los muchachos flirtean con las muchachas. Si un muchacho se siente atraído por una muchacha, él coquetea (flirts) con ella con los ojos (gives her the eye)—una costumbre llamada *dar cuerda* (to wind up). Durante el próximo paseo, que comienza cuando la banda vuelve a tocar, el muchacho se pone al lado de la muchacha que le atrae, y juntos se pasean alrededor de la plaza varias veces hasta que cesa la música. Entonces se separan otra vez. Si a la muchacha le gusta el muchacho, ella puede aceptar su invitación a tomar un refresco con él en un café cercano. Pero el muchacho tendrá que invitar también a las amigas de la muchacha.

Aunque la costumbre de la siesta ha disminuido en los últimos años, todavía se observa en muchos lugares, especialmente en los pueblos pequeños donde hace mucho calor por la tarde. Entre la una y las cuatro de la tarde (la duración varía de pueblo en pueblo), las tiendas se cierran y mucha gente vuelve a casa para tomar el almuerzo, que es generalmente una comida muy fuerte (heavy). Por lo general descansan o duermen después de almorzar.

Por todo México se celebran muchas fiestas, tanto religiosas como no religiosas. Casi todas se caracterizan por sus fuegos artificiales, desfiles y venta de comida y bebidas en puestos provisionales. Para añadir al ambiente festivo, hay tiovivos (merry-go-rounds) y varios tipos de juegos.

Un día de fiesta muy popular es el Día de los Difuntos, que se celebra el 2 de noviembre. En las panaderías aparecen los famosos "panes de muerto" que representan santos y calaveras. Las calaveras se hacen de azúcar, y cada una lleva un nombre en la frente escrito en letras hechas de dulces.

Aunque en algunos lugares—especialmente en las ciudades grandes—se conocen el árbol de Navidad y Santa Claus, para la mayoría de los mexicanos la Navidad es un acontecimiento religioso. La época de Navidad comienza en México con "las posadas", que representan la historia de José y María cuando buscaban posada en Belén (Bethlehem). Durante las nueve noches que preceden a la Navidad, colas de peregrinos andan por las calles, con velas en las manos, cantando villancicos que relatan la búsqueda de José y María. Por tradición llaman a ocho puertas cerradas

que nadie abre. Por fin, la novena puerta se abre y todos entran. En este momento empiezan las diversiones. El punto culminante de estas diversiones, especialmente para los niños, es el momento en que se rompe la "piñata". La piñata es una olla de barro grande, llena de dulces, frutas y juguetes, que cuelga del techo. La piñata está cubierta de papel en colores, y suele tener la figura de un toro, una oveja u otro animal. Todos los niños se reúnen debajo de la piñata. Uno de ellos, con los ojos vendados, trata de romper la piñata con un palo. Al romperse la piñata, todos se lanzan hacia ella para coger lo que puedan.

La víspera de Navidad, o sea la "Nochebuena", los miembros de la familia se reúnen para la cena especial de pavo (los mexicanos lo llaman "guajalote" o "guajolote"). Luego van a la iglesia para celebrar la Misa de Gallo (Midnight Mass).

El seis de enero ha sido tradicionalmente el día en que se dan regalos, aunque esta costumbre ha caído en desuso, a favor de la costumbre norteamericana de dar regalos el día de Navidad. El seis de enero se celebra el día en que los Tres Reyes Magos (Baltasar, Melchor y Gaspar) llegaron a Belén trayendo regalos para el niño Jesús. La noche anterior los niños ponen sus zapatos en la puerta antes de acostarse. Si han sido buenos durante el año, encontrarán juguetes dentro de los zapatos. Pero si no han sido buenos, encontrarán un pedazo de carbón.

Una discusión de los deportes de México tiene que empezar con la corrida de toros. La plaza de toros más grande del mundo (Plaza de Toros Monumental) está situada en la ciudad de México. Todos los domingos por la tarde, miles de aficionados van a la plaza para ver la corrida.

Otro deporte muy popular es la equitación, que data de los primeros años de la Reconquista. Los clubs de "charro" son grupos que montan a caballo.

El fútbol (soccer) es el deporte nacional de México. Los mejores jugadores de fútbol llegan a ser casi héroes nacionales, y los niños sueñan con hacerse famosos como ellos. En cualquier barrio se pueden ver grupos de niños jugando al fútbol.

Otros deportes populares en México son el béisbol, el boxeo y la lucha libre (wrestling).

CHAPTER 18
Interrogative and Relative Pronouns

An *interrogative* pronoun asks a question: *what? which? who? whom?* A *relative* pronoun refers to a preceding noun: "The girls *who* came in (*whom* you met) are my cousins."

1 The common Spanish interrogatives are **¿qué?** (what?), **¿cuál, -es?** (which? what?), **¿quién, -es?** (who?), **¿a quién, -es?** (whom?), and **¿de quién, -es?** (whose?):

> **¿A quién** hablaba Ud.?   To whom were you speaking?

2 The most common relative pronoun is **que** (that, which, who, whom), which may refer to persons or things:

> el libro **que** Ud. lee   the book that you are reading
> los hombres **que** vienen   the men who (that) are coming
> la muchacha **que*** viste   the girl whom (that) you saw

3 Relative Pronouns as Objects of Prepositions:

a. When **que** refers to persons, it changes to **quien(-es):**

> la señora **con quien** (los señores **con**   the lady (the gentlemen) with whom I
>   **quienes**) hablé   spoke

b. When **que** refers to things, it does not change:

> la raqueta **con que** juego   the racquet with which I play

c. Since Spanish sentences cannot end in a preposition, an English clause or sentence that ends in a preposition should be rephrased for easier conversion into Spanish by "relocating" the preposition: *the man I spoke with* = "the man with whom I spoke"; *the school I'm going to* = "the school to which I'm going."

---

*Instead of **que,** the personal **a** may be used with **quien:** "la muchacha **a quien** viste." The use of **a quien(-es)** in place of **que** as direct object is rare in spoken Spanish, however.

d. The relative pronoun is often omitted in English but *never* in Spanish:

la película **que** vi ayer   the film I saw yesterday

e. Whose? = **¿de quién(-es)?** but *whose* as a relative adjective = **cuyo, -a:**

¿De quién es ese coche?   Whose car is that?
El hombre **cuyo coche** admiras es   The man whose car you admire is my
mi hermano.   brother.

¿De quiénes son estas novelas?   Whose novels are these?
El escritor **cuyas novelas** lees es   The writer whose novels you're read-
mexicano.   ing is Mexican.

Note that **cuyo** agrees in number and gender with the noun that follows, not with the possessor.

4

a. What? = **¿qué?** but *what* in the sense of *that which* is expressed by **lo que:**

¿Qué quieres?   What do you want?
Lo que quieres es imposible.   What you want is impossible.
Muéstrame **lo que** tienes en la car-   Show me what you have in your brief-
tera.   case.

b. What? may be **¿qué?** or **¿cuál(-es)?** in accordance with the following rules:

(1) **¿Qué?** is used when requesting a definition or identification:

¿Qué es un tacómetro?   What is a tachometer?
¿Qué es su tío?   What is your uncle (= What is his oc-
    cupation)?

(2) **¿Cuál(-es)?** is used for selection or listing:

¿Cuál es la capital de España?   What is the capital of Spain? (Which
    city?)
¿Cuáles son los colores de nuestra   What are the colors of our flag?
bandera?   (Which colors are they?)
¿Cuáles son los meses del año?   What are the months of the year? (List
    them.)
¿Cuál es su tío?   Which (one) is your uncle?

5

a. Which? as a pronoun = **¿cuál(-es)?:**

¿Cuál de estos libros es tuyo?   Which of these books is yours?
¿Cuáles de estas revistas son mías?   Which of these magazines are mine?

b. Which? as an adjective = **¿qué?:**

> **¿Qué** libro lees? **¿Qué** revistas quieres?

> Which book are you reading? Which magazines do you want?

El Cual, La Cual, Los Cuales, Las Cuales

6 Consider the following sentence:

> La hermana de José, que toca el piano, es una amiga mía.

Who plays the piano—José or his sister? We can't be sure, since **que** (*who*) may refer to either one. If it is the sister who plays the piano, we can make this perfectly clear by saying:

> La hermana de José, **la cual** toca el piano,...

If a relative pronoun has two possible antecedents, you can avoid confusion by using a form of **el cual** to refer to the first, or more distant, antecedent (*La hermana*).

Note

a. At the beginning of a clause, the relative pronoun referring to persons may be either **que** or **quien(-es):**

> La hermana de José, **quien** toca el piano,...

> The sister of Joseph, who plays the piano,...

b. **El cual, la cual,** etc., have the alternate forms **el que, la que, los que, las que:**

> La hermana de José, **la que** toca el piano,...

> Joseph's sister, who plays the piano,...

Other examples:

> Los amigos de Susana, **quien (que)** va a la fiesta mañana, son muy simpáticos.

> The friends of Susan, who is going to the party tomorrow, are very nice.

> Los amigos de Susana, **los que (los cuales)*** van a la fiesta mañana,...

> Susan's friends, who are going to the party tomorrow,...

*One can also say "Los amigos de Susana, **quienes** van a la fiesta,..." The plural form **quienes** can only refer to the plural antecedent, **Los amigos**.

7 A form of **el cual** or **el que** must be used if the relative pronoun follows a preposition other than **a, de, con,** or **en,** regardless of the location of the antecedent:

La reunión **a que** asistí fue muy interesante.

The meeting that I attended was very
interesting.

But:

Quería hablar al comienzo de la
reunión, **para la cual (para la
que)** había preparado un informe.

I wanted to speak at the beginning of
the meeting, for which I had prepared a report.

Other examples:

Las calles **en que** viven tienen pocas
casas.

The streets in which they live have
few houses.

El edificio **de que** habló era muy
viejo.

The building of which he spoke (that
he talked about) was very old.

But:

Las calles **por las cuales (por las
que)** pasaban eran muy anchas.

The streets through which they were
passing were very narrow.

El edificio **cerca del cual (cerca del
que)** vivo es muy alto.

The building near which I live (that I
live near) is very tall.

Relative pronouns take the forms **el cual (el que), la cual (la que),** etc., after prepositions such as **para, por, sin, tras, hacia, durante,** and the compound prepositions **cerca de, lejos de,** etc.

Lo Cual, Lo Que

8 When *which* at the beginning of a clause refers not to a preceding noun but to the thought expressed by the preceding clause, its Spanish equivalent is **lo cual** or **lo que:**

Pedro no estudió anoche, **lo cual (lo
que)** disgustó a su padre.

Peter didn't study last night, which
displeased his father.

Pasaron la noche jugando a las cha-
radas, **lo que** fue muy divertido.

They spent the evening playing cha-
rades, which was lots of fun.

El Que, La Que, Los Que, Las Que

9 Note the use of the following expressions:

el que, he who ⎫
la que, she who ⎬ the one who

los que ⎫
las que ⎬ those who

El (La) que viene es mi primo(-a).
Los que quieren entradas deben venir temprano.

The one who is coming is my cousin.
Those who want tickets should come early.

Interrogative Pronouns Used in Indirect Questions

10 The interrogative pronouns **¿qué?, ¿quién(-es)?**, etc., retain their accent marks when used as indirect questions:

¿Qué hacen ellos?
What are they doing?

No sé **qué** hacen.
I don't know what they are doing.

¿Quién fue?
Who was it?

No me dijo **quién** fue.
She didn't tell me who it was.

¿Sabe Ud. **quién** es?
Do you know who he (she) is?

___ EJERCICIOS ___

A. Complete la oración con la palabra apropiada: *qué, cuál(-es), o quién(-es).*

1. No sabemos _____ tiene el dinero.

2. ¿_____ de estas dos revistas quieres leer?

3. No sé de _____ es ese paquete.

4. ¿_____ necesitan Uds.?

5. ¿Sabes _____ discos quieres comprar?

6. ¿A _____ esperas aquí?

7. ¿Saben Uds. _____ son esas mujeres?

8. ¿A _____ mandas el cheque?

9. ¿_____ son las selecciones?

10. ¿De _____ es esa casa extraña?

B. Éstas son respuestas. ¿Cuáles son las preguntas? Escriba una pregunta para cada respuesta, usando una de las palabras discutidas en esta lección.

> EJEMPLO: Me dio lo que le pedí.
> *¿Qué te dio ella?*

1. Es la chica con quien vino José. _____

2. Es de mi padre. _____

3. Quiero éste, no ése. _____

4. Yo busco a mi marido. _____

5. Todos nuestros parientes están aquí. _____

6. Me mostraron todo lo que trajeron. _____

7. Son de nuestros primos. _____

8. Es para mí. _____

9. No sé con quién se fue. _____

10. Dame éstos. _____

C. Combine las dos oraciones con la palabra *que*, empezando con las palabras dadas.

　　　EJEMPLO: Ese chico anda por la calle. Es mi primo.

　　　Ese chico _____*que anda por la calle es mi primo*_____ .

1. Esos parientes nos visitan hoy. Son mis tíos.

   Esos parientes _____ .

2. Ayer vi una casa. Estaba en malas condiciones.

   Ayer vi _____ .

3. El hombre vino hace poco. Lo saludamos.

   Saludamos _____ .

4. Arreglé la bicicleta. Estaba rota.

   Arreglé _____ .

5. Las mujeres pasan por nuestra casa. Son muy elegantes.

   Las mujeres _____ .

6. Vendí unos muebles. Eran viejos.

   Vendí _____ .

7. Leí tres libros. Los había comprado en Madrid.

   Leí _____ .

8. Bebimos el vino. Era delicioso.

   El vino _____ .

9. Mi madre ha recibido unas flores. Las compramos ayer.

   Mi madre _____ .

10. El señor acaba de llegar. Va a subir a su habitación.

    El señor _____ .

D. Combine las dos oraciones usando *quien* o *quienes* con una preposición apropiada. Empiece con las palabras dadas.

　　　EJEMPLO: Hablé con el hombre. Era mi abuelo.

　　　El hombre _____*con quien hablé era mi abuelo*_____ .

1. Le di el dinero a la mujer. Es mi amiga.

   La mujer _____ .

2. Compré este libro para mi amigo. Él lee mucho.

   El amigo _____ .

3. Hablamos de los chicos. Son muy corteses.

   Los chicos _____ .

4. José vino con un amigo. Se llama Roberto.

   El amigo _____ .

5. Les mandamos los regalos a los profesores. Los merecían.

   Los profesores _____ .

E. Cambie la forma de la oración a una que tenga una parte separada con comas, según se indica en el ejemplo.

> EJEMPLO: Mi tió viene mañana y trae regalos.
> *Mi tío, que viene mañana, trae regalos.*

1. El Sr. Santos es muy rico y nos prestará el dinero.

   _____

2. Nuestros abuelos viven en España y vienen a visitarnos.

   _____

3. Hablé ayer con la Sra. Robles y ella fue muy amable.

   La Sra. Robles, _____

4. Mi amigo Miguel tiene sólo 14 años y se conduce ya como un hombre maduro.

   _____

5. Nos fiábamos del Dr. Vega y él no cumplió con su palabra.

   El Dr. Vega, _____

F. Exprese la contestación en una oración completa comenzando con *Lo que*, según se indica en el ejemplo.

> EJEMPLO: "¿Qué llevas en la mano?" "Un paquete."
> *Lo que llevo en la mano es un paquete.*

1. "¿Qué tienes en tu cuarto?" "Mi televisor."

   _____

2. "¿Qué estudian Uds. esta noche?" "Un nuevo concepto."

   _____

3. "¿Qué hace él ahora?" "Su tarea."

   _____

4. "¿Qué canta Ud. en el concierto?" "Una canción vieja."

   _____

5. "¿Qué enseña la profesora hoy?" "Algo aburrido."

   _____

G. Empezando con *Todo lo que*, cambie la oración según se indica en el ejemplo.

> EJEMPLO: Ud. siempre dice algo interesante.
> *Todo lo que Ud. dice es interesante.*

1. Ellos han comprado algo caro.

   _____

2. Tú dijiste algo malo.

   _____

3. Los ladrones robaron algo de mucho valor.

   _____

4. Ella trajo algo bonito.

   _____

5. El viejo nos dijo algo increíble.

   _____

H. Complete las oraciones según se indica en el ejemplo:

> EJEMPLO: *a.* El primo de María, ____*que*____ es una buena amiga mía, es jugador de fútbol.
>
> *b.* El primo de María, ____*el cual*____ es jugador de fútbol, vive en aquella casa.

1. *a.* ¿Conoce Ud. a la esposa del Sr. Robles, _____ trabaja de enfermera?

   b. ¿Conoce Ud. a la esposa del Sr. Robles, _____ es un abogado famoso?

2. *a.* Los hermanos de Lupita, _____ son muy simpáticos, juegan al tenis los sábados.

   b. Los hermanos de Lupita, _____ es mi mejor amiga, van a la misma escuela.

3. *a.* La profesora de los muchachos, _____ tocan en la banda, es muy amable.

   b. La profesora de los muchachos, _____ es muy amable, vive en el mismo barrio.

4. *a.* ¿Has visto al bebé de Margarita, _____ se casó con Miguel el año pasado?

   b. ¿Has visto al bebé de Margarita, _____ se parece a su padre?

5. *a.* La amiga de Carlos, _____ prefiere seguir soltero, no desea casarse tampoco.

   b. La amiga de Carlos, _____ espera hacerse doctora, le dice que carece de ambición.

I. Empezando con *La persona*, cambie la oración según se indica en el ejemplo.

> EJEMPLO: Llevo la camisa de mi hermano.
> *La persona cuya camisa llevo es mi hermano.*

1. Uso el carro de mi tío.

   _____

2. Tengo los discos de Ana.

   _____

3. Traigo las cintas de mi padre.

   _____

4. Voy a vender el tocadiscos de mi hermana.

_____

5. Veo la casa de mi vecino.

_____

J. Conteste en una oración completa:

1. ¿Cree Ud. todo lo que lee en los periódicos?

_____

2. ¿Quién es el amigo en quien tiene más confianza?

_____

3. ¿Cuál es la asignatura que más le interesa a Ud.?

_____

4. ¿Hay un lugar en su ciudad desde el cual se pueda gozar de una vista panorámica?

_____

5. Describa Ud. la casa en que vive.

_____

6. ¿Cuál es la revista que Ud. prefiere leer?

_____

7. ¿Quién vive en la calle cerca de la cual Ud. vive?

_____

8. ¿Fue interesante lo que Uds. aprendieron ayer en la clase de español?

_____

9. ¿Qué canal de televisión es el que le gusta a Ud. poner con más frecuencia?

_____

10. ¿Cuál fue la última película que Ud. vio?

_____

K. Traduzca al español:

1. _a._ Who went to the concert with Mary? _____

_b._ I don't know who went there with her. _____

_c._ The spectators who were there came from several states. _____

_____

2. _a._ "What is the date of her birthday?" "It's January 9."

_____

_b._ "Isn't it next Tuesday?" "I don't know on what day it falls."

_____

_c._ "I'm sure it's Tuesday.* The date that you mentioned isn't correct."

_____

3. _a._ What does he want? _____

*See the _Note_ above §17 on page 82.

    b. I don't know what he wants. _____

    c. What he wants is impossible. _____

4. *a.* "Did they come to the party?" "Yes." "Whom did they come with?"

    _____

    b. The boys they came with were very nice. _____

    _____

5. *a.* For whom is this package? _____

    b. I don't know whom it's for. _____

    c. The person for whom they brought it left five minutes ago. _____

    _____

6. *a.* We got to class late, which annoyed the teacher. _____

    _____

    b. What doesn't annoy our teacher? _____

    c. What annoys him is lateness. _____

7. *a.* Those who have the tickets don't have to wait in line. _____

    _____

    b. Who is the one who has our tickets? _____

    c. The one who has our tickets is my sister. _____

    _____

8. *a.* John's mother, who is very nice, is preparing dinner for us. _____

    _____

    b. Mary's brothers, who are my friends, are in the living room. _____

    _____

9. *a.* Yesterday I saw the son of Mr. López, who is my Spanish teacher.

    _____

    b. Did you speak to Susan's brother, who played football with us yesterday? _____

    _____

10. Who is the woman whose gloves you found? _____

    _____

11. Whose coat is this? _____

12. *a.* What are you asking for? _____

    b. I can't give you what you're asking for. _____

13. *a.* Who are those gentlemen? _____

    b. I don't know who they are. _____

14. The people ("persons") you saw are our relatives. _____

_____

15. The statue we are standing in front of is very famous. _____

_____

16. The buildings towards which you (*Uds.*) are walking are old. _____

_____

17. The food I can't live without is sold in this store. _____

_____

18. We went to a boring lecture during which Paul fell asleep. _____

_____

19. What girl were they talking to? _____

20. The girl they were chatting with is my sister. _____

_____

Part 2
Activities

1 Practice in Speaking

A. Oral Questions to be Answered Orally

To the student: Prepare this exercise by writing your replies in Spanish to the questions that follow. After the answers have been corrected in class, put away your written copy and be ready to reply *orally* to the same questions when your teacher repeats them in class for practice in conversation.

1. *a.* ¿Qué hace usted al volver a casa después de las clases?
   b. ¿Qué hizo usted ayer cuando volvió a casa?
   c. ¿Qué hará usted mañana cuando vuelva a casa?

2. *a.* ¿Cómo llega usted por lo general a la escuela?
   b. ¿Cómo llegó usted esta mañana a la escuela?
   c. ¿Cómo llegará usted mañana a la escuela?

3. ¿Dónde se juega al béisbol?

4. *a.* ¿Cuál es su programa favorito de televisión?
   b. ¿Fue el mismo el año pasado?

5. *a.* ¿Con quiénes viene usted a la escuela por la mañana?
   b. ¿Con quién vino usted esta mañana?
   c. ¿Con quiénes vendrá usted mañana?

6. *a.* ¿Por qué se necesita una licencia de conducir?
   b. ¿La tiene usted?
   c. Si no la tiene, ¿quiere tenerla algún día?

7. *a.* ¿Cuántos años tendrá su padre el año próximo?
   b. ¿Cuántos años tenía usted cuando empezó a venir a esta escuela?

8. *a.* ¿Dónde prefiere usted hacer los ejercicios físicos?
   b. ¿Los hace usted todos los días?
   c. ¿Por qué?

9. ¿A qué edad anduvo usted por primera vez sin ayuda?

10. ¿Quién le enseñó a usted a comer con tenedor y cuchillo?

11. ¿Por qué es necesario votar en las elecciones?

12. *a.* ¿Qué clase de libros prefiere usted leer?
    b. ¿Los prefería usted cuando era niño(-a)?

13. *a.* ¿Qué clase de música preferiría usted oír en un concierto?
    b. ¿La prefería usted hace cinco años?

14. *a.* ¿Cómo se podría ir a la ciudad de México desde su ciudad?
    b. ¿Cómo se iba allí en el siglo diez y nueve?

15. Si usted estuviera en un cine y alguien gritara «¡Fuego!», ¿qué haría?

16. ¿Observa usted siempre los reglamentos de tránsito en su ciudad?

17. ¿Adónde se va para comprar sellos y echar cartas?

18. *a.* ¿Qué le gusta a usted hacer los sábados por la noche?
    b. ¿Qué prefiere usted hacer los domingos por la tarde?
    c. ¿Y los fines de semana?

19. ¿En que parte de su ciudad o pueblo se encuentran las tiendas más modernas?

20. *a.* ¿Adónde se va para esquiar?
    b. ¿Cuándo fue la última vez que usted fue a esquiar?

21. *a.* ¿Cuándo fue la última vez que usted fue a ver al médico?
    b. ¿Qué tenía?
    c. ¿Qué recetó el médico?
    d. ¿Se curó usted pronto o tardó algún tiempo en recobrar la salud?

22. ¿En qué actividades de su escuela prefiere usted tomar parte?

23. *a.* ¿Qué clase de trabajo le gustaría a usted hacer en el verano?
    b. ¿Trabajó usted el verano pasado?
    c. ¿Trabajará usted el verano próximo?

24. ¿Dónde prefiere su familia pasar las vacaciones?

25. ¿Cuál es su pasatiempo favorito?

26. ¿Cuáles son algunos recursos culturales de su comunidad?

27. *a.* ¿Cómo se celebra el cumpleaños de un miembro de su familia?
    b. ¿Cómo celebró usted su último cumpleaños?

28. *a.* ¿Le permiten a usted sus padres usar el teléfono sin restricciones?
    b. Si hay restricciones, ¿cuáles son?
    c. ¿Cómo las considera usted?

29. En su opinión, ¿cuál es la función principal de la policía?

30. Describa usted un centro comercial cerca de su casa: número y tipos de tiendas, restaurantes, tamaño del centro, horas de apertura, etc.

31. ¿Cuáles son los medios de transporte de su ciudad o pueblo?

32. *a.* ¿Le gusta a usted visitar los museos de arte?
    b. ¿Qué clase de arte prefiere usted?
    c. ¿Hay una gran variedad de museos en su ciudad o pueblo?

33. *a.* ¿Prefiere usted un tocadiscos o una grabadora?
    b. ¿Por qué?

34. *a.* Si usted pudiera votar, ¿qué partido político preferiría?
    b. ¿Quisiera usted ser candidato(-a) en las elecciones?

35. *a.* ¿Cuál es su plato favorito?
     b. ¿Quién lo prepara: su madre, su padre o usted mismo(-a)?
     c. ¿Adónde puede ir usted para conseguir ese plato si no se prepara en casa?

36. *a.* ¿Cuántas veces por semana va usted al cine?
     b. ¿Por qué va usted al cine?
     c. ¿Qué tipo de película prefiere usted ver?
     d. ¿Por qué?

B. Situations That Require Appropriate Responses

1. *To the student:* Your teacher will read aloud two or three sentences describing a situation to which you are expected to respond by saying something appropriate. Respond in Spanish, addressing your listener as *tú* or *usted*, depending on the situation.

2. *To the student:* Your teacher will read aloud two or three sentences describing a situation in which someone says something to you. Reply in Spanish, using *tú* or *usted* depending on your relation to the speaker.

C. Oral Reports

To the student: Prepare a short talk in Spanish, to be given in class, on one of the topics suggested below. The vocabularies offer some words and expressions that you may find helpful.

1. Tell about a day you spent shopping. Include the following: why you went shopping, with whom you went, when you left the house, where you went, how you got there, how long it took you to get there, which stores you visited, what you bought and how much it cost, what your companion thought of the things you bought, whether you took your purchases with you or had them sent.

Vocabulary

ir de compras } to go shopping
hacer compras }
el **centro comercial,** shopping center, mall
salir de casa, to leave the house
llegar allí, to arrive (get) there
en autobús (en carro, coche), by bus (car)
ir a pie, to walk
costar (ue), to cost

llevar, to take, carry
hacerlos mandar a casa, to have them sent home
estar de vuelta, to be back
a eso de (las ocho), at about (eight o'clock)
¿qué piensas de. . . ? what do you think of. . . ?
tardar en + *inf.:* **tardé una hora en llegar allí,** it took me an hour to get there
la **prenda de vestir,** article of clothing

2. Tell about a game (basketball, baseball, soccer, tennis) between your school team and the team of a rival school. Include the following: the names of the two schools, where the game was played, who the key players were, when the game began and ended, who won, some highlights of the game.

Vocabulary

el **partido (de fútbol),** (soccer) game
el **equipo,** team
el **jugador** ⎫
la **jugadora** ⎭ player
el **jugador de relevo,** relief player
el **campeón** ⎫
la **campeona** ⎭ champion
el **espectador** ⎫
la **espectadora** ⎭ spectator
ganar, to win
perder (ie) ⎫
ser vencido, -a ⎭ to lose
ganar puntos (tantos), to earn points
los **ganadores (vencedores),** winners
los **vencidos,** losers
el **marcador,** scoreboard

el **cuarto,** quarter
la **mitad,** half
el **árbitro,** referee, umpire
dar gritos, to shout
dar en, to hit
hacerse daño, to get hurt
tener la culpa, to be at fault
tener lugar, to take place
tener suerte, to be lucky
ser aficionado(-a) a, to be fond (a fan) of
a causa de, because of
a la derecha (izquierda), to the right (left)
a principios de, at the beginning of
al cabo de, at the end of
de pronto ⎫
de repente ⎭ suddenly

BASEBALL

el **béisbol,** baseball (game)
la **pelota,** ball
el **bate,** bat
el **jonrón,** homerun
el **batazo,** hit

la **base,** base
la **base del bateador,** home plate
la **carrera,** run
el **lanzador,** pitcher
el **receptor,** catcher

BASKETBALL

el **baloncesto (básquetbol),** basketball (game)
el **cesto** ⎫
la **canasta** ⎭ basket

el **balón,** ball
la **pista,** court

SOCCER

el **fútbol,** soccer
el **campo** ⎫
la **cancha** ⎭ field

el **balón,** ball
marcar un gol, to score a goal

TENNIS

el **tenis,** tennis
la **pista (cancha),** court
el **saque (servicio),** serve
servir (sacar), to serve

la **pelota,** ball
la **raqueta,** racquet
la **red,** net

3. Tell about a school day that was unusually interesting or exciting.

Vocabulary

el **día escolar,** school day

emocionante (excitante), exciting

distinto de ⎱
diferente a ⎰ different from

extraordinario, -a ⎱
insólito, -a ⎰ unusual

el **incidente,** incident

el **suceso,** event
los **detalles (pormenores),** details
resultar, to turn out (to be)
tener lugar, to take place

4. Tell about a school dance you attended. Include the following: when and where the dance took place, how many people attended, whether you went alone or with someone else, what kind of music was played, what refreshments were served, what time the dance ended, and how you went home.

Vocabulary

ir a un baile, to go to a dance
tocar música, to play music
sacar a bailar, to ask (someone) to dance: **la saqué
 a bailar,** I asked her to dance
el **disco,** record
la **cinta,** tape
la **música rock,** rock music

servir refrescos, to serve refreshments

divertirse (ie, i) ⎱
pasar un buen rato ⎰ to have a good time

volver en auto (en autobús), to return by car
 (bus)
volver a casa a pie, to walk home

5. Tell about a movie you saw recently. Include the following: where and when you saw it, with whom you went, how you went, how much the tickets cost, where you sat, the title of the film, a short summary of the plot, whether you enjoyed the film, what you ate or drank in the theater, what you did after the show, at what time you got home.

Vocabulary

ir al cine, to go to the movies
ir en carro (por metro), to go by car (by subway)
ir allí a pie, to walk there
hacer cola, to stand in line
sacar las entradas, to buy the tickets
la **pantalla,** screen
tratar de, to be about, deal with
los **dulces,** candy
las **palomitas de maíz,** popcorn
hacer el papel de, to play the role of
el **público,** audience
aplaudir, to applaud
la **función,** performance
actuar, to act
interpretar, to perform (a role)
el **actor,** actor
la **actriz,** actress

el **dibujo animado,** cartoon
la **película policíaca,** detective film
la **película de horror,** horror movie
el **cuento de amor,** love story
la **ciencia-ficción,** science-fiction

el **argumento** ⎱
la **trama** ⎰ plot

el **personaje,** character
el **protagonista,** main character
el **héroe,** hero
la **heroína,** heroine
enamorarse de, to fall in love with
parecerse a, to look like, resemble
ser aficionado(-a) a, to be fond of
hacerse tarde, to be getting late
de veras, really
en cuanto a, as for, with regard to

6. Describe your house. Include answers to the following questions: Is it a house or an apartment? Does it have a basement? A garage? How many rooms? Which are they? Do you have a balcony or a terrace? Where do you do your homework? Where does the family spend most of its time together? (If you live in an apartment, does the building have an elevator? On what floor do you live?) In what sort of neighborhood is your house situated?

Vocabulary

la **casa particular,** private house
la **casa de apartamentos (de pisos),** apartment house
el **apartamento,** apartment
el **ascensor,** elevator
la **escalera,** staircase
el **tejado,** roof
el **garaje,** garage
la **pieza (habitación),** room
la **cocina,** kitchen
el **comedor,** dining room
el **vestíbulo,** vestibule, entrance
la **sala (de estar),** living room
el **despacho,** den, office

el **dormitorio,** bedroom
el **cuarto de baño,** bathroom
el **jardín,** garden
el **lavadero,** laundry room
la **planta baja,** ground floor
el **primer piso,** first floor (one flight up)
la **terraza,** terrace
el **balcón,** balcony
la **piscina,** swimming pool
dar a, to face
asomarse a, to look out of
servir (i) de, to serve as, be used for
junto a, next to
a la derecha (izquierda), to the right (left)

7. Describe your city or town in Spanish. Include the following: its size and population, important places and buildings, places of interest to tourists, transportation within the city or town, places of entertainment.

Vocabulary

la **población,** population
los **habitantes,** inhabitants
el **sitio de interés,** place of interest
el **edificio histórico,** historic building
el **aeropuerto,** airport
el **puente,** bridge,
el **centro comercial,** shopping center, mall
el **metro,** subway
el **autobús,** bus
las **diversiones,** amusements
el **almacén,** department store
el **museo,** museum
la **biblioteca,** library
el **teatro,** theater

el **cine,** movie theater, movies
el **estadio,** stadium
el **zoo,** zoo
el **ayuntamiento,** city hall
dar a, to face
dar un paseo (una vuelta), to take a walk
tener lugar, to take place
gozar de, to enjoy
parecerse a, to resemble, look like
sacar fotos, to take pictures
a lo lejos, in the distance
el **concierto al aire libre,** outdoor concert
todo el mundo, everybody

8. The fourth-year Spanish class in your high school has been canceled because of insufficient enrollment. Persuade your bilingual principal to restore the class, speaking in Spanish to strengthen your argument. Include the following points:

a. You and your classmates need the advanced class because Spanish plays an important role in your plans for the future.

b. The three-year course in Spanish is not sufficient to master the language.

c. Your school allows small classes that serve special purposes—"band," gymnastics, etc.—but does not allow small classes for advanced students in important subjects like Spanish. This is unfair.

d. Many Hispanic students who have enrolled for the course need to study their language and heritage at an advanced level. They would be very upset if the class were canceled.

Vocabulary

anular (cancelar), to cancel
la **clase del cuarto año,** fourth-year class
el **director**
la **directora** } principal
la **falta de estudiantes,** lack of students
persuadir a uno a hacer algo, to persuade someone to do something
el **curso,** course

inscribirse (para), to enroll (in), register (for)
la **clase avanzada,** advanced class
los **compañeros de clase,** classmates
seguir estudiando, to continue studying
enterarse de, to find out about
perturbar, to upset (someone)
la **gimnasia,** gymnastics
el **propósito,** purpose

2 Listening Comprehension

To the teacher: The passages pertaining to this exercise will be found in the Answer-Key booklet.

To the student: Your teacher will read aloud some short passages in Spanish. Each passage will be read twice. After the second reading, circle the number of the response that best answers the question.

Group 1

1. What are these people doing to avoid trouble?
   1 They're getting to the airport early.
   2 They are packing their bags at night.
   3 They are calling the airport for information.

2. What is the reason for this request?
   1 They want to have peace and quiet.
   2 Their suitcases are still at the airport.
   3 They prefer a large room.

3. Why does this person wish to stop?
   1 He is tired.
   2 He sees someone he knows.
   3 He is thirsty.

4. What has frustrated these people's plans?
   1 They have bought the wrong items.
   2 They can't find any stores open.
   3 There are no stores in the neighborhood.

5. What are the intentions of these people?
   1 to buy a new automobile
   2 to take a car trip
   3 to consult a travel agent

6. Where does this scene take place?
   1 at a post office
   2 at the movies
   3 at an outdoor cafe

7. Where does this scene take place?
   1 in a school
   2 at the zoo
   3 in a department store

8. What does this person prefer to do?
   1 watch television with his friends
   2 go to the movies instead of staying home
   3 read a book rather than watch television

9. What has upset their plans?
   1 someone's illness
   2 lack of transportation
   3 the bad weather

10. What have these people decided to do?
    1 have dinner out
    2 stand in line for a movie
    3 exchange an article of clothing

11. What are these people looking for?
    1 an automobile
    2 an apartment
    3 a place to eat

12. Where does this speech take place?
    1 in a restaurant
    2 on a tour bus
    3 in a hotel dining room

13. Why is this person making the call?
    1 He was absent from school and needs information.
    2 He wants to get together with his friend.
    3 He forgot something in his Spanish class.

14. What does this person wish to do?
    1 get together with a friend
    2 take a trip to a foreign country
    3 learn a new sport

15. What is this person complaining about?
    1 He doesn't feel well.
    2 His mother is a bad cook.
    3 There's not enough food in the house.

16. What does this person want to do?
    1 leave the store
    2 exchange an article of clothing
    3 meet someone in the store

17. What is the cause of this person's complaint?
    1 inclement weather
    2 a bad concert
    3 an irritating friend

18. Who is talking here?
    1 a newspaper vendor
    2 a high-school teacher
    3 a radio announcer

19. To whom is the doctor speaking?
    1 a mother
    2 a teacher
    3 his wife

20. Why can't the boy have the car?
    1 It's not working well.
    2 He doesn't know how to drive well.
    3 His parents have to use it.

Group 2

1. ¿Dónde tiene lugar esta escena?
   1 en una estación de tren
   2 en un aeropuerto
   3 en una playa
   4 en un teatro

2. ¿Qué ha anunciado el director?
   1 Un grupo de estudiantes ha triunfado.
   2 El equipo perdió el partido.
   3 La escuela va a cerrarse al día siguiente.
   4 Habrá una excursión a un sitio de interés.

3. ¿Qué desea esta persona?
   1 ver una película
   2 ver tocar a los músicos
   3 comprar unos discos
   4 vender unos billetes

4. ¿Qué problema tiene Rosa?
   1 Prefiere quedarse en casa.
   2 Está muy enferma.
   3 No le gusta la escuela.
   4 No hace buenos progresos en una clase.

5. ¿De qué se queja esta persona?
   1 de no poder ver a su hijo
   2 de estar muy ocupada todo el tiempo
   3 de tener un hijo lejos de casa
   4 de no recibir llamadas de su hijo

6. ¿Por qué se necesitan en Madrid tantas habitaciones?
   1 Muchos habitantes se encuentran sin casa.
   2 Mucha gente va a visitar la ciudad.
   3 Nadie quiere visitar las otras ciudades.
   4 Madrid es más interesante que las otras ciudades.

7. ¿Qué tratan de hacer los americanos?
   1 proteger a los niños
   2 eliminar las casas abandonadas
   3 construir casas para los niños abandonados
   4 animar a los niños a jugar y saltar

8. ¿Qué ocurrió aquí?
   1 Un caballo fue gravemente herido.
   2 Hubo un accidente entre un animal y un vehículo.
   3 Un coche fue destruido por completo.
   4 Un hombre perdió su caballo en la calle.

9. ¿Por qué no puede venir a casa el joven?
   1 No tiene medio de transporte.
   2 Se ha encontrado con un amigo.
   3 Hace mal tiempo.
   4 Quiere ver una película.

10. ¿Qué no puede hacer esta persona?
    1 aprender a tocar el piano
    2 estudiar para sus clases
    3 abandonar su trabajo
    4 pasar el tiempo con sus compañeros

Group 3

1. Why is the teacher unhappy?
   1 His students have not done well on an exam.
   2 His students are very stupid.
   3 The exam was very difficult.
   4 No one pays attention to him in class.

2. What does Mónica Fernández do?
   1 She listens to the radio every morning.
   2 She hosts a radio program.
   3 She listens to records while she studies.
   4 She is the owner of a radio station.

3. Why did Ricardo Montalbán go to Barcelona?
   1 to visit his relatives
   2 to make a movie for television
   3 to see a television program
   4 to sign several documents

4. What are many people doing?
   1 They are looking for means of transportation.
   2 They are visiting a certain city.
   3 They are going back to work.
   4 They are going on vacation.

5. What is this machine used for?
   1 buying train tickets
   2 obtaining credit cards
   3 sending train tickets to other countries
   4 learning how to use the computer

6. What is Adela's profession?
   1 bus driver   3 tourists' guide
   2 English teacher   4 architect

7. What did the patient discover when he woke up?
   1 He could see again.
   2 He had to go to the hospital.
   3 The anesthetic had made him feel sick.
   4 The doctors had not cured him.

8. What do we know about the University of Salamanca?
   1 It's a place where the young people of Salamanca get together.
   2 Lots of celebrations take place there.
   3 It was established several centuries ago.
   4 It offers special courses for teachers.

9. What does the writer tell us about the market in La Paz?
   1 It's a place where people meet one another to socialize.
   2 People come there only to buy and sell.
   3 It's a place where many tourists get together.
   4 Parents go there with their children to have a good time.

10. How long did it take the United States to restore the Statue of Liberty?
    1 a few weeks   3 more than a year
    2 several months   4 almost a century

3 Reading Comprehension

A. Passages Followed by Queries

To the student: Each passage in this unit is followed by a question or an incomplete statement. Choose the word or expression that best answers the question or completes the statement in accordance with the meaning of the passage.

Group 1

1. Si usted está preocupado por sus amigos que viven en otros lugares, recibirá noticias muy gratas. En su trabajo pueden surgir dificultades, pero si utiliza la inteligencia es posible que salga adelante. No se deje sugestionar por personas que estén cerca de usted. Actúe por sí mismo con serenidad y cabeza fría.

What does this horoscope say?

a. Your friends will send you bad news.
b. You are going to fall ill.
c. Look for another job.
d. Be independent in your actions.

2. A partir de ahora, gracias a un aparato fabricado por una empresa de Hong Kong, resulta muy fácil cortarse el pelo en casa, ahorrándose así los gastos de la peluquería. Se trata de un cortador eléctrico, de hojas finas y afiladas, que funciona a gran velocidad para darle un corte limpio. El nuevo *peluquero* está hecho de plástico muy resistente; su motor, que gasta muy poca energía, funciona con pilas y puede estar en marcha una hora y media ininterrumpidamente.

How can this appliance save you money?

a. It can be used at home.
b. It's an electric appliance.
c. It is made in Hong Kong.
d. It is made of plastic.

3. Una compañía japonesa acaba de lanzar una nueva serie de coches, llamada *Bluebird*, que incorpora un microprocesador novedoso. Por la presión de las manos sobre el volante o los giros irregulares de las ruedas, el microprocesador determina un comportamiento incorrecto del conductor y su grado de cansancio. Las horas que lleva conduciendo se controlan en un panel luminoso. Una alarma luminosa suena cuando la marcha del automóvil resulta peligrosa, indicando al conductor que no debe seguir conduciendo.

The alarm in this car indicates that

a. it's prudent to stop and rest
b. the gas tank is almost empty
c. the engine is in danger
d. the driver should continue driving

4. El origen de las depresiones mentales no está en la mente, como se cree, sino en el estómago. Algunos médicos afirman que la sensibilidad de este órgano a ciertos alimentos provoca reacciones únicas en cada individuo. Esas reacciones difieren de un individuo a otro, como difiere también el tipo de alimento que las provoca, pero se manifiestan en la depresión, la fatiga y la irritabilidad.

According to this article, what may be the cause of mental depressions?

a. having neurotic friends
b. eating while you're tired
c. eating certain foods
d. speaking with a person who is in a bad mood

5. Hace 100 o 150 millones de años la Rioja fue un paraíso de los dinosaurios. Este edén, que incluía también parte de la actual provincia de Soria, fue un delta en la desembocadura de un gran río en el mar, donde vivía una enorme manada de saurios de familias muy diversas, unos acuáticos y terrestres otros.

About 100 million years ago the Rioja was

a. like a beautiful garden
b. inhabited by prehistoric animals
c. populated by many groups of people
d. an area in which millions of animals perished

6. El pionero de todos los puentes colgantes modernos fue el puente construido por Roebling para sustituir al viejo ferry que unía Brooklyn con la isla de Manhattan. Roebling murió antes de ver finalizada su obra, pero los métodos de construcción que empleó en el puente de Brooklyn le han inmortalizado.

Why didn't Roebling see the end of the construction of Brooklyn Bridge?

a. He lost interest in the project.
b. He had to take a trip far from Brooklyn.
c. He didn't live long enough.
d. He found work in another place.

7. La cuarta parte de los españoles está convencida de que, en alguna ocasión, hemos sido visitados por seres extraterrestres, aunque sólo una pequeña minoría, el 3,7 por ciento, afirma haber visto platillos volantes. Muchos otros, sin haberlos visto, creen en los ovnis* (35,7 por

*objetos volantes no identificados

ciento). En lo que más coinciden es en la creencia de que existe algún tipo de vida fuera de la Tierra. Y el 41,9 por ciento se atreve a declarar que esta vida extraterrestre se trataría de seres más inteligentes que los humanos.

What do some Spaniards believe?

a. There are human beings like ourselves on the other planets.
b. Some day we will encounter people from another planet.
c. Intelligent beings may exist on other planets.
d. There is more intelligence on earth than on other planets.

8. Aún quedan kilómetros de costa donde la capacidad turística española ofrece sol y sosiego. Alicante es uno de los puntos preferidos por españoles y extranjeros, y se calcula que casi cuatro millones de turistas pasan sus vacaciones de verano en aquella provincia.

Why do tourists go to Alicante?

a. Its beach is very popular.
b. It is only a few miles from the coast.
c. It has more sunshine.
d. There are no other beaches.

9. En 1969, Franco designó como sucesor suyo al Príncipe Juan Carlos de Borbón y Borbón, nieto del último Rey de España, Alfonso XIII. Franco dijo que Juan Carlos llevaría el título de Príncipe de España hasta el momento en que fuera llamado a ocupar el trono.

What would Juan Carlos become when Franco dies?

a. King of Spain   c. grandson of Alfonso XIII
b. Chief of State   d. Prince of Spain

10. Una visita a La Paz, Bolivia, no debe terminar dentro de los límites de la ciudad. Muy cerca hay un sitio que hay que ver: el misterioso Valle de la Luna, una vasta área de extrañísimas e imponentes formaciones geológicas que parecen un paisaje lunar. Hay muy buen camino para ir en auto, pero lo mejor es bajarse de éste y caminar junto a las impresionantes moles pétreas, respirando el purísimo aire del altiplano.

Why should one visit the Valley of the Moon?

a. Many residents of La Paz always go there.
b. It is very different from ordinary landscapes.
c. It is not far from La Paz.
d. Several astronauts have visited it.

Group 2

1. El famoso juego llamado *cubo de Rubik*, que se hizo muy popular hace unos años en todo el mundo, ha sido superado por el *cilindro mágico*. Este juego ofrece 26 variantes más que el anterior, y pueden jugar varias personas al mismo tiempo. El juego, además, contribuye al pensamiento matemático, lógico y hasta lingüístico. En la Unión Soviética, gracias a estas propiedades, el *cilindro* ha sido recomendado como material de enseñanza en las escuelas.

(*a*) Why is the magic cylinder superior to Rubik's cube?
  1 It is popular among the Russians.
  2 It's a lot of fun.
  3 More things can be done with it.
  4 American teachers recommend it.

(*b*) How is the cylinder used in the Soviet Union?
  1 to teach students
  2 as an amusing toy for teachers
  3 as a children's game
  4 as a substitute for teachers

2. La NASA, agencia espacial norteamericana, acaba de anunciar que dentro de unos años instalará en la Luna la primera colonia extraterrestre. En 1990 una estación espacial en la órbita terrestre abrirá paso a una base lunar que será el trampolín desde el que se saltará a otros planetas. Esta estación lunar permanente ofrece varias ventajas: el emprender investigaciones espaciales que serían imposibles desde la Tierra; la posibilidad de hacer un examen profundo sobre la Luna y sus recursos; el uso de éstos para la producción de oxígeno, carburante y otras formas de energía; y la posible obtención de materiales de construcción y metales esenciales para la exploración del espacio. El costo de la operación es de ocho mil millones de dólares.

(*a*) Why is the lunar base important?
  1 The earth can be more clearly observed from telescopes on the moon.
  2 Tourists will be able to stay at the base while visiting the moon.
  3 Permanent homes can be built there.
  4 It will be easier to explore the solar system from a base on the moon.

(*b*) What can be done in the lunar station?
  1 build schools for astronauts
  2 learn more about the moon
  3 bring materials from the earth
  4 study the possibility of living without oxygen

3. Al aparecer los primeros rayos del sol veraniego, nuestras calles y parques se llenan de niños consumiendo conos de helados multicolores. Rara es la persona a la que no le gusten los helados. Los americanos, por ejemplo, consumen al año el equivalente a tres cubos llenos de helado: ¡veintisiete litros! Cinco veces más que los italianos, reyes del helado, y diez veces más que nosotros los españoles. Paradójicamente el consumo de helados no guarda relación directa con el clima de los países sino con su nivel de vida. Aunque parezca curioso, los países del Norte son mucho más aficionados al helado que los países mediterráneos.

(*a*) This article says that
  1 Spaniards eat less ice cream than Americans
  1 it's mostly children who like ice cream
  3 in Italy ice cream is most popular in the summertime
  4 people who live in the North don't like ice cream very much

(*b*) In any country, the consumption of ice cream depends on
    1 the quality of the ice cream
    2 the tastes of the people
    3 the climate
    4 the standard of living

4. Durante los días de Navidad, la mayoría de las personas envían tarjetas a familiares y conocidos, manifestando sus buenos deseos para el nuevo año. Hay mucha actividad en todas las oficinas de correos. Las sacas salen llenas de correspondencia, sobre las largas mesas se alinean cartas y tarjetas y las máquinas automáticas de matar sellos trabajan a ritmo muy rápido. Sin embargo, todos los esfuerzos resultan insuficientes para dar entrada y salida a la numerosa correspondencia. Durante la semana anterior al día 25 de diciembre, se calcula que la Oficina Central de Correos de Madrid despacha unos diez millones de mensajes y la de Barcelona, ocho millones.

(*a*) What do many people do during Christmas?
    1 They celebrate by having parties in the post offices.
    2 They send presents to their relatives.
    3 They write to their friends.
    4 They visit various members of their families.

(*b*) What problem arises in Barcelona and Madrid?
    1 Many letters arrive after December 25.
    2 The post offices are not equipped to handle the enormous volume of mail.
    3 The post office employees don't want to work.
    4 There are not enough workers in the post offices.

5. En diversas regiones de España los caballos gozan de libertad durante todo el año y son recogidos al final de la primavera. Muy de mañana, los ganaderos propietarios salen en busca de los animales y trabajan hasta reunir todos los animales dispersos. Los animales que han nacido durante el año son marcados, y se procede también a la separación de los que han sido destinados para la doma y futura venta; el resto volverá de nuevo a sus valles para gozar de un año más de libertad.

(*a*) Whom do the cattlemen look for?
    1 some animals who live free
    2 the owners of horses
    3 some men who need work
    4 the people who are going to run the rodeo

(*b*) Which animals will remain free for a year?
    1 those that love freedom
    2 those that live in the valleys
    3 those that will not be sold
    4 all those that were rounded up by the cattlemen

6. En 1898, Morgan Robertson escribió una novela en la que describía el primer viaje de un gran transatlántico, el Titán. El barco se consideraba «insumergible» pero se hundió en una noche de abril, tras chocar con un iceberg en el Atlántico. Catorce años después, el Titanic naufragaba en idénticas circunstancias a las anunciadas por Robertson, cuyo imaginario buque tenía numerosas características similares a las del Titanic. En 1935, William Reeves—que había nacido el día que desapareció el Titanic—montaba guardia en el Titanian. Movido por un insoportable presentimiento, ordenó detener el barco cuando llegaron al lugar donde se habían hundido los otros dos, evitando así ser arrollados por un iceberg.

(*a*) What did the *Titán* and the *Titanic* have in common?
    1 They were commanded by the same captain.
    2 They suffered the same fate.
    3 They were built in the same year.
    4 Some passengers had traveled on both ships.

(*b*) Why did William Reeves order his ship stopped?
    1 He had read Morgan Robertson's book.
    2 He saw an iceberg in front of the ship.
    3 He had been a passenger on the *Titanic*.
    4 He sensed that something bad was going to happen.

7. En la región de Patagonia, en la Argentina, al sur del pueblo de Calafate, se encuentra el Lago Argentino, bautizado así por Francisco P. Moreno (1852-1919) el 15 de febrero de 1877. Alrededor de esa fecha, Moreno y sus compañeros habían remontado el Río Santa Cruz desde el Atlántico, por espacio de un mes. Ellos eran de los primeros (a excepción de los indios tehuelches) en ver el lago.

En 1834, el capitán Robert Fitz-Roy, el célebre naturalista inglés Charles Darwin y veinticinco tripulantes a bordo del *Beagle* (el mismo navío empleado en la conocida expedición de Darwin a las Islas Galápagos), intentaron un viaje similar, pero regresaron después de veinte días de trayecto a causa del cansancio y de la falta de provisiones, sin haber descubierto el nacimiento del Río Santa Cruz.

(*a*) What did Francisco Moreno do?
    1 He joined the Tehuelche Indians.
    2 He spent a month sailing the Atlantic Ocean.
    3 He discovered a lake.
    4 He conquered a tribe of Indians.

(*b*) Why were Fitz-Roy and Darwin unable to complete their journey upriver?
    1 They were tired and didn't have enough to eat.
    2 They didn't know the territory very well.
    3 The ship was in poor condition.
    4 They were attacked by Indians.

Group 3

1. Desde la conquista española en el siglo XVI hasta mediados del XIX se sabía muy poco sobre la historia maya antes del descubrimiento de América. Fue durante la década de 1840 a 1850 que las exploraciones de dos viajeros norteamericanos, John Lloyd Stephens y su compañero-artista Frederick Catherwood, llamaron la atención del público a las ruinas de Copán, Palenque y Chichén-Itzá. Poco después, un grupo de exploradores y profesores inició un gran esfuerzo para descifrar los enigmas de la civilización maya, y ese esfuerzo sigue hoy día. Mientras más se aprendía acerca de los mayas, tanto los arqueólogos como las personas no expertas se asombraban de sus maravillosos talentos. Sin tener herramientas de metal, animales de carga, ni la rueda, los mayas erigieron centenares de centros ceremoniales y ciudades llenas de plazas, caminos, acrópolis y templos de piedra, pirámides, palacios y santuarios. Durante la «Edad de Oro»—el período clásico (d. de C. 250–800)—algunas de estas ciudades tenían 40.000 habitantes, con estructuras que satisfacían las necesidades tanto religiosas como seculares.

(*a*) ¿Cómo se descubrió lo que hoy sabemos acerca de la antigua civilización maya?
  1 Las ruinas de la civilización maya revelan mucho sobre su historia y manera de vivir.
  2 Los conquistadores españoles nos dejaron muchos informes sobre los mayas.
  3 Los mayas de hoy nos han contado mucho sobre la historia de sus antepasados.
  4 Las personas no expertas han descubierto muchos hechos sobre sus maravillosos talentos.

(*b*) ¿Qué hizo John Lloyd Stephens?
  1 Estableció una residencia en Chichén-Itzá.
  2 Luchó por la libertad de los indios.
  3 Exploró las tierras mayas acompañado de un amigo.
  4 Hizo un viaje a los Estados Unidos.

(*c*) ¿Por qué nos asombran todavía los mayas antiguos?
  1 Descubrieron minas de oro.
  2 Establecieron una religión extraordinaria.
  3 Encontraron sitios arqueológicos.
  4 Lograron construir muchas estructuras imponentes.

2. El 25 de diciembre, Navidad de 1884, habría de ser un día trágico en la historia de Andalucía. Según un relato del señor Félix Vallaure, de Linares (Jaén), a las 20 horas 55 minutos de la noche hubo una primera sacudida de gran violencia, que se repitió a las 23.44. Estaba con algunos amigos en el comedor de su casa cuando oyeron un ruido semejante al de un carruaje que se acerca. Inmediatamente sintieron un balanceo como el de un buque, y empezaron a moverse los muebles, cristalería y lámparas de gas. Pareció que la casa iba a derrumbarse y vacilaron entre huir o permanecer quietos.

(*a*) ¿Qué pasó el 25 de diciembre de 1884 en Andalucía?
  1 Félix Vallaure se murió.
  2 Hubo un temblor de tierra.
  3 Había una gran celebración en Linares.
  4 Unas personas se pusieron violentas.

(*b*) El incidente ocurrió
  1 por la tarde
  2 a la medianoche en punto
  3 antes de la medianoche
  4 durante una cena

(*c*) ¿Qué problema tuvieron los que estaban presentes?
  1 No sabían qué hacer.
  2 Trataron de controlar el movimiento.
  3 Uno de ellos se cayó.
  4 No podían salir de la casa.

3. Los Wright—Wilbur (1867–1912) y Orville (1871–1948)—eran los dos hijos menores de los cinco que tenía un clérigo protestante que en las últimas décadas del siglo XIX vivía en Dayton (Ohio). El interés de los dos hermanos por las cosas del aire prendió un día de 1878 (Wilbur tenía once años, y siete Orville), cuando su padre les regaló un pequeño «avión-juguete» del estilo de los que Pénaud diseñaba en Francia. Ni que decir tiene que lo probaron, desmontaron y volvieron a montar infinidad de veces, dedicándose desde entonces, en sus ratos de ocio, a construir aparatos similares, cometas y pequeños planeadores. En 1890 ambos hermanos establecieron un taller de bicicletas con el que rápidamente obtuvieron prósperos resultados. Esto les ayudó a convertirse en expertos mecánicos, a la vez que les proporcionaba los medios económicos para sus experimentos aeronáuticos ya a mayor escala. Vivamente impresionados por las noticias que les llegaban de Europa relativas a los vuelos planeados de Lilienthal, se dedicaron, ya seriamente, al estudio de la Aerodinámica.

(*a*) ¿Cuándo comenzaron a interesarse los hermanos Wright en cosas que volaban?
  1 cuando volaron con su padre
  2 cuando fueron a Francia
  3 en el cumpleaños de Wilbur
  4 al recibir un regalo de su padre

(*b*) ¿Cómo se hicieron buenos mecánicos los dos hermanos?
  1 construyendo pequeños aviones-juguetes
  2 observando a su padre
  3 correspondiendo con Pénaud
  4 trabajando en bicicletas

(*c*) ¿Qué les impresionaba a los dos hermanos?
  1 los aeroplanos de otros expertos norteamericanos
  2 los modos de ganar dinero
  3 la construcción de nuevos tipos de bicicletas
  4 el trabajo de un aviador europeo

4. «Año nuevo, vida nueva.» Después de los días navideños se recibe también con alegría la despedida del año. La fiesta de Nochevieja tiene ya menos sentido familiar; se abandona la casa para beber champaña o consumir las uvas de la suerte en otros lugares. Éste es un viejo rito cuyo origen se pierde en el tiempo. A las doce de la noche, toda España come las doce uvas blancas—una por cada campanada del reloj. La última uva se come a la medianoche en punto. Las calles animadas hasta ya entrada la madrugada están llenas de personas que cantan acompañadas de guitarras y otros instrumentos. En la vieja Puerta del Sol medio Madrid contempla la última vez que la bola dorada del reloj desciende durante el año viejo. Se organizan mesas en los hoteles, en los comedores de lujosos o modestos restaurantes, en las salas de fiestas. Las uvas también se comen en teatros, cines y toda sala de espectáculos. Después se baila hasta bien entrado el día del año recién nacido.

(*a*) ¿Cuándo ocurren estas escenas?
  1 durante las vacaciones de verano
  2 antes de la Navidad
  3 en la primavera
  4 el 31 de diciembre

(*b*) ¿Qué se nota en las calles?
    1 Todos desaparecen a medianoche.
    2 La gente celebra una vieja costumbre.
    3 Toda la ciudad mira un reloj.
    4 Pasan muchos automóviles.

(*c*) ¿Hasta cuándo baila la gente?
    1 hasta el fin de semana
    2 hasta la mañana del primero de enero
    3 hasta la noche del día siguiente
    4 hasta comer todas las uvas blancas

5. En la noche del 5 al 6 de enero, fieles a su cita con los niños de España, los Reyes Magos de Oriente hacen su entrada triunfal en todas las ciudades españolas. En esa noche, sus Majestades llegan a todas las ventanas del país. El juguete pedido llega siempre. A esto contribuyen los padres, encargados de enviar las cartas a los Reyes Magos. Cada año se gastan en estas fechas millones de pesetas en juguetes. Los vehículos dirigidos por control remoto o por control eléctrico son populares este año, en gran cantidad y variedad, en los escaparates de las tiendas de juguetes.

(*a*) ¿Por qué es tan importante para los niños la noche del 5 al 6 de enero?
    1 No tienen que ir a la escuela.
    2 Van a visitar a los Reyes Magos.
    3 Se reúnen con sus amigos.
    4 Van a recibir regalos.

(*b*) En realidad, ¿de dónde vienen los juguetes?
    1 de los padres de los niños
    2 de los Reyes del Oriente
    3 del gobierno
    4 del Rey de España

(*c*) ¿Qué regalos son los más populares entre los niños?
    1 los coches caros
    2 los juguetes eléctricos
    3 las figuras de los Reyes Magos
    4 cartas de los Reyes

6. A las siete y media de la mañana del 22 de noviembre de 1682, un joven inglés observaba por un telescopio desde su casa, en las afueras de Londres, la aparición de un intrigante cuerpo celeste. Apenas hacía tres meses que un astrónomo alemán, Georg Samuel Dorffel, había alertado a todos sus colegas europeos de la presencia de un nuevo «cometa», nombre que habían dado los griegos a unos peculiares astros que, por su aspecto, semejaban la larga cabellera de una mujer: *astron kometes*. Edmund Halley tenía 26 años cuando vislumbró por primera vez el cometa que había de llevar su nombre. Era hijo de un próspero fabricante de jabones que había intuido muy pronto los talentos de su hijo, su genio prometedor, y le había llenado de libros y maestros, e incluso le había comprado uno de aquellos «curiosos aparatos» con que observar las estrellas y planetas, inventados por un par de ópticos holandeses en 1608. En la escuela de San Pablo, donde hizo Edmund sus estudios, se interesó de inmediato por la nueva filosofía de la ciencia, que no era ni más ni menos que la más vieja de todas. Como él mismo contaría años más tarde: «Desde mi más tierna edad, me entregué enteramente a la consideración de la Astronomía.»

(*a*) ¿Qué hacía el joven inglés una mañana?
1 Miraba un objeto en el cielo.
2 Viajaba fuera de Londres.
3 Estudiaba para un examen.
4 Se preparaba para ir a Alemania.

(*b*) ¿Por qué le daba libros el padre de Halley?
1 Era su cumpleaños.
2 Eran muy baratos.
3 Conocía su talento.
4 Trabajaba bien en la fábrica.

(*c*) Según Halley, ¿cuándo empezó su interés en la astronomía?
1 a la edad de 26 años
2 cuando era muy joven
3 al ver un cometa
4 en 1608

7. Teodoro de Jesús Villarué, musculoso, delgado, moreno—más conocido por su apodo profesional de Yoyo—es un artista primitivo cuyo medio no es ni la acuarela ni el óleo, sino el esmalte para exteriores. Yoyo, que fue maestro de escuela en la ciudad de Panamá, desde hace 35 años pinta vehículos comerciales—a veces hasta dos taxis diarios—para ganarse la vida y pagarle los estudios universitarios a Anel, su hijo menor, y un sueldo a Danilo, su hijo mayor, que lo ayuda con la pintura. Lo que más le gusta a Yoyo es pintar autobuses de colores primarios brillantes. Las escenas primitivas de seres extraterrestres que vienen a este mundo y las casitas acogedoras rodeadas de árboles de follaje otoñal son características del estilo de Yoyo.

Nadie sabe exactamente cómo la pintura de autobuses empezó en Panamá. Al principio, el color se usaba en los vehículos—que son particulares—para indicar las rutas: la ruta roja indicaba un lugar de destino, la azul otro.

(*a*) ¿Qué trabajo hacía Yoyo antes de ser pintor?
1 Era chofer de un taxi.
2 Enseñaba a niños.
3 Conducía autobuses.
4 No tenía trabajo fijo.

(*b*) En cuanto a la pintura de los autobuses, se podría decir que
1 no se sabe cómo se originó en Panamá
2 Teodoro de Jesús Villarué fue el primero en hacerlo
3 varios pintores lo habían hecho en los Estados Unidos
4 se pintan no sólo los autobuses sino también los carros privados

(*c*) Una de las razones por las cuales Yoyo hace este tipo de trabajo es:
1 divertirse con sus hijos
2 hacer viajes en su autobús
3 satisfacer las demandas del gobierno
4 pagar la educación de uno de sus hijos

Group 4

1. Científicos norteamericanos han diseñado unos robots* para que jueguen con los niños. Están mucho más humanizados que los que se han creado hasta ahora, y además emiten música. La idea original fue la del compositor inglés Peter Shelley, que vio cómo, a pesar de estar entrando en la era de las computadoras, los robots seguían siendo una cosa extraña para la mayoría de la gente. Ante esto, pensó dar a los niños unos dinámicos amigos de la era espacial, que les ayudasen a prepararse para el futuro. El resultado de la idea es un grupo de robots compuesto por *Robotman* y sus amigos: *Stellar*, una robot lista, inventiva y muy femenina, *Opss*, el pequeño del grupo, y *Lintb*, la mascota. Lo más original de estos robots es que tienen como única función hacer felices a los niños. Su medio de comunicación preferido es la música y el amor, sin el que pierden rápidamente su energía, ya que viven gracias a las caricias de los niños.

(a) ¿Para qué se han creado los robots?
   1 para divertir a los adultos
   2 para enseñar música a los niños
   3 para ser compañeros de los niños
   4 para sustituir a los maestros

(b) ¿Qué piensan muchas personas de los robots?
   1 No les gustan.
   2 No los comprenden muy bien.
   3 Creen que no son apropiados para los niños.
   4 Quieren jugar con ellos.

(c) ¿Para qué sirven estos robots?
   1 para divertir a los niños
   2 para ayudar a los adultos a cuidar a los niños
   3 para acompañar a los niños a la escuela
   4 para entretener a todo el mundo

(d) ¿De qué dependen los robots?
   1 de la energía espacial
   2 de la música
   3 de las computadoras
   4 del cariño de los niños

2. Todos sabemos que la policía inglesa es conocida por el nombre de Scotland Yard, y que en inglés Scotland es el nombre de Escocia. Hay que remontarse[†] al siglo XIII, nada menos, para encontrar el origen. En aquella época, cuando los reyes de Escocia bajaban a Londres para renovar su fidelidad al rey de Inglaterra, se alojaban en una residencia que habían construido en una gran finca o «yard». El palacio desapareció con el paso de los años, pero la calle adyacente recibió el nombre de «Great Scotland Yard». En 1829 Sir Robert Peel decidió la creación de la actual policía inglesa, que en 1840 instaló su cuartel general en un gran edificio situado en aquella calle. Los policías bautizaron su cuartel como «Scotland Yard», y así fue conocido desde entonces, lo mismo el edificio que la policía.

---

*In Spanish, this word is pronounced "robó" in both the singular and the plural. The endings -*t* and -*ts* are silent.
†volver

(a) Los reyes de Escocia iban a Londres para
   1 tomar parte en la construcción de una finca
   2 ver Scotland Yard
   3 encontrar el origen de la policía inglesa
   4 mostrar su lealtad a la corona inglesa

(b) ¿Qué se sabe del palacio?
   1 Se convirtió en una residencia para policías.
   2 Ya no existe.
   3 Llegó a ser Scotland Yard.
   4 Se hizo un famoso edificio.

(c) ¿Qué hizo Sir Robert Peel?
   1 Llegó a ser jefe de la policía de Londres.
   2 Se fue a vivir a Scotland Yard.
   3 Se instaló en la calle de "Great Scotland Yard".
   4 Estableció el presente cuerpo de policía de Inglaterra.

(d) ¿Quiénes dieron el nombre de Scotland Yard a la policía de Inglaterra?
   1 los reyes de Inglaterra   3 los habitantes de Escocia
   2 los policías mismos   4 No se sabe.

3. Ya descubierta la electricidad por Volta y sus continuadores y el telégrafo eléctrico por Morse (Baltimore, 1843), alguien había de pensar que si el alambre eléctrico podía transmitir a distancia impulsos que produjesen al otro extremo del hilo signos a voluntad, era lógico que algún día el hilo transmitiese sonidos, letras y finalmente palabras. Este hombre fue el escocés Alejandro Graham Bell, inmigrante en Boston, el año 1876. Allí, en su taller de Court Street 109, logra el día 10 de marzo del citado año transmitir palabras por un hilo electrificado de 16 pies y una placa vibratoria de cobre. Las primeras palabras transmitidas no tuvieron la menor solemnidad. Fueron las que Bell dijo a su fiel colaborador Watson, en el otro extremo del hilo: «Señor Watson, haga el favor de venir. Le necesito.» Así, tan sencillamente, nacía el gran auxiliar de la vida y de la civilización moderna: el teléfono. En ese momento empezaba en un taller de Boston el proceso técnico que llegaría a enlazar todo el mundo por medio de las ondas y los satélites artificiales puestos en órbita terrestre.

(a) ¿Dónde nació el teléfono?
   1 en la casa de Watson   3 en Baltimore
   2 en Boston   4 en un taller escocés

(b) ¿Cómo pudo comunicarse Bell con Watson?
   1 por un aparato nuevo   3 en persona
   2 por telégrafo   4 por radio

(c) ¿Qué le pidió Bell a Watson?
   1 que le trajera un teléfono
   2 que le comprara un teléfono
   3 que pasara a su taller
   4 que se pusiera en órbita terrestre

(d) Cuando recibió el mensaje de Bell, Watson estaba
   1 en otra habitación   3 en otro país
   2 al otro extremo de la ciudad 4 dormido

4. En el centro cultural de Madrid se celebra una exposición de arqueología taína, con piezas que hasta ahora nunca habían salido de Santo Domingo. Las cuatrocientas cincuenta piezas que se exhiben pertenecen al Museo del Hombre Dominicano, en la capital de la República Dominicana. Según el director del Museo, José Antonio Caro Álvarez, los taínos fueron los aborígenes que encontró Colón a su llegada a Santo Domingo en 1492. Esta colección se exhibe por primera vez en el mundo y la han traído a España por la gran fraternidad y similitud de carácter que existe entre los dos países. La cultura taína duró desde el año 600 hasta 1492. Algunas de las palabras taínas—*tabaco, cacique, hamaca* y otras—se han incorporado al vocabulario español.

(*a*) ¿De dónde vienen las piezas para la exhibición?
  1 de Centroamérica
  2 de Madrid
  3 No se sabe.
  4 de la República Dominicana

(*b*) ¿Quién es José Antonio Caro Álvarez?
  1 un profesor español
  2 el jefe de un museo
  3 un indio taíno
  4 un descendiente de Colón

(*c*) ¿Quiénes fueron los taínos?
  1 los aborígenes de España
  2 una tribu de indios de Santo Domingo
  3 los directores de un museo de Madrid
  4 los ciudadanos de la República Dominicana

(*d*) ¿Cuánto tiempo duró la cultura de los taínos?
  1 casi 900 años
  2 un siglo
  3 600 años
  4 menos de 500 años

5. El hallazgo de vestigios de una ciudadela preínca en la selva amazónica peruana, acaso más extensa que la de Machu Picchu y con más de veintitrés mil edificaciones construidas en ciento sesenta kilómetros cuadrados, fue anunciado por el explorador norteamericano Gene Savoy.

Estas ruinas, según Savoy, pertenecieron a una cultura originaria de la selva peruana a la cual ha denominado «Los Chachapoyas».

Las exploraciones realizadas ratifican la teoría de que el hombre peruano no sólo vivió en la costa y en la sierra sino que una gran cultura con características propias y definidas se desarrolló en la selva.

La ciudadela fue explorada por una expedición peruano-norteamericana y fue bautizada con el nombre de «Gran Vilaya».

El explorador norteamericano añade que todas estas edificaciones están unidas por caminos de piedra.

Según su teoría, estas construcciones formarían parte de una muralla construida por los «Chachapoyas» para defenderse de los ataques de los incas.

(*a*) ¿Qué encontró Gene Savoy?
  1 restos de una civilización antigua
  2 la selva del Perú
  3 los descendientes de una tribu perdida
  4 el origen de Machu Picchu

(b) ¿Qué se cree como resultado de estos hallazgos?
    1 Machu Picchu ocupa más territorio que la tierra de los Chachapoyas.
    2 Las antiguas tribus del Perú emigraron a otros países.
    3 Los indios peruanos hicieron muchas exploraciones.
    4 Los peruanos antiguos vivían en diferentes partes del país.

(c) ¿Quiénes colaboraron en estas exploraciones?
    1 grupos de indios y norteamericanos
    2 exploradores de los Estados Unidos y del Perú
    3 Savoy y miembros de su familia
    4 los Chachapoyas y los habitantes de otra región

(d) ¿Por qué se cree que existían estas construcciones?
    1 Conducían de un camino a otro.
    2 Servían de casas para los Chachapoyas.
    3 Una tribu de indios necesitaba protección contra otra.
    4 De allí los Chachapoyas sacaban piedras preciosas.

6. En las costas volcánicas de las Islas Galápagos, en Ecuador, vive un curioso reptil cuya horrible apariencia causaría pánico en cualquier calle de Lima o Caracas. No sólo su monstruosa figura y gran tamaño—algunos de hasta un metro y medio de largo—nos evocan a los antiguos animales prehistóricos sino que, además, echa «humo» por la boca y la nariz. Es una especie de «dragón moderno». Se trata de la iguana marina.

Pero no es su grotesca forma lo que ha llamado la atención de los científicos, sino el hecho de que es la única iguana en el mundo que se ha adaptado al mar. Se alimenta de algas, semillas y otras plantas acuáticas. Además, bebe agua salada y nada tan bien como cualquier pez.

Desde el punto de vista cardíaco, este reptil acuático es una de las criaturas más interesantes del mundo animal. No sólo es capaz de reducir la frecuencia de los latidos del corazón, sino que, además, puede voluntariamente detener totalmente el funcionamiento de ese órgano por largos períodos, con el objeto de que los tiburones no la detecten debajo del agua.

Las iguanas marinas poseen una extraordinaria capacidad de orientación. Experimentalmente se les ha retirado uno o dos kilómetros del área donde viven e invariablemente regresan a su hogar.

(a) ¿Qué es lo que caracteriza a la iguana marina?
    1 Puede asustar a la gente que la ve.
    2 Vive en los alrededores de ciertas ciudades.
    3 Data de los tiempos prehistóricos.
    4 Se adapta mal a los experimentos científicos.

(b) ¿Qué distingue a la iguana marina de las otras iguanas?
    1 No le gusta nadar.   3 Puede existir en el agua.
    2 Tiene un aspecto muy feo.   4 Come sólo plantas.

(c) ¿Por qué es tan interesante la iguana marina?
    1 Es capaz de encontrar otros animales debajo del agua.
    2 Ayuda a los otros animales en momentos de peligro.
    3 No necesita el corazón para vivir.
    4 Puede controlar los movimientos del corazón.

(d) Se podría decir que la iguana marina
    1 prefiere ir en busca de tiburones   3 se mueve muy despacio
    2 no se pierde fácilmente   4 viaja lejos de su sitio de origen

Group 5

1. El mural «Guernica» fue encargado a Picasso por el gobierno de la República Española durante la Guerra Civil, para el pabellón español de la Exposición Universal de París que iba a celebrarse en los jardines del Trocadero y del Campo de Marte de aquella ciudad. Picasso lo comenzó a pintar en los primeros días de mayo de 1937, una semana después del bombardeo de aquella población[1] vasca por la aviación alemana. En su taller de la calle «Grands Augustins» número 7 de París, donde entonces vivía en compañía de la pintora y fotógrafa Dora Maar, realizó ocho bosquejos[2] previos para llenar el gran espacio disponible de 3,50 metros de altura por 7,85 de anchura antes de concluir la obra definitiva, hecho que tuvo lugar el 4 de junio de aquel año, según ha contado el propio Picasso.

La entrega del cuadro tuvo lugar poco después y pudo ser exhibido en la Exposición a la que iba destinado. Más tarde fue presentado en la Retrospectiva de Picasso en Nueva York (1939), volvió a París (Museo de las Artes Decorativas), otra vez a los Estados Unidos (Museum of Modern Art de New York), y recientemente ha venido a España para su instalación y exhibición definitiva.

(*a*) ¿Qué es «Guernica»?

   1 una batalla   3 un jardín de París

   2 la madre de Picasso   4 un cuadro famoso

(*b*) ¿Quiénes bombardearon a Guernica?

   1 los vascos   3 los franceses

   2 los españoles   4 los alemanes

(*c*) ¿Dónde realizó Picasso su gran obra de arte?

   1 en los jardines del Trocadero

   2 en el pabellón español

   3 en su taller en París

   4 en España

(*d*) ¿Cuánto tiempo tardó Picasso en terminar su obra?

   1 un año   3 cuatro meses

   2 unos treinta días   4 ocho días

(*e*) ¿Por qué se ha traído «Guernica» a España?

   1 para ser finalmente instalado en un lugar

   2 para ser exhibido en varios lugares

   3 para ser restaurado

   4 para recibir un premio

2. Cada vez que un miembro de la familia Rabosa se encontraba con uno de la familia Casporra, había disputas e insultos. Todo el vecindario temía que sucediera algo malo. El alcalde pedía que las dos familias hiciesen las paces, y el cura iba de una casa a otra recomendando el olvido de las ofensas.

En otro tiempo habían sido buenos amigos, y sus casas estaban separadas por una pared baja. Después de 30 años de lucha, en casa de los Casporra sólo quedaba una viuda con tres hijos bien fuertes. En la otra estaba el tío Rabosa, de 80 años, inmóvil en un sillón, con las piernas paralizadas, quien vivía con sus dos nietos. Ya no disputaban como antes, pero tampoco se buscaban ni se hablaban al encontrarse en la calle.

[1]pueblo   [2]*sketches*

Una tarde sonaron las campanas del pueblo. Había un incendio en casa del tío Rabosa, que estaba solo. El pobre viejo no podía moverse. Los nietos estaban lejos, en la huerta. La gente reunida en la calle trataba de entrar en la casa para salvar al viejo, pero les era imposible a causa del denso humo que llenaba la casa y salía por puertas y ventanas.

De pronto los tres muchachos de la familia Casporra corrieron hacia la casa y se arrojaron en el enorme fuego. Toda la gente les aplaudió al verlos salir llevando en alto al tío Rabosa en su sillón. Los chicos habían pensado que, aunque se trataba de una familia enemiga, el tío era un pobre viejo que debía ser salvado.

Y el pobre paralítico besó las manos de los tres chicos, llorando sin cesar. Se destruyó la casa, pero antes de que comenzaran a construir otra, los nietos de Rabosa tenían que hacer un trabajo urgente: derribar la pared maldita que habían erigido entre las dos casas.

(a) ¿Qué pasaba entre las dos familias?
  1 Había malas relaciones.
  2 Organizaban juegos entre los hijos de las dos familias.
  3 Realizaban encuentros amistosos entre los nietos.
  4 Había un matrimonio infeliz.

(b) El alcalde y el cura
  1 eran buenos amigos de las dos familias
  2 visitaban las dos casas todos los días
  3 querían que las dos familias pusieran fin a sus disputas
  4 construyeron una pared entre las dos casas

(c) El tío Rabosa
  1 no podía caminar
  2 siempre se disputaba con la viuda de Casporra
  3 tenía ganas de hablar con los hijos de Casporra
  4 buscaba otra casa en que vivir

(d) ¿Por qué estaba en peligro el tío Rabosa?
  1 Los bomberos no podían entrar en la casa.
  2 Un ladrón quería entrar para robarle.
  3 Sus parientes le habían abandonado para siempre.
  4 No podía salir de la casa.

(e) ¿Quiénes salvaron al tío Rabosa?
  1 sus propios hijos
  2 unos miembros de la familia enemiga
  3 los nietos del viejo
  4 algunas personas de otro pueblo

3. Cuando el tren se detuvo en la pequeña estación, casi todos los viajeros de segunda y tercera clase se quedaron durmiendo dentro de los coches, porque el frío penetrante de la madrugada no invitaba a pasear por el andén abandonado. El único viajero de primera clase que venía en el tren bajó de prisa y, dirigiéndose a los empleados, les preguntó si aquélla era la estación de Villahorrenda.

—En Villahorrenda estamos —contestó el conductor—. Se me había olvidado llamarle a usted, señor De Rey. Creo que ahí le esperan a usted con los caballos.

—¡Pero hace aquí tanto frío! —dijo el viajero, envolviéndose en su manta. —¿No hay aquí algún sitio donde descansar y reponerse antes de empezar un viaje a caballo por esta región tan fría?

(a) Los viajeros
   1 bajaron en seguida del tren
   2 hablaban con el señor De Rey
   3 se durmieron en el andén
   4 querían quedarse en el tren

(b) Villahorrenda era el nombre
   1 del pueblo donde se detuvo el tren
   2 del hotel del pueblo
   3 de uno de los viajeros
   4 del conductor del tren

(c) ¿Qué buscaba el señor De Rey?
   1 algo de comer
   2 un lugar donde descansar un rato
   3 un poco de luz
   4 la estación del ferrocarril

(d) ¿Qué tiempo hacía?
   1 Hacía buen tiempo.   3 Llovía.
   2 Nevaba.   4 Hacía mucho frío.

(e) ¿Cómo iba a salir el viajero de la estación?
   1 en automóvil   3 a caballo
   2 en taxi   4 a pie

4. El siglo XX, que ha inventado el plástico y las fibras sintéticas, no ha sido capaz de encontrar ningún material que iguale las propiedades del cuero. Los materiales artificiales han sustituido a la piel y han rebajado el precio de los productos. Pero no es lo mismo. Cuando se llevan zapatos de plástico o de goma, los pies sudan excesivamente por falta de aire y sufren malos efectos. El cuero no es otra cosa que la piel de los animales tratada con sustancias químicas que actúan de conservantes. Posee poros y unas fibras de albúmina que dejan pasar el aire. Se trata del mismo material que cubre nuestro cuerpo. A pesar de su condición de *transpirable,* el cuero no deja penetrar el agua.

No se sabe cuándo y qué pueblo utilizó el cuero por primera vez, pero los sistemas de conservación de las pieles tienen sus orígines en la Prehistoria, y se han mantenido hasta el siglo pasado, cuando la industria química descubrió nuevas formas de trabajo. Aunque no hay datos precisos ni definitivos, hay teorías que sostienen que el hombre prehistórico conocía el modo de fabricar el cuero, y es lógico que lo usase para preservarse de las inclemencias del tiempo.

(a) Según este artículo, el cuero
   1 es difícil de encontrar hoy día
   2 fue descubierto antes del siglo XX
   3 es igual a los materiales artificiales
   4 es superior a las fibras sintéticas

(b) ¿Qué defecto tienen los zapatos de goma?
1 No se pueden llevar en el verano.
2 No pueden sustituir al plástico.
3 Reaccionan mal a las sustancias químicas.
4 No entra suficiente aire.

(c) La piel de los animales
1 tiene sustancias químicas
2 no conserva las fibras y los poros
3 es semejante a la piel del cuerpo humano
4 permite que el agua entre por sus poros

(d) ¿Qué se sabe con respecto al uso del cuero?
1 No existía antes del desarrollo de la industria química.
2 Los pueblos prehistóricos sabían fabricar esta sustancia.
3 Se descubrieron todos los usos modernos en el siglo XIX.
4 Los hombres de la Prehistoria no sabían aprovecharse de las pieles de animales.

(e) Se supone que los hombres primitivos
1 no se interesaban en las pieles de animales
2 usaban el cuero para protegerse de los elementos
3 se servían del cuero para protegerse contra sus enemigos
4 creaban artefactos y ornamentos de cuero

5. Un buen día al hombre se le ocurrió contar, y con esto cambió su vida y tal vez su suerte. Debió de haber comenzado del modo más parecido a un juego infantil. Probablemente, ese hombre primitivo se puso a mirar sus manos y descubrió algo sorprendente: las dos tenían la misma cantidad de dedos; y no sólo las suyas sino también las de los demás.

Los antropólogos no están de acuerdo sobre la fecha en que el hombre se hizo consciente de los números. Unos sitúan este momento antes de la invención del lenguaje, aproximadamente 300.000 años antes de nuestra era. Otros creen que ocurrió con el principio de la época de las pinturas rupestres (en las paredes de las cuevas)—35.000 años atrás. Un desarrollo similar se puede ver hoy en los niños entre el quinto y séptimo año de su vida: en sus dibujos aparecen por vez primera seres cuyas manos tienen cinco dedos. Esto indica que los niños han comenzado a darse cuenta de que todas las cosas son contables. Cuando se comparan esos dibujos con otros hechos por niños más pequeños—de tres a cinco años—la evolución aparece aún más clara: las manos tienen un número indeterminado y variable de dedos. Del mismo modo, en las pinturas rupestres, figuras humanas aparecen con tres, cuatro o cinco dedos.

(a) Cuando el hombre aprendió a contar,
1 dejó de tener buena suerte
2 ocurrieron cambios en su modo de vivir
3 empezó a poner más énfasis en los juegos de niños
4 perdió sus maneras primitivas

(b) Al examinar sus manos, el hombre primitivo
1 se dio cuenta de que eran iguales con respecto al número de dedos
2 vio que eran distintas de las de otros seres humanos

3 quiso usarlas para destruir la naturaleza

4 no notó nada extraño con respecto al tamaño de los dedos

(c) Los antropólogos disputan sobre

1 el año en que aparecieron los números en las paredes pintadas por los primitivos

2 el uso de los números por los hombres

3 el empleo de los números en el lenguaje del ser humano

4 cuándo los hombres se dieron cuenta de la existencia de los números

(d) ¿De qué se dan cuenta los niños entre cinco y siete años de edad?

1 Todos los seres se desarrollan de igual manera.

2 Cada mano consiste en cinco dedos.

3 Es posible contar todo.

4 El número de dedos de las manos se puede variar.

(e) ¿Qué se ha descubierto en las cuevas primitivas?

1 figuras sin manos ni pies

2 pinturas de niños con cinco dedos en cada mano

3 dibujos de personas con diferente número de dedos en las manos

4 huesos de niños primitivos

6. Después de pasar el pueblo de Amecameca, muy cerca de la capital de México—unos 40 kilómetros aproximadamente—entramos en el camino que nos lleva al Popocatépetl. Aunque salimos a las cuatro de la tarde, nos ha tomado la noche—nos enredamos con las «horas pico» y el enorme tráfico del Distrito Federal. Llueve mucho y el frío se siente en todas partes. La niebla es espesa—mejor, así no vemos las curvas peligrosas ni los precipicios que se abren en la cuesta. Sin embargo, la carretera que nos conduce hasta el hotel es magnífica y segura, aunque el ascenso es fatigoso por la enorme cantidad de vueltas que debemos dar antes de llegar al campamento del Socorro Alpino de México. Nuestra intencíon era escalar el Popocatépetl, el famoso volcán del sur de la Sierra Nevada, cuya altura es de unos 5.452 metros.

Me habían dicho que el «Popo» se podía escalar sin muchos requisitos técnicos—algo fundamental en mi caso, pues no soy alpinista. La singular posibilidad de poder realizar «el sueño de una vida», como anuncian siempre los agentes de viaje, me mantenía excitado, e ingenuamente pensé que si estaba bien equipado y contaba con un buen guía podría emprender el ascenso sin mayores dificultades.

(a) ¿Por qué han tardado estas personas en llegar a Amecameca?

1 El pueblo estaba muy lejos de la capital.

2 Había muchos autos en el camino.

3 El chofer conducía mal.

4 No conocían bien la carretera.

(b) ¿Qué querían hacer estas personas?

1 subir un volcán conocido

2 pasar sus vacaciones en un hotel

3 visitar a unos amigos en un campamento

4 construir una carretera nueva

(c) El narrador creía que
  1 no necesitaba los servicios de un guía
  2 tendría que dormir antes de salir del hotel
  3 el volcán no era muy alto
  4 su tarea no sería difícil

(d) ¿Qué problema encontraba el grupo en el camino?
  1 dificultad para encontrar un hotel
  2 mucha gente andando por la carretera
  3 el mal tiempo que hacía
  4 muchas curvas

(e) ¿Por qué estaba excitado el narrador?
  1 Esperaba hacer lo que tanto había deseado.
  2 Iba a conocer a mucha gente nueva.
  3 Le gustaba mucho el hotel.
  4 Alguien le dio buen equipo para la excursión.

B. Slot Completion

To the student: Read each passage carefully, then choose the words or expressions on the right that make the best sense when inserted in the blanks. Circle the letter of your choice for each blank.

Group 1

1. Cristóbal Colón llamó erróneamente indios a los pobladores america-nos, pues pensaba que había desembarcado en la India. Más tarde, se les denominó "pieles rojas" debido al _____ del tinte con que se pintaban el rostro. Su piel era pardoamarillenta, pero nunca roja.

  a. color
  b. creador
  c. medio
  d. sello

2. Las crónicas históricas mencionan sólo un reducido número de mu-jeres piratas y heroínas de los mares. La navegante más famosa de todos los tiempos fue sin duda la reina Artemisa de Halicarnaso, la primera al-mirante femenina que estuvo al mando de una flota de guerra. Aliados a los persas, sus _____ lucharon contra Atenas en la batalla de Salamina (480 antes de Cristo).

  a. viajes
  b. barcos
  c. funciones
  d. barrios

3. Se está estudiando la posibilidad de la construcción de un túnel bajo el estrecho de Gibraltar. No es la primera vez que se ha considerado la idea; después de la primera Guerra Mundial, tanto España como Francia se mos-traron muy interesadas, aunque nunca se llevó a cabo. El enorme _____ de viajeros y vehículos que existe entre Algeciras y los puertos marroquíes hace que sea claramente útil la construcción de un túnel bajo el estrecho de Gibraltar.

  a. coche
  b. extranjero
  c. remedio
  d. tráfico

Group 2

1. Casi todas las carreteras del estado están identificadas con un número. Se emplean formas y colores distintos para identificar las carreteras federales, inter-estatales y estatales. Antes de iniciar un ___(1)___, es prudente consultar un mapa de carreteras para ___(2)___ la ruta por los números de carreteras que deberán seguirse.

(1)
  a. estado
  b. automóvil
  c. viaje
  d tipo

(2)
  a. volar
  b. usar
  c. conducir
  d. trazar

2. Júpiter es el más brillante de los planetas. Se encuentra a una distancia media de la Tierra de 778 millones de kilómetros. Su diámetro mide 142.700 kilómetros, más de once ___(1)___ el de la Tierra. Hoy conocemos muy bien a Júpiter gracias a las misiones Voyager 1 y 2 que en marzo y julio de 1979 pasaron cerca del planeta. Por ellas sabemos que los vientos atmosféricos pueden alcanzar ___(2)___ de más de 500 kilómetros por hora.

(1)
  a. veces
  b. tiempos
  c. horas
  d. metros

(2)
  a. reuniones
  b. velocidades
  c. viajes
  d. experiencias

3. Pablo Martínez, de ochenta y dos años de edad, posee un vicio: andar. Nació en Madrid, tuvo diez y ocho hermanos, nueve hijos y catorce nietos. El pasado 22 de junio ___(1)___ Madrid a pie hacia Barcelona (unos 600 kilómetros de distancia), donde había de llegar a las seis y cuarto de la tarde del día treinta. Su ___(2)___ era ver un partido de fútbol. Él dice: «Muchas personas me llaman loco, pero hago lo que me gusta hacer y no hago mal a nadie.»

(1)
  a. atacó a
  b. salió de
  c. voló a
  d. se acordó de

(2)
  a. esposa
  b. muerte
  c. viaje
  d. motivo

Group 3

1. Cristóbal Colón ha sido uno de los más eminentes entre los navegantes y descubridores que han existido en el mundo. Según la mayoría de sus ___(1)___, nació Cristóbal Colón en Génova (Italia) hacia el año 1436; algunos historiadores le han supuesto nacido en España, en Galicia según unos, y en Cataluña según otros. Fue marino desde muy temprana edad, y de 1470 a 1483 hizo diversos viajes por el Atlántico, llegando hasta Islandia y la Guinea. Después fijó su ___(2)___ en Portugal, donde se casó con la hija de un célebre marino llamado Pedestrello. Se fue a Génova para exponer sus planes de ___(3)___ nuevas tierras, pero no encontró la ayuda que necesitaba, como tampoco la encontró luego en Portugal ni en Inglaterra. Entonces decidió ofrecerse a los Reyes Católicos de España, esperando que ellos le ayudaran en su empresa.

(1)
  a. marinos
  b. edades
  c. biógrafos
  d. títulos

(2)
  a. residencia
  b. excursión
  c. nacimiento
  d. vuelo

(3)
  a. destruir
  b. descubrir
  c. empezar
  d. contener

2. Gretchen Kathryn Gross-Kettler, «turista diez millones» de España, ha llegado al aeropuerto de Barajas en vuelo «charter», procedente de Nueva York. La señorita Gross-Kettler tiene diecisiete años, es rubia y cursó en Pensilvania los ____(1)____ preparatorios a su ingreso en la Universidad. Ha llegado a España con un grupo de ciento cincuenta estudiantes que ____(2)____ nuestro país durante un mes, en un viaje de estudios. La «turista diez millones» de este año es hija de un profesor de un centro universitario de Maryland. Aunque no ha estado nunca en España, Gretchen asegura haber leído mucho sobre nuestro país, pues—según afirmó—en Estados Unidos existe un gran ____(3)____ por España.

(1)   *a.* campos
      b. temas
      c. placeres
      d. estudios

(2)   *a.* borrarán
      b. recorrerán
      c. cortarán
      d. poseerán

(3)   *a.* puerto
      b. examen
      c. interés
      d. viaje

3. En el famoso Capitolio de Washington, donde se reúne el Congreso de los Estados Unidos, hay una puerta bien conocida que lleva el nombre de «Puerta de España» o «Puerta de Colón». Por ella entraron los Reyes de España cuando fueron ____(1)____ por todo el Congreso de los Estados Unidos. Eran huéspedes de honor para la conmemoración del segundo centenario de la ____(2)____ de ese país, a cuya libertad tanto contribuyó España con dinero, con hombres, con barcos y con armas. La famosa puerta fue modelada en bronce por Randolph Rogers en 1858, y contiene bajorrelieves (bas-reliefs) que ilustran diversas escenas del ____(3)____ de América.

(1)   *a.* recibidos
      b. encarcelados
      c. atropellados
      d. dirigidos

(2)   *a.* caída
      b. huida
      c. independencia
      d. falta

(3)   *a.* relato
      b. descubrimiento
      c. Congreso
      d. teatro

Group 4

1. Julio Reol, mecánico de vuelo de la compañía Iberia, fabricó un Sorenai II en el garaje de su casa. Algo más de un año y medio tardó en ____(1)____ un avión de algo más de cuatro metros de fuselaje que alcanza una ____(2)____ de 170 kilómetros por hora, con una autonomía de cuatro horas. El motor es de un coche Volkswagen. El adaptar el motor de un coche a un avión fue una de las cosas que más le costó. Todo ____(3)____ en diciembre de 1981 cuando regresó de Wisconsin con los planos debajo del brazo; el 10 de agosto de 1983 el Sorenai II se estrenó en Robledillo, pilotado por Rafael Vecino Gallego. Julio Reol era aficionado a aeromodelismo de vuelo circular, más tarde de radio control, cuando tuvo la idea de ____(4)____ su propio avión.

(1)   *a.* destruir
      b. comprar
      c. fabricar
      d. volar

(2)   *a.* llegada
      b. velocidad
      c. altura
      d. tierra

(3)   *a.* empezó
      b. funcionó
      c. tomó
      d. abrió

(4)   *a.* llamarse
      b. transmitirse
      c. construirse
      d. venderse

2. El esquí acuático, aparte de un deporte, es una gran diversión. Se puede practicar en casi todas las playas y lagos, casi siempre con las motoras fuera-borda que pueden arrastrar a uno o más deportistas. Se trata de un deporte que ofrece gran cantidad de atractivos por los juegos y acrobacias, no sólo para el que lo practica sino también para los ___(1)___ . Desde que el mundo es mundo, el hombre ha tenido dos grandes ilusiones: poder ___(2)___ como lo hacen los pájaros y poder dominar el agua, no hundirse en ella, como hoy hacen los barcos. Fue en 1921, en el lago de Annecy, cuando a un aficionado al esquí sobre nieve se le ocurrió que podía deslizarse sobre la ___(3)___ del agua si se ponía los esquíes. Lo hizo y, a pesar de que se hundió pronto, comprendió que aquella idea era posible, con algunas ___(4)___ en las tablas preparadas para la nieve.

(1) *a.* espectadores
b. jugadores
c. barcos
d. obreros

(2) *a.* manejar
b. entrenar
c. sobrevivir
d. volar

(3) *a.* superficie
b. estampilla
c. arena
d. tempestad

(4) *a.* fotografías
b. ferias
c. modificaciones
d. piedras

3. Puerto Rico se vistió de luto por tres días por la muerte del cellista más grande de este siglo, el célebre maestro Pablo Casals, fallecido a la edad de 96 años por un fallo cardio-respiratorio. «Don Pablo», como le ___(1)___ cariñosamente sus amigos y admiradores, había sufrido un ataque cardíaco el 30 de septiembre cuando jugaba una partida de dominó en casa de un amigo. Su estado fue ___(2)___ durante más de una semana, y los médicos y familiares opinaban que su existencia se prolongaba gracias a la fortaleza física del maestro, quien tenía un gran amor por la ___(3)___ . El famoso cellista español legó a Puerto Rico el famoso Festival de música que lleva su ___(4)___ , así como la Orquesta sinfónica y el Conservatorio de Música de Puerto Rico, fundados por él.

(1) *a.* presentaban
b. servían
c. llamaban
d. daban

(2) *a.* crítico
b. famoso
c. ajeno
d. fuerte

(3) *a.* pintura
b. noche
c. comida
d. vida

(4) *a.* crítica
b. compañía
c. nombre
d. presentación

4. Desde hace tiempo sabemos que, de todas las criaturas del mar, los delfines son nuestros mejores amigos. Y también son animales de extraordinaria ___(1)___ . Para probar hasta qué grado son capaces de reaccionar a un entrenamiento programado de aprendizaje, son varios los acuarios que llevan a cabo notables ___(2)___ con los delfines.

Uno de estos centros es el estanque *Kewalo*, del Laboratorio Marino para entrenamiento de mamíferos acuáticos, perteneciente a la Universidad de Hawaii. En ese lugar, un grupo de pacientes biólogos marinos

(1) *a.* palabra
b. frecuencia
c. inteligencia
d. industria

(2) *a.* experimentos
b. honores
c. cantidades
d. escuelas

llevan a cabo, diariamente, un proyecto muy importante: ___(3)___ a hablar a dos delfines.

    Aunque el entrenamiento diario de estos delfines se realiza con prudente discreción, se sabe que ellos ya dominan un número impresionante de palabras. Los expertos de *Kewala* no esperan que los delfines logren aprender un vocabulario extenso. No obstante, sí consideran que estos animales tienen el potencial de inteligencia necesario para comprender y ejecutar muchas órdenes, y por eso tal vez podrían ser ___(4)___ en misiones navales de carácter secreto.

(3) *a.* dar
    b. enfrentar
    c. volver
    d. enseñar

(4) *a.* hechos
    b. utilizados
    c. vistos
    d. tenidos

Group 5

1. Yo era niño cuando me alejaron de mi casa para que empezara mis estudios en el famoso colegio de Bogotá. La noche anterior a mi ___(1)___, entró en mi cuarto una de mis hermanas, y sin decirme una sola palabra cariñosa, porque el llanto no le permitía hablar, cortó de mi cabeza unos cabellos. Cuando ella salió, todavía estaba ___(2)___.

    Me dormí llorando y sentí que iba a sufrir mucho en el futuro. Mientras dormía, ___(3)___ todos los sitios donde yo había pasado, sin comprenderlo, las horas más felices de mi vida.

    A la mañana siguiente mi padre insistía en que mi madre dejase de abrazarme. Mis hermanas, al decirme sus adioses, me besaban sin cesar. María esperaba humildemente su turno, sintiendo mucho ___(4)___, y le fue muy difícil darme su despedida.

    Pocos momentos después seguía yo a mi padre, que ocultaba la cara a mis miradas. Subimos al coche cuyos caballos nos ___(5)___ con impaciencia. En unos segundos estábamos en marcha.

(1) *a.* clase
    b. viaje
    c. juego
    d. premio

(2) *a.* llorando
    b. pidiendo
    c. bostezando
    d. andando

(3) *a.* hablaba de
    b. confirmaba
    c. olvidaba
    d. soñaba con

(4) *a.* odio
    b. contento
    c. tamaño
    d. dolor

(5) *a.* esperaban
    b. derrotaban
    c. huían
    d. amaban

2. En el año 2000 La población mundial viajará tanto que la exigencia de una lengua común se habrá convertido en una necesidad urgente. El dominio de un idioma universal para ___(1)___ ya no será un privilegio gozado únicamente por ciertas personas cultas. Tendremos que ___(2)___ cuál será esta lengua: una lengua sin fronteras que no estará pensada para nuestra generación sino para las generaciones futuras.

    La Organización de Naciones Unidas (ONU) utiliza cinco idiomas oficiales: inglés, español, ruso, chino y francés; y no hay suficientes tra-

(1) *a.* alegrarse
    b. quejarse
    c. quedarse
    d. comunicarse

(2) *a.* sufrir
    b. decidir
    c. componer
    d. realizar

ductores profesionales. Se podría escribir una enciclopedia con los _____(3)_____ de interpretación que se cometen.

En la Tierra se hablan aproximadamente 3.000 lenguas. La mitad de la _____(4)_____ mundial se comunica en chino-mandarín, inglés, español, ruso, árabe, hindú y portugués. El comercio internacional, el turismo, la política, los descubrimientos científicos … han impuesto ya la intercomunicación entre hombres de distintas _____(5)_____ y áreas lingüísticas. Hoy se necesita la introducción de una lengua para la humanidad. Sin embargo, esta idea no resulta tan fácil de llevar a la práctica.

(3) *a.* errores
    b. rasgos
    c. pasos
    d. nombres

(4) *a.* alimentación
    b. parte
    c. nación
    d. población

(5) *a.* combinaciones
    b. culturas
    c. palabras
    d. guerras

3. Aún en nuestros días nos fascinan las hazañas prodigiosas de Hernán Cortés, cuyas conquistas _____(1)_____ enormemente la extensión del imperio español en América. En el año 1519 Cortés llegó a México con menos de 600 soldados, marchó a Tenochtitlán, la capital azteca, e hizo prisionero al emperador Moctezuma. ¿Cómo se explica la _____(2)_____ de un imperio poderoso al que defendían miles de guerreros valientes que habrían podido aplastar a los españoles en el primer encuentro con ellos? Esta pregunta no tiene respuesta sencilla.

Moctezuma creía que Cortés era la encarnación del dios Quetzalcoatl, quien habría vuelto a México para vengarse del maltrato que, según una _____(3)_____ azteca, había sufrido en un pasado lejano. El emperador trató de aplacar a este dios extraño de cara blanca y barba gruesa; al acercarse los españoles a Tenochtitlán, Moctezuma salió a recibirlos con regalos muy ricos, pero no pudo disuadirlos de entrar en la ciudad. Sus guerreros, que nunca habían visto caballos, se _____(4)_____ al ver a los españoles montados a caballo porque les parecía que caballo y jinete eran dos partes de un mismo cuerpo monstruoso. Pronto se dieron cuenta de que los españoles eran hombres como ellos, y algunas veces pudieron _____(5)_____ por la fuerza de los números, pero la valentía sola no pudo vencer los mosquetes y cañones de los españoles ni la astucia de Cortés, quien sabía explotar la superstición de los aztecas y el odio que les tenían sus enemigos—algunas tribus indígenas que sufrían el dominio opresivo de Moctezuma y que llegaron a ser aliadas de los conquistadores.

(1) *a.* disminuyeron
    b. aumentaron
    c. bajaron
    d. perdieron

(2) *a.* caída
    b. victoria
    c. calidad
    d. belleza

(3) *a.* fiesta
    b. cocina
    c. lectura
    d. leyenda

(4) *a.* alegraron
    b. sentaron
    c. asustaron
    d. lavaron

(5) *a.* vencerlos
    b. invitarlos
    c. conocerlos
    d. traerlos

4
Writing Practice

A. Pictures

To the student: Write a story in Spanish suggested by what you see in each picture. Do not merely describe the picture. Your teacher will tell you how many words, clauses, or sentences each story will require.

The vocabulary below each picture offers some words and expressions that you may find helpful in writing your story.

1.

Vocabulary

conducir } to drive
manejar

la **autoescuela** } driving school
la **escuela de manejar**

la **lección de manejar,** driving lesson
el **instructor de conducción,** driving instructor
el **parabrisas,** windshield
el **asiento delantero,** front seat
el **asiento trasero,** back seat
el **conductor** } driver
la **conductora**

la **licencia de manejar,** driver's license
tener su turno, to have his (her) turn
abrocharse el cinturón de seguridad, to fasten one's seat belt

hacer arrancar el motor, to start the engine
ponerse en marcha, to start out
aprobar (ue) el examen, to pass the test
salir mal en el examen, to flunk the test
el **espejo retrovisor,** rear-view mirror
ajustar, to adjust
soltar (ue) el freno de emergencia, to loosen the emergency brake
el **coche (carro, auto),** car
pasearse en coche, to drive, go for a car ride
la **luz** } traffic light
el **semáforo**

pararse ante la señal de "stop," to stop at the stop sign

2.

Vocabulary

la **parada de autobús,** bus stop
llover a cántaros, to rain cats and dogs (to rain heavily)
el **paraguas roto,** the broken umbrella
coger un taxi, to get a cab

el **impermeable,** raincoat
estar de pie, to be standing
estar mojado(-a) hasta los huesos, to be drenched to the skin
hacer viento, to be windy

3.

Vocabulary

hablar por teléfono, to talk on the phone
estar echado(-a) en la cama, to be stretched out on the bed
estar aburrido(-a), to be bored

el **televisor,** TV set
pedir una cita, to ask for a date
apoyarse en, to lean against

4.

Vocabulary

el **cartero,** mailman
acabar de + *inf.,* to have just
entregar una carta, to deliver a letter

estar preocupado, -a, to be worried
acercarse a, to approach
recibir noticias de, to hear from

5.

Vocabulary

la **habitación de hospital,** hospital room
la **cama de ruedas,** hospital bed
el **enfermero** ⎫
la **enfermera** ⎬ nurse
la **mesa de cama,** bed table
el **médico** ⎫
la **médica** ⎬ doctor
el **televisor,** TV set

radiografiar, to X-ray
la **pierna enyesada,** leg in a plaster cast
guardar cama, to stay in bed
hacer una visita, to pay a visit
el **enfermo,** the male patient
hacerse daño ⎫
herirse ⎬ to hurt oneself

B. Informal Notes

To the student: Write a note in Spanish consisting of three or four sentences that convey the message indicated. The vocabulary lists offer some words and expressions that you may find helpful in writing your messages.

1. Tell your parents at what time you will be coming home this evening, and explain why you will be back so late.

Vocabulary

Querida mamá, dear mom
Querido papá, dear dad
Queridos padres, dear parents
sentir, to be sorry

llegar tarde (temprano), to arrive late (early)
quedarse, to stay
tener una cita con, to have an appointment with
tratar de telefonear, to try to telephone

2. Tell your teacher why you were late or absent.

Vocabulary

estar ausente, to be absent
la **ausencia,** absence
llegar tarde, to be late

la **tardanza,** lateness
hacer un recado, to do (run) an errand
perdonar, dispensar, excusar, to excuse

3. Tell your boss why you won't be able to come to work on a certain day.

Vocabulary

cuidar a un niño, to take care of a child   **sentirse mal,** to feel sick

4. You are expecting a package but will not be home to receive it. Ask your mailman to deliver the package to your neighbor.

Vocabulary

el vecino (la vecina) de al lado (de enfrente),   **tener permiso para** + *inf.*, to have permission to
  the neighbor next door (across the street)

5. Thank a relative for a gift that he or she has sent you.

Vocabulary

regalar, to give as a gift: **ella me regaló un disco,**   **mandar, enviar,** to send
  she gave me a record as a gift   **dar las gracias por,** to thank for
el **regalo,** gift, present

6. Tell your friend to buy, pick up, or return something for you when he or she is downtown.

Vocabulary

conseguir⎱ to get, obtain   el **recibo,** receipt
obtener⎰   el **dependiente,** sales clerk
ir al centro, to go downtown   el **almacén,** department store
devolver, to return, give back

7. Invite a friend to your birthday party.

Vocabulary

invitar a alguien a una fiesta de cumpleaños,   **no traer un regalo,** not to bring a gift
  to invite someone to a birthday party   **el sábado, 20 de abril, a las ocho de la noche,**
cumplir . . . años, to reach one's . . . birthday: **Voy**   on Saturday, April 20th, at 8 P.M.
  a cumplir dieciséis años, I'm going to be 16
  years old

C. Letters

To the student: The Vocabulary lists below offer words and expressions that you may find useful in writing the letters.

1. Write a letter to a friend in a Hispanic country telling her or him about a recent illness from which you've just recovered. Include the following information: how it began (the symptoms); how soon you visited the doctor; the doctor's diagnosis and prescribed treatment; how long the illness lasted; how long you stayed out of school; how you feel now.

Vocabulary

la **enfermedad,** illness
estar **enfermo,-a,** to be sick
padecer, to suffer
el **resfriado,** cold
la **pulmonía,** pneumonia
la **gripe (influenza),** flu
la **fiebre,** fever
el **dolor de estómago,** stomachache
el **dolor de cabeza (garganta),** headache (sore throat)
tener mucha sed y poca hambre, to be very thirsty and not very hungry
la **tos,** cough
toser, to cough
estornudar, to sneeze
las **glándulas hinchadas,** swollen glands
el **diagnóstico,** diagnosis
la **receta,** prescription

recetar, to prescribe
los **medicamentos,** medication
la **píldora,** pill
la **pastilla,** tablet
las **gotas para los ojos (la nariz)** eye (nose) drops
el **jarabe para la tos,** cough syrup
guardar cama, to stay in bed
sentirse (ie, i) mejor, to feel better
recobrar la salud } to recover, get better
reponerse
cuidar, to take care of
tardar (mucho tiempo) en, to take (a long time) to; **tardé una semana en reponerme,** it took me a week to recover
no tener prisa para volver a la escuela, not to be in a hurry to go back to school

2. You have recently attended a dinner party given by the parents of a Spanish-speaking classmate. Write a letter of thanks to the parents of your friend. Include the following: how much you enjoyed yourself, how gracious your hosts were, how glad you are to have their son or daughter for a friend, your parents send their regards and thanks.

Vocabulary

asistir a una cena, attend a dinner
agradecer } to thank
dar las gracias
invitar (convidar), to invite
pasar una noche agradable, to spend a pleasant evening

los **anfitriones,** hosts
gozar de, to enjoy
mandar (dar) recuerdos
quiero agradecerles (quiero darles las gracias por) su bondad, I want to thank you for your kindness

3. You and your Mexican friend Alicia* attended high school together. She has returned to Mexico with her parents, leaving her Mexican address with you. Write to her, telling her you miss her, how much you enjoyed her friendship, how much Spanish you learned in her company and during visits with her family, that you hope you and she will remain friends by writing regularly to each other, that you and she will meet again some day. Close by asking her to give your regards to her parents.

Vocabulary

gozar de, to enjoy; **gocé de nuestra amistad,** I enjoyed our friendship
volver a encontrarse, to meet again
pasar buenos ratos juntos(-as), to spend good times together
echar de menos, to miss; **te echo (mucho) de menos,** I miss you (very much)
pensar (ie) + *inf.,* to intend (to)

acordarse (ue) de } to remember
recordar (ue)
a menudo } often
muchas veces
de veras, really, truly
de vez en cuando, from time to time
dar recuerdos a, to give regards to

*If you prefer a male friend, call him Alberto.

4. Your Spanish teacher assigned for homework a composition that was due in class a week ago. You finished yours only yesterday. Write a note to your teacher, to be clipped to your composition when you drop it on her desk, explaining why you were unable to hand in your work on time. Tell her:

a. You work after school and on weekends and, for that reason, you don't have enough time to do all your homework.

b. However, you plan to quit your job this weekend. After next Monday, you will be able to hand in all your homework on time.

c. You thank her for her patience.

Vocabulary

sentir (ie, i), to be sorry
dejar de + *inf.*, to fail to
entregar, to hand in
a tiempo, on time
el **tema**
la **composición** } composition
el **ensayo,** essay
después de las clases, after school

el fin de semana, weekend
dejar el empleo (el trabajo), to quit one's job
darse cuenta de (que), to realize (that)
de hoy en adelante, from now on
de veras, really, truly
tratar de + *inf.*, to try to
le agradezco (gracias por) su paciencia, thanks for your patience

5. You have been entertaining your Peruvian pen-pal Raúl,* who is visiting the United States. He is staying with relatives, but tonight you and he have a date to meet at your house to go to the movies together. This afternoon your parents are sending you on an errand, and you can't be sure you will be back home in time to keep your appointment. Assume that Raúl speaks no English and your parents speak no Spanish. Write a note, to be left with your mother, explaining the situation. Tell him you are very sorry but you may not be back home in time, ask him to wait for you, and suggest other ways of spending the evening if you return too late for the movie.

Vocabulary

hacer un recado, to do an errand
sentir (ie, i), to be sorry
tardar . . . en, to take (*time interval*) to; **tardaré una hora en volver,** it will take me an hour to get back
volver (estar de vuelta) a tiempo, to return (to be back) on time

volver muy tarde para, to return too late to (for)
esperar, to wait for
tratar de + *inf.*, to try to
a eso de, (at) about; **a eso de las ocho,** (at) about 8 o'clock
cuanto antes
lo más pronto posible } as soon as possible

D. Persuasion

You are a member of the Spanish Club at your school. The club wants to have lunch at a Spanish restaurant during a school day, but it would take an hour to get there by bus. Your

*If you prefer a female pen-pal, call her Anita.

principal, Mrs. Contreras, is reluctant to give you the permission you need because you would miss too many classes while you were gone from school that day. Write her a letter in Spanish to persuade her to allow the club to take the trip. Include the following points:

a. The purpose of the trip (to practice speaking Spanish and to become familiar with Spanish cooking).

b. How you and your fellow club members could make up the classwork you missed.

c. The lunch would have educational value.

d. The members of the club would behave themselves well and be a credit to the school (*le haría honor a la escuela*).

Vocabulary

dirigirse a, to go to see (address oneself to) (someone)

el club (círculo) de español, Spanish Club

el miembro, (male or female) member

hacer una excursión, to take a trip

tardaremos una hora en llegar allí, it will take us an hour to get there

estar poco dispuesto(-a) a conceder permiso, to be reluctant to grant permission

perder (ie) instrucción, to miss instruction

el propósito, purpose

sacar (mucho) provecho de, to benefit (greatly) from

recuperar el tiempo perdido, to make up for the lost (missed) time

portarse bien, to behave well

consentir (ie, i) en, to consent to

estar de vuelta, to be back

tratar de + *inf.,* to try to

la cocina, cooking

familiarizarse con, to familiarize oneself with

E. Inquiry

You are answering an advertisement for a summer job as baby-sitter for a Spanish-speaking family in your neighborhood. In your letter, include the following data: your age and sex, experience with children of different ages, what school you attend, your grades, teacher-references, the phone numbers of other parents whose children you have cared for.

Vocabulary

el empleo de verano, summer job

el anuncio, advertisement

el guardián }
la guardiana } **de niños,** baby-sitter

cuidar, to take care of

vigilar, to watch over

tener buenas referencias, to have good references

la solicitud, application

solicitar, to apply for

llenar los requisitos del puesto, to have the qualifications for the job

servir (i) de, to serve as

confiar en, to rely on

preocuparse de (por), to worry about: **no se preocupe Ud. por nada,** don't worry about anything

sacar buenas notas, to get good grades (marks)

a tiempo, on time

de buena gana, gladly, willingly

de día, during the day

de noche, at night

APPENDIX

PART 1
SUMMARY OF VERB FORMS

To the student: Part 1 of the Appendix comprises the following sections:

I. Derivation of verb forms in all tenses.

II. Paradigms (lists of forms) of regular -AR, -ER, and -IR verbs in all tenses.

III. Paradigms of irregular verbs, that is, verbs that have irregular forms in certain tenses. This section does not include stem-changing verbs and verbs with spelling changes.

IV. Stem-changing verbs.

V. Verbs with spelling changes (orthographic-changing verbs) and verbs that have both stem changes and spelling changes.

Information given in one section may be repeated in another—for example, some verb forms displayed in section I may appear again in section II—but such duplication is unavoidable.

If you are looking for a certain verb form and are not sure in which section you will find it, look up the verb in the Spanish-English Vocabulary at the end of the book. The Vocabulary will indicate whether the verb is irregular, stem-changing, or has a spelling change. If it is regular in all tenses, no indication is given, and you should refer to section II.

I
Verb Forms in All Tenses

The Present Tense (see chapter 1)

I go, am going; does he speak? is he speaking?

REGULAR VERBS

Drop the **-ar, -er,** or **-ir** ending of the infinitive and add the appropriate endings for each conjugation:

> **cantar:** cant**o, -as, -a, -amos, -áis, -an**
> **beber:** beb**o, -es, -e, -emos, -éis, -en**
> **vivir:** viv**o, -es, -e, -imos, -ís, -en**

IRREGULAR VERBS

A. *Verbs that are irregular only in the first person singular*

-go forms		*other forms*	
caer	*caigo*	caber	*quepo*
hacer	*hago*	conducir	*conduzco*
poner	*pongo*	conocer	*conozco*
salir	*salgo*	dar	*doy*
traer	*traigo*	saber	*sé*
valer	*valgo*	ver	*veo*

B. *Verbs that are irregular in all forms except those for **nosotros** and **vosotros***

decir:	*digo*	*dices*	*dice*	decimos	decís	*dicen*
estar:	*estoy*	*estás*	*está*	estamos	estáis	*están*
oír:	*oigo*	*oyes*	*oye*	oímos	oís	*oyen*
poder:*	*puedo*	*puedes*	*puede*	podemos	podéis	*pueden*
querer:*	*quiero*	*quieres*	*quiere*	queremos	queréis	*quieren*
tener:	*tengo*	*tienes*	*tiene*	tenemos	tenéis	*tienen*
venir:	*vengo*	*vienes*	*viene*	venimos	venís	*vienen*

C. *Verbs that are irregular in all six forms*

ser:	*soy*	*eres*	*es*	*somos*	*sois*	*son*
ir:	*voy*	*vas*	*va*	*vamos*	*vais*	*van*

STEM-CHANGING VERBS

A. *Stem vowel **o** changes to **ue** in four forms (all three conjugations)*

contar:	c**ue**nto	c**ue**ntas	c**ue**nta	contamos	contáis	c**ue**ntan
volver:	v**ue**lvo	v**ue**lves	v**ue**lve	volvemos	volvéis	v**ue**lven
dormir:	d**ue**rmo	d**ue**rmes	d**ue**rme	dormimos	dormís	d**ue**rmen

Jugar belongs to this group:

j**ue**go	j**ue**gas	j**ue**ga	jugamos	jugáis	j**ue**gan

*__Poder__ and **querer** in the present tense actually belong among the stem-changing verbs, but they are included in this list because of their irregularities in other tenses.

B. *Stem vowel **e** changes to **ie** in four forms (all three conjugations)*

pensar:	p*ie*nso	p*ie*nsas	p*ie*nsa	pensamos	pensáis	p*ie*nsan
entender:	ent*ie*ndo	ent*ie*ndes	ent*ie*nde	entendemos	entendéis	ent*ie*nden
preferir:	pref*ie*ro	pref*ie*res	pref*ie*re	preferimos	preferís	pref*ie*ren

C. *Stem vowel **e** changes to **i** in four forms (-IR verbs only)*

| **repetir:** | rep*i*to | rep*i*tes | rep*i*te | repetimos | repetís | rep*i*ten |

Note the conjugation of **reír** (and **sonreír**): r*í*o, r*í*es, r*í*e, reímos, reís, r*í*en
A list of common stem-changing verbs appears in section IV.

Verbs with Spelling Changes

A. *Verbs with infinitives that end in **-ger, -gir**, and **-guir***

In this group, a consonant changes to preserve the original sound.

> -**ger** changes **g** to **j** before **o** and **a**
> -**gir** changes **g** to **j** before **o** and **a** } in the first person singular only
> -**guir** changes **gu** to **g** before **o** and **a**

prote*g*er: prote*j*o, proteges, etc.
diri*g*ir: diri*j*o, diriges, etc.
se*gu*ir: si*g*o, sigues, etc.   Note that **seguir** is also a stem-changing verb.

B. *Verbs with infinitives that end in **-ecer, -ocer**, and **-ucir***

The **c** changes to **zc** in the first person singular only:

apare*c*er: apare*zc*o, apareces etc.
cono*c*er: cono*zc*o, conoces etc.
condu*c*ir: condu*zc*o, conduces etc.

The verb **vencer** has a consonant before the **-cer** ending, and is therefore conjugated as follows: ven*z*o, vences, etc.

C. *A few verbs with infinitives that end in **-iar** and **-uar***

The **i** in **-iar** and the **u** in **-uar** take an accent mark, except for the **nosotros** and **vosotros** forms:

| contin**u**ar: | contin*ú*o | contin*ú*as | contin*ú*a | continuamos | continuáis | contin*ú*an |
| env**i**ar: | env*í*o | env*í*as | env*í*a | enviamos | enviáis | env*í*an |

Common verbs in this category are **continuar, graduarse, enviar,** and **guiar.**

Exceptions: the following verbs do *not* belong in this category: **anunciar, cambiar, copiar, estudiar, pronunciar, averiguar.** (When in doubt, always check the verb in the Vocabulary or in a dictionary.)

D. *Verbs with infinitives that end in **-uir** (BUT NOT **-guir**)*

The **i** in **-uir** changes to **y** in all forms except those for **nosotros** and **vosotros**:

construir: constru*yo* constru*yes* constru*ye* construimos construís constru*yen*

SOME VERBS THAT HAVE BOTH STEM CHANGES AND SPELLING CHANGES IN THE PRESENT TENSE

seguir: *sigo, sigues,* etc.
torcer: *tuerzo, tuerces,* etc.

For spelling changes that occur only in the present subjunctive and polite commands, see section D, page 247.

The Preterite Tense (see chapter 2)

I went; did she speak?

REGULAR PRETERITES

Drop the **-ar, -er,** or **-ir** ending of the infinitive and add the appropriate preterite endings:

-AR verbs: **-é, -aste, -ó, -amos, -asteis, -aron**
-ER and -IR verbs: **-í, -iste, -ió, -imos, -isteis, -ieron**

cantar:	cant*é*	cant*aste*	cant*ó*	cant*amos*	cant*asteis*	cant*aron*
pensar (ie):	pens*é*	pens*aste*	pens*ó*	pens*amos*	pens*asteis*	pens*aron*
comer:	com*í*	com*iste*	com*ió*	com*imos*	com*isteis*	com*ieron*
volver (ue):	volv*í*	volv*iste*	volv*ió*	volv*imos*	volv*isteis*	volv*ieron*
recibir:	recib*í*	recib*iste*	recib*ió*	recib*imos*	recib*isteis*	recib*ieron*

See section D, pages 241–242, for preterite stem changes in -IR stem-changing verbs.

IRREGULAR PRETERITES

Verbs that are irregular in the preterite tense can be grouped as follows:

A. *Verbs with preterite forms that keep the "regular" pronunciation but have the third-person endings **-yo** and **-yeron.*** All other endings have accented **i.**

caer:	*caí*	*caíste*	*cayó*	*caímos*	*caísteis*	*cayeron*
creer:	*creí*	*creíste*	*creyó*	*creímos*	*creísteis*	*creyeron*
leer:	*leí, leíste,* etc.					
oír:	*oí, oíste,* etc.					

B. *Verbs with special preterite stems.* These forms have no accent marks. The endings that are added to their special stems are:

-e, -iste, -o, -imos, -isteis, -ieron (**-eron** after the letter **j**)

-U- Stems

andar (*anduv-*):	*anduve*	*anduviste*	*anduvo*	*anduvimos*	*anduvisteis* *anduvieron*
caber (*cup-*):	*cupe*	*cupiste*	*cupo*	*cupimos*	*cupisteis* *cupieron*
estar (*estuv-*):	*estuve, estuviste,* etc.				
poder (*pud-*):	pude, pudiste, etc.				
poner (*pus-*):	puse, pusiste, etc.				
saber (*sup-*):	supe, supiste, etc.				
tener (*tuv-*):	tuve, tuviste, etc.				

-I- Stems

hacer (*hic-*):	*hice*	*hiciste*	*hizo*[1]	*hicimos*	*hicisteis* *hicieron*
querer (*quis-*):	*quise, quisiste,* etc.				
venir (*vin-*):	*vine, viniste,* etc.				

-J- Stems

The verbs **conducir** (all verbs that end in **-ducir**), **decir,** and **traer** have preterite stems that end in **j.** The ending **-ieron** becomes **-eron.**

conducir (*conduj-*):

conduje	*condujiste*	*condujo*	*condujimos*	*condujisteis*	*condujeron*

decir (*dij-*):

dije	*dijiste*	*dijo*	*dijimos*	*dijisteis*	*dijeron*

traer (*traj-*):

traje	*trajiste*	*trajo*	*trajimos*	*trajisteis*	*trajeron*

C. *The verbs* **dar***,* **ser***, and* **ir**

The verb **dar** is conjugated in the preterite as if it were an -ER or -IR verb:

di[2]	**diste**	**dio**[2]	**dimos**	**disteis**	**dieron**

Ser and **ir** have identical preterites:

fui[2]	**fuiste**	**fue**[2]	**fuimos**	**fuisteis**	**fueron**

D. *Stem-changing verbs ending in* **-ir**

Two verbs in this group have the stem vowel **o: dormir** and **morir.** All others have the stem vowel **e,** for example, **pedir, preferir, repetir,** and **sentir.** These verbs change only in the third person singular and plural of the preterite:

[1]In the third person singular, the **c** changes to **z** to represent the same sound before the letter **o.**

[2]Since these forms are monosyllables, they do not need an accent mark.

dormir:	dormí	dormiste	d**u**rmió	dormimos	dormisteis	d**u**rmieron
pedir:	pedí	pediste	p**i**dió	pedimos	pedisteis	p**i**dieron
sentir:	sentí	sentiste	s**i**ntió	sentimos	sentisteis	s**i**ntieron

The verb **reír** (and **sonreír**) is conjugated as follows:

| **reí** | **reíste** | **rió** | **reímos** | **reísteis** | **rieron** |

A list of verbs in this group appears in section IV.

E. *Verbs with spelling changes*

1. Verbs whose infinitives end in **-car, -gar,** and **-zar.** The spelling change affects the consonant preceding the **-ar** infinitive ending.

> **-car** changes **c** to **qu** before **e** ⎫
> **-gar** changes **g** to **gu** before **e** ⎬ in the first person singular,
> **-zar** changes **z** to **c** before **e** ⎭ preterite tense

Examples: **tocar:** to**qu**é, tocaste, tocó, etc.
pagar: pa**gu**é, pagaste, pagó, etc.
gozar: go**c**é, gozaste, gozó, etc.

2. Verbs whose infinitives end in **-uir** (but not **-guir**). The third person singular and plural have the endings **-yo** and **-yeron.** Note, for example, the preterite forms of the verb **construir:**

> construí construiste constru**y**ó construimos construiste constru**y**eron

3. Verbs whose infinitives end in **-guar.** Two dots (called a dieresis) are placed over the **u** in the first person singular. The most common verb in this group is **averiguar:**

> averig**ü**é, averiguaste, averiguó, etc.

The dieresis is used to preserve the **u**-sound ("-gway").

The Imperfect Tense (see chapter 3)

I was going; she used to sing

Except for **ser, ir,** and **ver,** all Spanish verbs form the imperfect tense by adding the following endings to the stem of the infinitive:

-AR Verbs: add **-aba, -abas, -aba, -ábamos, -abais, -aban**

For example:

| **tomar:** | tom**aba** | tom**abas** | tom**aba** | tom**ábamos** | tom**abais** | tom**aban** |

-ER and -IR Verbs: add **-ía, -ías, -ía, -íamos, -íais, -ían**

For example:

poder: pod**ía**   pod**ías**   pod**ía**   pod**íamos**   pod**íais**   pod**ían**
dormir: dorm**ía**   dorm**ías**   dorm**ía**   dorm**íamos**   dorm**íais**   dorm**ían**

The three verbs that are irregular in the imperfect are conjugated as follows:

> **ir:** *iba ibas iba íbamos ibais iban*
> **ser:** *era eras era éramos erais eran*
> **ver:** *veía veías veía veíamos veíais veían*

Note that the first person plural of **ser** and **ir** takes a written accent over the first letter, and the second person plural forms have no accent marks. **Ver** is irregular in that it retains the **e** of the infinitive ending.

The Future Tense and the Conditional
I will study   *I would go*
(see chapter 4)

A. REGULAR VERBS

With twelve exceptions, all Spanish verbs form the future tense and the conditional by adding the following endings to the full infinitive form:

> Future: **-é, -ás, -á, -emos, -éis, -án**
> Conditional: **-ía, -ías, -ía, -íamos, -íais, -ían**

Examples:

contar: future   contar**é**   contar**ás**   contar**á**   contar**emos**   contar**éis**   contar**án**
           conditional   contar**ía**   contar**ías**   contar**ía**   contar**íamos**   contar**íais**   contar**ían**

leer: future   leer**é**   leer**ás**   leer**á**   leer**emos**   leer**éis**   leer**án**
       conditional   leer**ía**   leer**ías**   leer**ía**   leer**íamos**   leer**ías**   leer**ían**

ir: future   ir**é**   ir**ás**   ir**á**   ir**emos**   ir**éis**   ir**án**
       conditional   ir**ía**   ir**ías**   ir**ía**   ir**íamos**   ir**íais**   ir**ían**

B. IRREGULAR VERBS

Irregular verbs in the future and the conditional have regular endings but irregular stems. They can be divided into three groups:

1. Verbs that drop the **e** of the infinitive ending:

	Future		*Conditional*
caber:	*cabr*é, -ás -á, -emos, -éis, -án		*cabr*ía, -ías, -ía, -íamos, -íais, -ían
haber:	*habr*é, etc.		*habr*ía, etc.
poder:	*podr*é, etc.		*podr*ía, etc.
querer:	*querr*é, etc.		*querr*ía, etc.
saber:	*sabr*é, etc.		*sabr*ía, etc.

2. Verbs that change the **e** or **i** of the infinitive ending to **d:**

poner:	*pondr*é, etc.		*pondr*ía, etc.
salir:	*saldr*é, etc.		*saldr*ía, etc.
tener:	*tendr*é, etc.		*tendr*ía, etc.
valer:	*valdr*é, etc.		*valdr*ía, etc.
venir:	*vendr*é, etc.		*vendr*ía, etc.

3. The verbs **decir** (*dir-*) and **hacer** (*har-*):

decir:	*dir*é etc.		*dir*ía etc.
hacer:	*har*é etc.		*har*ía etc.

The Compound Tenses (see chapter 5)

The compound tenses consist of a form of **haber** + a past participle.

A. *Regular past participles.* These are formed by adding the following endings to the stem of the infinitive:

> -AR verbs: add **-ado**   -ER and -IR verbs: add **-ido**
>
> am**ar**   ten**er**   sal**ir**
>
> am***ado***   ten***ido***   sal***ido***

B. *Past participles ending in* **-***ído***

INFINITIVE	PAST PARTICIPLE	INFINITIVE	PAST PARTICIPLE
caer	*caído*	**oír**	*oído*
creer	*creído*	**reír (sonreír)**	*reído (sonreído)*
leer	*leído*	**traer**	*traído*

C. *Irregular past participles*

INFINITIVE	PAST PARTICIPLE
abrir	*abierto*
cubrir (descubrir)	*cubierto (descubierto)*
decir	*dicho*
escribir (describir)	*escrito (descrito)*
hacer	*hecho*
morir	*muerto*

INFINITIVE	PAST PARTICIPLE
poner	*puesto*
resolver	*resuelto*
romper	*roto*
ver	*visto*
volver (devolver)	*vuelto (devuelto)*

THE PRESENT PERFECT

present tense of **haber**
+ past participle

I have taken, eaten, written

he
has
ha
hemos } tomado, comido, escrito
habéis
han

THE PLUPERFECT (PAST PERFECT)

imperfect tense of **haber**
+ past participle

I had loved, drunk, lived, opened

había
habías
había
habíamos } amado, bebido, vivido, abierto
habíais
habían

THE FUTURE PERFECT

future tense of **haber**
+ past participle

I will have arrived, returned, read

habré
habrás
habrá
habremos } llegado, vuelto, leído
habréis
habrán

THE CONDITIONAL PERFECT

conditional of **haber**
+ past participle

I would have answered, heard, broken

habría
habrías
habría
habríamos } contestado, oído, roto
habríais
habrían

The Present Participle (el Gerundio) (see chapter 6)

speaking, going, selling

The *gerundio* generally corresponds to the English present participle, which ends in *-ing*. Its spelling does not change for gender or number.

A. REGULAR PRESENT PARTICIPLES

Form the regular *gerundio* by adding the following endings to the stem of the infinitive:

-AR verbs: add **-ando**
   comenz**ar**
   comenz**ando**

-ER and -IR verbs: add **-iendo**
   respond**er**   viv**ir**
   respond**iendo**   viv**iendo**

B. Irregular Present Participles

1. *Gerundios* that end in **-yendo**

caer	*cayendo*	**oír**	*oyendo*
creer	*creyendo*	**traer**	*trayendo*
leer	*leyendo*		

Included in this group are verbs with infinitives that end in **-uir** (but not **-guir**):

construir   *construyendo*

2. Other irregular *gerundios*

decir	*diciendo*
ir	*yendo*
poder	*pudiendo*

3. *Gerundios* of -IR verbs that have a stem change in the preterite. The *gerundios* of such verbs take their stem from the third person plural of the preterite tense:

reír—*ri* eron	**sentir—*sint*** ieron
ri endo	***sint*** iendo
repetir—*repit* ieron	**dormir—*durm*** ieron
repit iendo	***durm*** iendo

Tenses of the Subjunctive (see chapters 7 and 8)

The Present Subjunctive

The present subjunctive is formed in the same way as the polite commands, that is, by using the first person singular (the **yo** form) of the present indicative as the base. To conjugate a verb in the present subjunctive, drop the **-o** ending of the **yo** form and add the following endings:

-AR verbs: **-e, -es, -e, -emos, -éis, -en**
-ER and -IR verbs: **-a, -as, -a, -amos, -áis, -an**

The only verbs that are irregular in the present subjunctive (that is, whose subjunctive forms cannot be derived from the **yo** form) are **dar, estar, haber, ir,** and **ser.** (See § E, page 247.)

Examples:

A. *Verbs with regular **yo** stems*

preguntar—pregunto**—pregunt-:** pregunt*e,* **-es, -e, -emos,** *éis,* **-en**
beber—bebo**—beb-:** beb*a,* **-as, -a, -amos, -áis, -an**
recibir—recibo**—recib-:** recib*a,* **-as, -a, -amos, -áis, -an**

B. *Stem-changing verbs*

1. -AR and -ER verbs. Their subjunctive forms have the same stem changes as the indicative:

   recordar—recuerdo—recuerd-: rec*ue*rde, rec*ue*rdes, rec*ue*rde, recordemos, recor-déis, rec*ue*rden

   perder—pierdo—pierd-: p*ie*rda, p*ie*rdas, p*ie*rda, perdamos, perdáis, p*ie*rdan

2. -IR verbs. The stem change **e** to **ie** becomes **e** to **i,** and **o** to **ue** becomes **o** to **u,** in the **nosotros** and **vosotros** forms of the subjunctive. Otherwise, the stem changes in the indicative and the subjunctive are identical:

   preferir—prefiero—prefier-: pref*ie*ra, pref*ie*ras, pref*ie*ra, pref*i*ramos, pref*i*ráis, pref*ie*ran

   repetir—repito—repit-: rep*i*ta, rep*i*tas, rep*i*ta, rep*i*tamos, rep*i*táis, rep*i*tan

   reír—río—rí-: r*í*a, r*í*as, r*í*a, r*i*amos, r*i*áis, r*í*an

   dormir—duermo—duerm-: d*ue*rma, d*ue*rmas, d*ue*rma, d*u*rmamos, d*u*rmáis, d*ue*rman

C. *Verbs with irregular* ***yo*** *forms*

   salir—salgo—salg-: salg*a*, *-as, -a, -amos, -áis, -an*
   ver—veo—ve-: *vea, veas, vea, veamos, veáis, vean*
   conocer—conozco—conozc-: conozc*a*, *-as, -a, -amos, -áis, -an*
   proteger—protejo—protej-: protej*a*, *-as, -a, -amos, -áis, -an*
   construir—construyo—construy-: construy*a-*, *-as, -a, -amos, -áis, -an*

D. *Verbs with spelling changes*

   In these verbs, the stem of the present indicative ends in a consonant that changes in the present subjunctive to retain the same pronunciation. (See also section V.)

   almorzar—almuerzo—almuerz-: almuer*c*e, almuer*c*es, almuer*c*e, etc.
   comenzar—comienzo—comienz-: comien*c*e, comien*c*es, comien*c*e, etc.
   jugar—juego—jueg-: jue*gu*e, jue*gu*es, jue*gu*e, etc.
   pagar—pago—pag-: pa*gu*e, pa*gu*es, pa*gu*e, etc.
   sacar—saco—sac-: sa*qu*e, sa*qu*es, sa*qu*e, etc.
   alzar—alzo—alz-: al*c*e, al*c*es, al*c*e, etc.

   In the list above, note that the first three verbs are also stem-changing.

E. *Verbs that are irregular in the present subjunctive*

dar:	*dé, des, dé, demos, deis, den*
estar:	*esté, estés, esté, estemos, estéis, estén*
haber:	*haya, hayas, haya, hayamos, hayáis, hayan*
ir:	*vaya, vayas, vaya, vayamos, vayáis, vayan*
ser:	*sea, seas, sea, seamos, seáis, sean*

THE IMPERFECT SUBJUNCTIVE

The imperfect subjunctive derives its forms from the third person plural of the preterite tense. It has two forms. To obtain them, replace the **-ron** ending of the preterite with the endings shown in the following examples:

comenzar: comenza**ron**—**comenza-**:		
	comenza**ra**	comenza**se**
	comenza**ras**	comenza**ses**
	comenza**ra**	comenza**se**
	comenzá**ramos**	comenzá**semos**
	comenza**rais**	comenza**seis**
	comenza**ran**	comenza**sen**

leer: leye**ron**—**leye-**:		
	leye**ra**	leye**se**
	leye**ras**	leye**ses**
	leye**ra**	leye**se**
	leyé**ramos**	leyé**semos**
	leye**rais**	leye**seis**
	leye**ran**	leye**sen**

ir: fue**ron**—**fue-**:		
	fue**ra**	fue**se**
	fue**ras**	fue**ses**
	fue**ra**	fue**se**
	fué**ramos**	fué**semos**
	fue**rais**	fue**seis**
	fue**ran**	fue**sen**

decir: dije**ron**—**dije-**:		
	dije**ra**	dije**se**
	dije**ras**	dije**ses**
	dije**ra**	dije**se**
	dijé**ramos**	dijé**semos**
	dije**rais**	dije**seis**
	dije**ran**	dije**sen**

Similarly:

morir: murie**ron**—**murie-**: murie**ra**, murie**ras**, murie**ra**, etc.
muriе**se**, murie**ses**, murie**se**, etc.

poner: pusie**ron**—**pusie-**: pusie**ra**, pusie**ras**, pusie**ra**, etc.
pusie**se**, pusie**ses**, pusie**se**, etc.

dar: die**ron**—**die-**: die**ra**, die**ras**, die**ra**, etc.
die**se**, die**ses**, die**se**, etc.

THE PERFECT (PRESENT PERFECT) SUBJUNCTIVE

The perfect subjunctive is formed like the perfect (or present perfect) indicative, except that the present-subjunctive forms of the verb **haber** are used before the past participle:

abrir: *haya* **abierto,** *hayas* **abierto,** *haya* **abierto,** etc.
formar: *haya* **formado,** *hayas* **formado,** *haya* **formado,** etc.

THE PLUPERFECT SUBJUNCTIVE

The pluperfect subjunctive consists of the imperfect subjunctive of **haber** + a past participle:

comer: *hubiera (hubiese)* **comido,** *hubieras (hubieses)* **comido,** etc.
volver: *hubiera (hubiese)* **vuelto,** *hubieras (hubieses)* **vuelto,** etc.

II Paradigms of Regular Verbs in All Tenses

INFINITIVE

trabajar to work   **comer** to eat   **recibir** to receive

PRESENT PARTICIPLE (GERUNDIO)

trabajando working   **comiendo** eating   **recibiendo** receiving

PAST PARTICIPLE

trabajado (have) worked   **comido** (have) eaten   **recibido** (have) received

INDICATIVE

PRESENT

trabaj**o** I work, am working	com**o** I eat, etc.	recib**o** I receive, etc.
trabaj**as**	com**es**	recib**es**
trabaj**a**	com**e**	recib**e**
trabaj**amos**	com**emos**	recib**imos**
trabaj**áis**	com**éis**	recib**ís**
trabaj**an**	com**en**	recib**en**

PRETERITE

trabaj**é** I worked	com**í** I ate	recib**í** I received
trabaj**aste**	com**iste**	recib**iste**
trabaj**ó**	com**ió**	recib**ió**
trabaj**amos**	com**imos**	recib**imos**
trabaj**asteis**	com**isteis**	recib**isteis**
trabaj**aron**	com**ieron**	recib**ieron**

IMPERFECT

trabaj**aba** I was working, used to work	com**ía** I was eating, etc.	recib**ía** I was receiving, etc.
trabaj**abas**	com**ías**	recib**ías**
trabaj**aba**	com**ía**	recib**ía**
trabaj**ábamos**	com**íamos**	recib**íamos**
trabaj**abais**	com**íais**	recib**íais**
trabaj**aban**	com**ían**	recib**ían**

FUTURE

trabajar**é** I will work	comer**é** I will eat	recibir**é** I will receive
trabajar**ás**	comer**ás**	recibir**ás**
trabajar**á**	comer**á**	recibir**á**
trabajar**emos**	comer**emos**	recibir**emos**
trabajar**éis**	comer**éis**	recibir**éis**
trabajar**án**	comer**án**	recibir**án**

CONDITIONAL

trabajar**ía** I would work	comer**ía** I would eat	recibir**ía** I would receive
trabajar**ías**	comer**ías**	recibir**ías**
trabajar**ía**	comer**ía**	recibir**ía**
trabajar**íamos**	comer**íamos**	recibir**íamos**
trabajar**íais**	comer**íais**	recibir**íais**
trabajar**ían**	comer**ían**	recibir**ían**

PERFECT (PRESENT PERFECT)

I have worked	I have eaten	I have received
he **has** **ha** **hemos** **habéis** **han** **trabajado**	**. . .comido**	**. . .recibido**

PLUPERFECT (PAST PERFECT)

I had worked	I had eaten	I had received
había **habías** **había** **habíamos** **habíais** **habían** **trabajado**	**. . .comido**	**. . .recibido**

FUTURE PERFECT

I will have worked	I will have eaten	I will have received
habré habrás habrá habremos habréis habrán trabajado	. . . comido	. . . recibido

CONDITIONAL PERFECT

I would have worked	I would have eaten	I would have received
habría habrías habría habríamos habríais habrían trabajado	. . . comido	. . . recibido

SUBJUNCTIVE

PRESENT SUBJUNCTIVE

trabaje	coma	reciba
trabajes	comas	recibas
trabaje	coma	reciba
trabajemos	comamos	recibamos
trabajéis	comáis	recibáis
trabajen	coman	reciban

IMPERFECT SUBJUNCTIVE

trabajara–trabajase	comiera–comiese	recibiera–recibiese
trabajaras–trabajases	comieras–comieses	recibieras–recibieses
trabajara–trabajase	comiera–comiese	recibiera–recibiese
trabajáramos–trabajásemos	comiéramos–comiésemos	recibiéramos–recibiésemos
trabajarais–trabajaseis	comierais–comieseis	recibierais–recibieseis
trabajaran–trabajasen	comieran–comiesen	recibieran–recibiesen

PERFECT (PRESENT PERFECT) SUBJUNCTIVE

haya hayas haya hayamos hayáis hayan trabajado	. . . comido	. . . recibido

PLUPERFECT SUBJUNCTIVE

hubiera–hubiese
hubieras–hubieses
hubiera–hubiese
hubiéramos–hubiésemos
hubierais–hubieseis
hubieran–hubiesen
} **trabajado** . . .**comido** . . .**recibido**

FAMILIAR IMPERATIVE (COMMAND)

habla (tú)
no hables (tú)
hablad (vosotros)
no habléis (vosotros)

come (tú)
no comas (tú)
comed (vosotros)
no comáis (vosotros)

recibe (tú)
no recibas (tú)
recibid (vosotros)
no recibáis (vosotros)

Paradigms of Irregular Verbs

Note: (1) Except for the forms needed to complete a conjugation, only irregular forms are displayed in this section.

(2) Only three verbs are irregular in the imperfect indicative:

ir:	*iba, ibas, iba, íbamos, ibais, iban*
ser:	*era, eras, era, éramos, erais, eran*
ver:	*veía, veías, veía, veíamos, veíais, veían*

(3) The future indicative and the conditional have the same stem. For that reason, no conditional forms are shown in this section.

(4) The formal commands and the negative **tú** commands are the same as the corresponding forms of the present subjunctive.

Key: *a.* present indicative   *d.* present subjunctive
      b. preterite   *e.* imperfect subjunctive
      c. future   *f.* affirmative familiar singular (**tú**) command

1. **andar**
   b. **anduve, anduviste, anduvo, anduvimos, anduvisteis, auduvieron**
   e. **anduviera(-se), anduvieras(-ses), anduviera(-se), anduviéramos(-semos), anduvierais(-seis), anduvieran(-sen)**

2. **caber**
   a. **quepo,** cabes, cabe, cabemos, cabéis, caben
   b. **cupe, cupiste, cupo, cupimos, cupisteis, cupieron**
   c. **cabré, cabrás, cabrá, cabremos, cabréis, cabrán**
   d. **quepa, quepas, quepa, quepamos, quepáis, quepan**
   e. **cupiera(-se), cupieras(-ses), cupiera(-se), cupiéramos(-semos), cupierais(-seis), cupieran(-sen)**

3. **caer**
   pres. part. **cayendo;** *past part.* **caído**
   a. **caigo,** caes, cae, caemos, caéis, caen
   b. **caí, caíste, cayó, caímos, caísteis, cayeron**
   d. **caiga, caigas, caiga, caigamos, caigáis, caigan**
   e. **cayera(-se), cayeras(-ses), cayera(-se), cayéramos(-semos), cayerais(-seis), cayeran(-sen)**

4. **creer**
   pres. part. **creyendo;** *past part.* **creído**
   b. creí, **creíste, creyó, creímos, creísteis, creyeron**
   e. **creyera(-se), creyeras(-ses), creyera(-se), creyéramos(-semos), creyerais(-seis), creyeran(-sen)**

5. **dar**
    a. **doy,** das, da, damos, **dais,** dan
    b. **di, diste, dio, dimos, disteis, dieron**
    d. **dé,** des, **dé,** demos, **deis,** den
    e. **diera(-se), dieras(-ses), diera(-se), diéramos(-semos), dierais(-seis), dieran(-sen)**

6. **decir**
    pres. part. **diciendo;** *past part.* **dicho**
    a. **digo, dices, dice,** decimos, decís, **dicen**
    b. **dije, dijiste, dijo, dijimos, dijisteis, dijeron**
    c. **diré, dirás, dirá, diremos, diréis, dirán**
    d. **diga, digas, diga, digamos, digáis, digan**
    e. **dijera(-se), dijeras(-ses), dijera(-se), dijéramos(-semos), dijerais(-seis), dijeran(-sen)**
    f. **di**

7. **estar**
    a. **estoy, estás, está,** estamos, estáis, **están**
    b. **estuve, estuviste, estuvo, estuvimos, estuvisteis, estuvieron**
    d. **esté, estés, esté,** estemos, estéis, **estén**
    e. **estuviera(-se), estuvieras(-ses), estuviera(-se), estuviéramos(-semos), estuvierais(-seis), estuvieran(-sen)**
    f. **está**

8. **haber**
    a. **he, has, ha, hemos,** habéis, **han**
    b. **hube, hubiste, hubo, hubimos, hubisteis, hubieron**
    c. **habré, habrás, habrá, habremos, habréis, habrán**
    d. **haya, hayas, haya, hayamos, hayáis, hayan**
    e. **hubiera(-se), hubieras(-ses), hubiera(-se), hubiéramos(-semos), hubierais(-seis), hubieran(-sen)**

9. **hacer**
    past part. **hecho**
    a. **hago,** haces, hace, hacemos, hacéis, hacen
    b. **hice, hiciste, hizo, hicimos, hicisteis, hicieron**
    c. **haré, harás, hará, haremos, haréis, harán**
    d. **haga, hagas, haga, hagamos, hagáis, hagan**
    e. **hiciera(-se), hicieras(-ses), hiciera(-se), hiciéramos(-semos), hicierais(-seis), hicieran(-sen)**
    f. **haz**

10. **ir**
    pres. part. **yendo**
    a. **voy, vas, va, vamos, vais, van**
    b. **fui, fuiste, fue, fuimos, fuisteis, fueron**
    d. **vaya, vayas, vaya, vayamos, vayáis, vayan**
    e. **fuera(-se), fueras(-ses), fuera(-se), fuéramos(-semos), fuerais(-seis), fueran(-sen)**
    f. **ve**

11. **oír**
    pres. part. **oyendo;** *past part.* **oído**
    a. **oigo, oyes, oye, oímos,** oís, **oyen**
    b. oí, **oíste, oyó, oímos, oísteis, oyeron**

    c. **oiré, oirás, oirá, oiremos, oiréis, oirán**
    d. **oiga, oigas, oiga, oigamos, oigáis, oigan**
    e. **oyera(-se), oyeras(-ses), oyera(-se), oyéramos(-semos), oyerais(-seis), oyeran(-sen)**
    f. **oye**

12. **poder**   *pres. part.* **pudiendo**
    a. **puedo, puedes, puede,** podemos, podéis, **pueden**
    b. **pude, pudiste, pudo, pudimos, pudisteis, pudieron**
    c. **podré, podrás, podrá, podremos, podréis, podrán**
    d. **pueda, puedas, pueda,** podamos, podáis, **puedan**
    e. **pudiera(-se), pudieras(-ses), pudiera(-se), pudiéramos(-semos), pudierais(-seis), pudieran(-sen)**

13. **poner**   *past part.* **puesto**
    a. **pongo,** pones, pone, ponemos, ponéis, ponen
    b. **puse, pusiste, puso, pusimos, pusisteis, pusieron**
    c. **pondré, pondrás, pondrá, pondremos, pondréis, pondrán**
    d. **ponga, pongas, ponga, pongamos, pongáis, pongan**
    e. **pusiera(-se), pusieras(-ses), pusiera(-se), pusiéramos(-semos), pusierais(-seis), pusieran**
    f. **pon**

14. **querer**   *a.* **quiero, quieres, quiere,** queremos, queréis, **quieren**
    b. **quise, quisiste, quiso, quisimos, quisisteis, quisieron**
    c. **querré, querrás, querrá, querremos, querréis, querrán**
    d. **quiera, quieras, quiera,** queramos, queráis, **quieran**
    e. **quisiera(-se), quisieras(-ses), quisiera(-se), quisiéramos(-semos), quisierais(-seis), quisieran(-sen)**
    f. **quiere**

15. **saber**   *a.* **sé,** sabes, sabe, sabemos, sabéis, saben
    b. **supe, supiste, supo, supimos, supisteis, supieron**
    c. **sabré, sabrás, sabrá, sabremos, sabréis, sabrán**
    d. **sepa, sepas, sepa, sepamos, sepáis, sepan**
    e. **supiera(-se), supieras(-ses), supiera(-se), supiéramos(-semos), supierais(-seis), supieran(-sen)**

16. **salir**   *a.* **salgo,** sales, sale, salimos, salís, salen
    c. **saldré, saldrás, saldrá, saldremos, saldréis, saldrán**
    d. **salga, salgas, salga, salgamos, salgáis, salgan**
    f. **sal**

17. **ser**   *a.* **soy, eres, es, somos, sois, son**
    b. **fui, fuiste, fue, fuimos, fuisteis, fueron**
    d. **sea, seas, sea, seamos, seáis, sean**
    e. **fuera(-se), fueras(-ses), fuera(-se), fuéramos(-semos), fuerais(-seis), fueran(-sen)**
    f. **sé**

18. **tener**   *a.* **tengo, tienes, tiene,** tenemos, tenéis, **tienen**
                  b. **tuve, tuviste, tuvo, tuvimos, tuvisteis, tuvieron**
                  c. **tendré, tendrás, tendrá, tendremos, tendréis, tendrán**
                  d. **tenga, tengas, tenga, tengamos, tengáis, tengan**
                  e. **tuviera(-se), tuvieras(-ses), tuviera(-se), tuviéramos(-semos),**
                  tuvierais(-seis), tuvieran(-sen)
                  f. **ten**

19. **traducir** *a.* **traduzco,** traduces, traduce, traducimos, traducís, traducen
                  b. **traduje, tradujiste, tradujo, tradujimos, tradujisteis, tradujeron**
                  d. **traduzca, traduzcas, traduzca, traduzcamos, traduzcáis,**
                  traduzcan
                  e. **tradujera(-se), tradujeras(-ses), tradujera(-se), tradujéra-**
                  mos(-semos), tradujerais(-seis), tradujeran(-sen)

20. **traer**   *pres. part.* **trayendo;** *past part.* **traído**
                  a. **traigo,** traes, trae, traemos, traéis, traen
                  b. **traje, trajiste, trajo, trajimos, trajisteis, trajeron**
                  d. **traiga, traigas, traiga, traigamos, traigáis, traigan**
                  e. **trajera(-se), trajeras(-ses), trajera(-se), trajéramos(-semos),**
                  trajerais(-seis), trajeran(-sen)

21. **valer**   *a.* **valgo,** vales, vale, valemos, valéis, valen
                  c. **valdré, valdrás, valdrá, valdremos, valdréis, valdrán**
                  d. **valga, valgas, valga, valgamos, valgáis, valgan**

22. **venir**   *pres. part.* **viniendo**
                  a. **vengo, vienes, viene,** venimos, venís, **vienen**
                  b. **vine, viniste, vino, vinimos, vinisteis, vinieron**
                  c. **vendré, vendrás, vendrá, vendremos, vendréis, vendrán**
                  d. **venga, vengas, venga, vengamos, vengáis, vengan**
                  e. **viniera(-se), vinieras(-ses), viniera(-se), viniéramos(-semos),**
                  vinierais(-seis), vinieran(-sen)
                  f. **ven**

23. **ver**   *past part.* **visto**
                  a. **veo,** ves, ve, vemos, veis, ven
                  b. **vea, veas, vea, veamos, veáis, vean**

IV Stem-Changing Verbs

In stem-changing verbs, the stem vowel undergoes changes in the following tenses and forms: the present indicative and subjunctive, the preterite indicative, the imperfect subjunctive, the present participle (or *gerundio*), and the familiar and formal commands. Stem-changing verbs may be arranged in three groups:

1. -AR and -ER verbs in which the stem vowel changes from **o** to **ue** or from **e** to **ie.**

2. -IR verbs in which the stem vowel changes from **e** to **ie** and sometimes from **e** to **i,** and -IR verbs in which the stem vowel changes from **o** to **ue** and sometimes from **o** to **u.**

3. -IR verbs whose stem vowel changes to **i.**

Group 1, -AR and -ER verbs. The stem vowel **e** changes to **ie** and **o** changes to **ue** in the following forms of the present indicative and subjunctive: first, second, and third person singular; third person plural. The following commands take changes: **Ud.** and **Uds.,** affirmative and negative; **tú,** affirmative and negative.

Examples:

	pres. ind.	*pres. subj.*	*formal command*	*familiar command*
recordar	rec**ue**rdo	rec**ue**rde	(no) rec**ue**rde Ud.	rec**ue**rda tú
	rec**ue**rdas	rec**ue**rdes	(no) rec**ue**rden Uds.	no rec**ue**rdes tú
	rec**ue**rda	rec**ue**rde		
	recordamos	recordemos		
	recordáis	recordéis		
	rec**ue**rdan	rec**ue**rden		
devolver	dev**ue**lvo	dev**ue**lva	(no) dev**ue**lva Ud.	dev**ue**lve tú
	dev**ue**lves	dev**ue**lvas	(no) dev**ue**lvan Uds.	no dev**ue**lvas tú
	dev**ue**lve	dev**ue**lva		
	devolvemos	devolvamos		
	devolvéis	devolváis		
	dev**ue**lven	dev**ue**lvan		

	pres. ind.	*pres. subj.*	*formal command*	*familiar command*
cerrar	cierro	cierre	(no) cierre Ud.	cierra tú
	cierras	cierres	(no) cierren Uds.	no cierres tú
	cierra	cierre		
	cerramos	cerremos		
	cerráis	cerréis		
	cierran	cierren		
entender	entiendo	entienda	(no) entienda Ud.	entiende tú
	entiendes	entiendas	(no) entiendan Uds.	no entiendas tú
	entiende	entienda		
	entendemos	entendamos		
	entendéis	entendáis		
	entienden	entiendan		

Group 2, -IR verbs with stem vowel e. The stem vowel changes to **ie** in the *present indicative and subjunctive,* first, second, third person singular and third person plural, and in the *commands,* **Ud., Uds., tú,** affirmative and negative.

The stem vowel changes to **i** in the *present subjunctive,* first and second person plural; the *preterite,* third person singular and plural; the *imperfect subjunctive,* all forms; the *present participle (gerundio);* and the *negative* **vosotros** command.

The stem vowel of **dormir** and **morir** changes from **o** to **ue** or **u** in the same verb forms as those just mentioned.

Examples:

	pres. ind.	*pres. subj.*	*preterite*	*imperf. subj. and gerundio*	*commands*
mentir	miento	mienta	mentí	mintiera	(no) mienta Ud.
	mientes	mientas	mentiste	(mintiese)	(no) mientan Uds.
	miente	mienta	mintió	etc.	miente tú
	mentimos	mintamos	mentimos		no mientas tú
	mentís	mintáis	mentisteis	mintiendo	no mintáis vosotros
	mienten	mientan	mintieron		
dormir	duermo	duerma	dormí	durmiera	(no) duerma Ud.
	duermes	duermas	dormiste	(durmiese)	(no) duerman Uds.
	duerme	duerma	durmió	etc.	duerme tú
	dormimos	durmamos	dormimos		no duermas tú
	dormís	durmáis	dormisteis	durmiendo	no durmáis vosotros
	duermen	duerman	durmieron		

Group 3, -IR verbs with stem vowel e. In this group, the stem vowel changes to **i** only. The stem changes occur in the same forms that are specified for the verbs of Group 2 (see above).

Example:

	pres. ind.	pres. subj.	preterite	imperf. subj. and gerundio	commands
pedir	p*i*do	p*i*da	pedí	p*i*diera	(no) p*i*da Ud.
	p*i*des	p*i*das	pediste	(p*i*diese)	(no) p*i*dan Uds.
	p*i*de	p*i*da	p*i*dió	etc.	p*i*de tú
	pedimos	p*i*damos	pedimos		no p*i*das tú
	pedís	p*i*dáis	pedisteis	p*i*diendo	no p*i*dáis vosotros
	p*i*den	p*i*dan	p*i*dieron		

Note the forms of **reír** (and **sonreír**):

río	**ría**	**reí**	**riera (riese)**	(no) **ría** Ud.
ríes	**rías**	**reíste**	etc.	(no) **rían** Uds.
ríe	**ría**	**rió**		**ríe** tú
reímos	**riamos**	**reímos**	**riendo**	**no rías** tú
reís	**riáis**	**reísteis**		**no riáis** vosotros
ríen	**rían**	**rieron**		

COMMON STEM-CHANGING VERBS

Starred verbs (*) also have spelling changes. **Llover** and **nevar** occur only in the third person singular.

Group 1

o→ue		**e→ie**	
acostarse	devolver	cerrar	defender
almorzar	llover	comenzar*	encender
contar	morder	confesar	entender
costar	mover(se)	despertar(se)	perder
encontrar	oler (huelo)	empezar*	
jugar* (u→ue)	resolver	nevar	
mostrar	soler	pensar	
recordar	volver	sentarse	
sonar			
soñar			
volar			

Group 2

e→ie and e→i	**o→ue and o→u**
convertir	dormir(se)
divertirse	morir(se)
mentir	
preferir	
sentir(se)	

Group 3

e→i	
conseguir*	repetir
despedirse	seguir*
impedir	servir
pedir	sonreír
reír(se)	vestir(se)

V Verbs with Spelling Changes

Note: This section includes verbs that also have stem changes. For spelling changes in the familiar commands, see page 265.

In most of these verbs, the spelling changes affect the consonant immediately before the **-ar, -er,** or **-ir** infinitive ending.

GROUP A: VERBS WITH INFINITIVES THAT END IN **-car, -gar, -zar**

-car changes **c** to **qu** before **e** ⎞ in the preterite first
-gar changes **g** to **gu** before **e** ⎬ person singular and in
-zar changes **z** to **c** before **e** ⎠ formal commands

Common **-car** verbs: **acercarse, atacar, buscar, explicar, sacar, tocar.**

Spelling changes in **tocar:**

	Preterite		*Formal Commands*
toqué	tocamos		toque Ud.
tocaste	tocasteis		toquen Uds.
tocó	tocaron		

Common **-gar** verbs: **castigar, entregar, jugar (ue), juzgar, llegar, pagar.**

Spelling changes in **llegar:**

	Preterite		*Formal Commands*
llegué	llegamos		llegue Ud.
llegaste	llegasteis		lleguen Uds.
llegó	llegaron		

Common **-zar** verbs: **abrazar, almorzar (ue), comenzar (ie), cruzar, empezar (ie), gozar.**

Spelling changes in **gozar:** *Preterite* *Formal Commands*

gocé	gozamos
gozaste	gozasteis
gozó	gozaron

goce Ud.
gocen Uds.

Note the formal commands of verbs that are stem-changing as well as orthographic-changing:

jugar:	**juegue** Ud.
	jueguen Uds.
almorzar:	**almuerce** Ud.
	almuercen Uds.
comenzar:	**comience** Ud.
	comiencen Uds.

GROUP B: VERBS WITH INFINITIVES THAT END IN **-ger, -gir, -guir**

-ger changes **g** to **j** before **o** and **a** ⎞ in the first person singular
-gir changes **g** to **j** before **o** and **a** ⎬ of the present tense
-guir changes **gu** to **g** before **o** and **a** ⎠ and in formal commands

Common **-ger** verbs: **coger, escoger, proteger, recoger.**

Spelling changes in **escoger:** *Present Tense* *Formal Commands*

escojo	escogemos
escoges	escogéis
escoge	escogen

escoja Ud.
escojan Uds.

Common **-gir** verbs: **corregir (i), dirigir**

Spelling changes in **dirigir:** *Present Tense* *Formal Commands*

dirijo	dirigimos
diriges	dirigís
dirige	dirigen

dirija Ud.
dirijan Uds.

Note the irregular forms of **corregir,** which is also stem-changing: yo **corrijo, corrija** Ud., **corrijan** Uds.

Common **-guir** verbs: **conseguir (i), seguir (i)**

Spelling changes in **conseguir:**

Present Tense

consigo	conseguimos
consigues	conseguís
consigue	consiguen

Formal Commands

consiga Ud.

consigan Uds.

GROUP C: VERBS WITH INFINITIVES THAT END IN **-ecer, -ocer, -ucir**

In these endings, **c** changes to **zc** in the first person singular of the present tense and in the formal commands.

Common verbs in this group:
agradecer, aparecer, conocer, desaparecer, merecer, nacer, obedecer, ofrecer, parecer, permanecer, reconocer; conducir, producir, reducir, traducir

Spelling changes in **merecer** and **traducir:**

Present Tense

merezco	mereces	merece	merecemos	merecéis	merecen
traduzco	traduces	traduce	traducimos	traducís	traducen

Formal Commands

merezca Ud.	merezcan Uds.
traduzca Ud.	traduzcan Uds.

The preterite forms of verbs ending in **-ducir** change **c** to **j:**

Preterite of traducir

traduje	tradujiste	tradujo	tradujimos	tradujisteis	tradujeron

Note: The verb **vencer** has a consonant before the **-cer** ending, and is therefore conjugated as follows:

Present Tense

venzo	vencemos
vences	vencéis
vence	vencen

Formal Commands

venza Ud.

venzan Uds.

GROUP D: SOME VERBS WITH INFINITIVES THAT END IN **-iar** AND **-uar**

In verbs of this group, the **i** in **-iar** and the **u** in **-uar** take an accent mark in the present tense, except for the **nosotros** and **vosotros** forms. These accent marks also occur in the formal commands and the present subjunctive.

Common **-iar** verbs in this group: **enviar, guiar.**
Common **-uar** verbs in this group: **continuar, graduarse.**

Accented forms in **enviar** and **continuar:**

Present Tense

envío	envías	envía	enviamos	enviáis	envían
continúo	continúas	continúa	continuamos	continuáis	continúan

Formal Commands

envíe Ud.	envíen Uds.
continúe Ud.	continúen Uds.

Several common verbs ending in **-iar** and **-uar** do not belong in this group: see page 239, §C, *Exceptions*. The verb **averiguar** takes a dieresis in the formal commands (averigüe Ud.), the present subjunctive, and the **yo** form of the preterite (see page 242, §3).

GROUP E: VERBS WITH INFINITIVES THAT END IN **-uir** (BUT NOT **-guir**)

In verbs of this group, the **i** in **-uir** changes to **y** in the following cases: (*a*) the present tense, except for the **nosotros** and **vosotros** forms; (*b*) the formal commands; (*c*) the third-person forms of the preterite; and (*d*) the present participle.

Common verbs in this group: **concluir, construir, contribuir, destruir, distribuir.**

Spelling changes in **concluir:**

Present Tense

concluyo	
concluyes	
concluye	concluyen

Formal Commands

concluya Ud.
concluyan Uds.

Preterite

concluí	concluimos
concluiste	concluisteis
concluyó	concluyeron

Present Participle

concluyendo

SPELLING CHANGES IN THE FAMILIAR COMMANDS

tocar	toca tú	no to**qu**es tú	tocad vosotros	no to**qu**éis vosotros
llegar	llega tú	no lle**gu**es tú	llegad	no lle**gu**éis
gozar	goza tú	no go**c**es tú	gozad	no go**c**éis
jugar	juega tú	no jue**gu**es tú	jugad	no ju**gu**éis
almorzar	almuerza	no almuer**c**es	almorzad	no almor**c**éis
comenzar	comienza	no comien**c**es	comenzad	no comen**c**éis
escoger	escoge	no esco**j**as	escoged	no esco**j**áis
dirigir	dirige	no diri**j**as	dirigid	no diri**j**áis
conseguir	consigue	no consi**g**as	conseguid	no consi**g**áis
merecer	merece	no mere**zc**as	mereced	no mere**zc**áis
traducir	traduce	no tradu**zc**as	traducid	no tradu**zc**áis
vencer	vence	no ven**z**as	venced	no ven**z**áis
enviar	env**í**a	no env**í**es	enviad	no enviéis
continuar	contin**ú**a	no contin**ú**es	continuad	no continuéis
concluir	conclu**ye**	no conclu**ya**s	concluid	no conclu**yá**is

PART 2
Other Topics

1. Cardinal Numbers

0 to 99

0	cero	21	veinte y uno (veintiuno)
1	uno, un, una	22	veinte y dos (veintidós)
2	dos	23	veinte y tres (veintitrés)
3	tres	24	veinte y cuatro (veinticuatro)
4	cuatro	25	veinte y cinco (veinticinco)
5	cinco	26	veinte y seis (veintiséis)
6	seis	27	veinte y siete (veintisiete)
7	siete	28	veinte y ocho (veintiocho)
8	ocho	29	veinte y nueve (veintinueve)
9	nueve	30	treinta
10	diez	31	treinta y uno
11	once	40	cuarenta
12	doce	42	cuarenta y dos
13	trece	50	cincuenta
14	catorce	53	cincuenta y tres
15	quince	60	sesenta
16	diez y seis (dieciséis)	67	sesenta y siete
17	diez y siete (diecisiete)	70	setenta
18	diez y ocho (dieciocho)	80	ochenta
19	diez y nueve (diecinueve)	90	noventa
20	veinte	99	noventa y nueve

100 to 1000

100	ciento, cien	400	cuatrocientos(-as)
104	ciento cuatro	500	quinientos(-as)
185	ciento ochenta y cinco	600	seiscientos(-as)
200	doscientos(-as)	700	setecientos(-as)
217	doscientos(-as) diecisiete	800	ochocientos(-as)
300	trescientos(-as)	900	novecientos(-as)
308	trescientos(-as) ocho	1000	mil

1,001 to 100,000,000

1001	**mil uno**	*31.578	**treinta y un mil quinientos setenta y ocho**
1006	**mil seis**		
1022	**mil veinte y dos**	501.010	**quinientos un mil diez**
1174	**mil ciento setenta y cuatro**	713.102	**setecientos trece mil ciento dos**
1508	**mil quinientos ocho**	1.000.000	**un millón**
1776	**mil setecientos setenta y seis**	2.000.000	**dos millones**
1945	**mil novecientos cuarenta y cinco**	35.046.007	**treinta y cinco millones cuarenta y seis mil siete**
2000	**dos mil**		
7001	**siete mil uno**	100.000.000	**cien millones**
8012	**ocho mil doce**		

UN, UNO, UNA

¿Tienes **un** libro?	Do you have a book?
Sí, tengo **uno.**	Yes, I have one.
¿Cuántas pesetas tienes?	How many pesetas do you have?
Tengo **una** peseta. (Tengo **una.**)	I have *one* peseta. (I have *one*.)
¿Cuántos hombres hay aquí?	How many men are there here?
Hay **veintiún** hombres.	There are twenty-one men.
Hay **veintiuno.**	There are twenty-one.
¿Cuántos billetes tienes?	How many tickets do you have?
Tengo cincuenta y **un** billetes.	I have fifty-one tickets.
Tengo cincuenta y **uno.**	I have fifty-one.

1. **Uno** becomes **un** before a masculine noun. The form **uno** is used if the masculine noun is not expressed.

CIEN, CIENTO

Tenemos **ciento un** dólares.	We have 101 dollars.
Tenemos **ciento** ochenta y **un** dólares.	We have 181 dollars.

    But:

Tenemos **cien** dólares.	We have a hundred dollars.
Tenemos **cien.**	We have a hundred.

2. **Ciento** becomes **cien** before a noun or when used alone.

DOSCIENTOS(-AS), TRESCIENTOS(-AS), ETC.

doscient**os** chic**os**	quinient**os** trece **hombres**
doscient**as** chic**as**	quinient**as** trece **mujeres**

ochocient**os** cuarenta y un **edificios**

ochocient**as** cuarenta y una **casas**

*Spanish notation uses a period instead of a comma to indicate thousands. The comma is used to set off decimal fractions; for example, 5.16 ("five point sixteen") = 5,16 ("cinco coma dieciséis").

3. In **doscientos, trescientos,** etc., the ending **-os** becomes **-as** before a feminine noun— even when it is separated from the feminine noun by another number-word.

NUMBERS EXPRESSED WITH *Y*

4. The conjunction **y** is used only between the digits of two-digit numbers (where the second digit is not zero), that is, in the numbers from 16 to 19, from 21 to 29, from 31 to 39, etc:

cuarenta **y** tres   forty-three

NUMBERS 16 TO 19 AND 21 TO 29

5. These numbers may be written either as one word or as three words; for example, 24 = **veinticuatro** or **veinte y cuatro.** All other two-digit numbers must be written as three words; for example, 63 = **sesenta y tres.**

MILLÓN, MILLONES

6. These words are used with **de** when followed by the noun they modify:

a million dollars = un millón **de** dólares
five million inhabitants = cinco millones **de** habitantes

2. Ordinal Numbers

primero (primer), primera, first
segundo, segunda, second
tercero (tercer), tercera, third
cuarto, cuarta, fourth
quinto, quinta, fifth

sexto, sexta, sixth
séptimo, séptima, seventh
octavo, octava, eighth
noveno, novena, ninth
décimo, décima, tenth

1. The ordinal numbers are adjectives and agree in gender and number with the noun they modify. They may either precede or follow the noun:

la **segunda** lección *or* la lección **segunda**
los **primeros** capítulos *or* los capítulos **primeros**

2. The ordinal numbers are not ordinarily used beyond the tenth:

la lección **once**   the eleventh lesson
el siglo **veinte**   the twentieth century

3. Days of the Week

el **lunes,** Monday
el **martes,** Tuesday
el **miércoles,** Wednesday
el **jueves,** Thursday

el **viernes,** Friday
el **sábado,** Saturday
el **domingo,** Sunday

1. The Spanish names for the days of the week generally begin with small (lower-case) letters.

2. The article **el** means *on:*

Te veré **el** lunes.   I'll see you on Monday.

3. *On* is translated as **los** when the days of the week are used in the plural:

No vamos a la escuela **los** domingo**s.**   We don't go to school on Sundays.

Los viernes vamos al cine.   On Fridays we go to the movies.

Caution: In English, the singular form of the day is often used with plural meaning. Before translating into Spanish, decide whether the singular or the plural is meant:

We are going downtown on Tuesday.   Vamos al centro **el** martes.

     But:

We go downtown on Tuesday   Vamos al centro **los** martes.
(= on Tuesday*s,* every Tuesday).

4. Months of the Year

enero, January	**julio,** July
febrero, February	**agosto,** August
marzo, March	**septiembre,** September
abril, April	**octubre,** October
mayo, May	**noviembre,** November
junio, June	**diciembre,** December

The Spanish names for the months are not capitalized.

5. Expressing Dates

¿Cuál es la fecha de hoy?   What is today's date?
Hoy es **el primero de mayo.**   Today is May 1.
Es **el dos de abril.**   It is April 2.
Es **el catorce de octubre.**   It is October 14.
Vamos **el ocho de junio.**   We are going on June 8.
Ayer fue domingo, **el veinte de julio de**   Yesterday was Sunday, July 20, 1989.
  mil novecientos ochenta y nueve.

1. Except for **el primero,** the cardinal numbers (**dos, tres, cuatro,** etc.) are used in dates.

2. The preposition **de** is used to separate the month from the number; for example, November 21 = el veintiuno **de** noviembre.

3. *On* is expressed in Spanish by **el;** for example, *on* January 1 = **el** primero de enero.

4. In Spanish, the year is expressed in thousands and hundreds; for example, 1921 = **mil novecientos veintiuno** (literally "one thousand nine hundred twenty-one").

6. Telling Time

¿Qué hora es?	What time is it?
Es la una.	It is one o'clock.
Son las dos.	It is two o'clock.
Son las tres y cuarto (y quince).	It is 3:15.
Son las siete y media (y treinta).	It is 7:30.
Son las ocho y diez.	It is 8:10.
Son las diez menos cuarto.	It is 9:45 (a quarter to ten).
Son las tres menos veinte.	It is 2:40 (twenty minutes to three).
Es mediodía.	It is noon.
Es medianoche.	It is midnight.
Son las nueve y media de la mañana.	It is 9:30 A.M.
Es la una y cuarto de la tarde.	It is 1:15 P.M.
Son las diez menos cinco de la noche.	It is 9:55 P.M.
¿A qué hora empieza la clase?	At what time does the class begin?
La clase empieza **a las once menos diez de la mañana.**	The class begins at ten minutes to eleven in the morning (at 10:50 A.M.)
Salimos de la escuela **a las tres de la tarde.**	We leave school at three o'clock in the afternoon (at 3:00 P.M.)

1. To tell time in Spanish, start with **son las** and add the number of the hour. The exception is one o'clock: **Es la una.**

2. To express a quarter past the hour, add **y cuarto** to the hour. To express half past the hour, add **y media** to the hour.

3. To express time past the hour (but not beyond the half hour), add **y** and the number of minutes.

4. To express time after the half hour, start with the *next* hour and subtract the number of minutes from that hour. "It is 4:50" is the same as "It is ten minutes to five": **Son las cinco menos diez.** *

5. To indicate A.M., we add **de la mañana.**

6. To express P.M., we add **de la tarde** between 12:01 P.M. (one minute after 12 noon) and nightfall. From nightfall to midnight, we add **de la noche.**

7. In Spanish-speaking countries, it is actual darkness that determines whether the afternoon has ended. Thus, if it is still light, we express 7:45 P.M. as "las ocho menos cuarto **de la tarde.**"

---

*It is also correct to express clock-time in the same way as we often do in English: *it is 4:50* = **son las cuatro y cincuenta.**

8. Do not confuse **son las tres** with **a las tres.** The expression **son las tres** means "*it is* 3 o'clock," whereas **a las tres** means "*at* 3 o'clock."

OTHER TIME EXPRESSIONS

Es la una **en punto.**	It is one o'clock *sharp.*
Venga Ud. **a tiempo.**	Come *on time.*
Llegaron **a eso de** las ocho.	They arrived *at about* 8 o'clock.
Es tarde.	It is late.
Se hace tarde.	It is getting late.
No es temprano.	It is not early.
Jugamos **por la tarde (por la noche, por la mañana).**	We play *in the afternoon (in the evening, in the morning).*

9. The expressions **por la mañana, por la tarde,** and **por la noche** refer to parts of the day and are not used after expressions of clock time (see §5 and §6 on page 270).

7. Special Uses of *Tener, Hacer,* and *Haber*

A. *TENER*

The verb **tener** means *to have,* but it is translated as *to be* in several idiomatic expressions:

¿Cuántos años **tiene** ella?	How old is she?
Ella **tiene** quince años.	She is 15 years old.
Tengo (mucho) calor.	I am (very) warm.
¿**Tiene** Ud. sueño?	Are you sleepy?

SOME COMMON IDIOMS WITH **tener**

tener . . . años	to be . . . years old
tener (mucho) calor	to be (very) warm
tener (mucho) cuidado	to be (very) careful
tener (mucho) éxito	to be (very) successful
tener (mucho) frío	to be (very) cold
tener (mucho) gusto en + *inf.*	to be (very) glad to
tener (mucha) hambre	to be (very) hungry
tener (mucho) miedo a	to be (very) afraid of (someone)
tener (mucho) miedo de + *inf.*	to be (very) afraid to
tener (mucha) prisa	to be in a (great) hurry
tener razón	to be right
no tener razón	to be wrong
tener (mucha) sed	to be (very) thirsty

B. *HACER*

1. **Hacer** in weather expressions is used only in the third person singular:

Hoy **hace** frío.	Today it is cold.
Ayer **hizo** calor.	Yesterday it was warm.
Mañana **hará** mucho sol.	Tomorrow it will be very sunny.

OTHER WEATHER EXPRESSIONS

¿Qué tiempo hace?	How is the weather?
Hace buen tiempo.	The weather is good.
Hace mal tiempo.	The weather is bad.
Hace (mucho) calor.	It is (very) warm.
Hace (mucho) fresco.	It is (very) cool.
Hace (mucho) frío.	It is (very) cold.
Hace (mucho) sol.	It is (very) sunny.
Hace (mucho) viento.	It is (very) windy.

2. The third person singular is also used to express the passage of time:

Hace una semana que Elena nos hizo una visita.	Helen visited us a week ago.
—**¿Cuánto tiempo hace** que estudias español?	"How long have you been studying Spanish?"
—**Hace** tres años que lo estudio.	"I have been studying it for three years."
Hacía una hora que jugábamos al tenis cuando empezó a llover.	We had been playing tennis for an hour when it began to rain.

C. *HABER*

Haber has the special form **hay,** *there is, there are.* When used in other tenses, this idiom is expressed by the forms of **haber** in the third person singular—even when the subject is in the plural:

Hay mucho trabajo hoy.	*There is* a lot of work today.
¿Hay cuadros en el cuarto?	*Are there* pictures in the room?
No **había** nada que hacer.	*There was* nothing to do.
Había veinte personas allí.	*There were* 20 people there.
¿Hubo refrescos en el baile?	*Were there* refreshments at the dance?
No **hubo** dinero.	*There was* no money.
Habrá una reunión mañana.	*There will be* a meeting tomorrow.
¿Habrá muchas cosas que hacer?	*Will there be* many things to do?

Ella contestó que **habría** treinta personas en la fiesta.

She answered that *there would be* 30 people at the party.

Ha habido una tormenta.

There has been a storm.

Ha habido cuatro tormentas.

There have been four storms.

8. *Por and Para*

A. By / For $\}$ = **por** or **para**, depending on the sense in which the preposition is used:

By

El puente fue construido **por** los romanos.
The bridge was built by the Romans.

Envió el paquete **por** avión.
He sent the package by airmail.

Lo terminará **para** el lunes a más tardar.
He will finish it by Monday at the latest.

Habrán salido **para** entonces.
They will have left by then.

For

1. = *in exchange for*

Pagué tres dólares **por** el reloj.
I paid three dollars for the watch.

2. = *for the sake of*

¿Quieres ir al correo **por** mí?
Will you go to the post office for me?

3. = *for the period of*

Estudió **por** dos horas.
He studied for two hours.

4. = *to get, go for*

Lo mandé **por** el paquete.
I sent him for the package.

1. = *meant or intended for*

Este regalo es **para** Susana.
This gift is for Susan.

El andar es bueno **para** el corazón.
Walking is good for your heart.

2. = *bound for*

Ayer partieron **para** México.
Yesterday they left for Mexico.

3. = *considering (that)* . . .

Es muy alta **para** su edad.
She is very tall for her age.

B. Other uses of **por:**

= *through*
Miró **por** la ventana.

He looked through the window.

= *along*
Se pasearon **por** la avenida.

They strolled along the avenue.

= *because of*

Los trenes dejaron de circular **por** la huelga.	The trains stopped running because of the strike.

= *in* or *at* (= *during*)

Visitaban a sus amigos . . .	They used to visit their friends . . .
. . . **por** la mañana.	. . . in the morning.
. . . **por** la tarde.	. . . in the afternoon.
. . . **por** la noche.	. . . in the evening, at night.

C. **Para** + *infinitive* = *to, in order to:*

Salimos temprano **para** evitar la muchedumbre.	We left early to avoid the crowds.

9. *Gustar* and Other Verbs That Are Used Like *Gustar*

Review the Spanish indirect object pronouns, pages 142–144.

A. *To like* is expressed in Spanish by using the verb gustar, *to please.* Thus, *I like the house* becomes "The house pleases me": **La casa me gusta,** or, more commonly, **Me gusta la casa.**

B. The subject of **gustar** often *follows* the verb:

We like the pictures = "The pictures please us."
Los cuadros nos gustan.

or, more commonly: *Nos gustan los cuadros.*

C. The object of the verb *to like* becomes the subject of **gustar,** and the subject of *to like* becomes the *indirect* object of **gustar:**

No **les** gustaron **los cuadros**.	You (They) did not like the pictures.
indirect object subject	subject object

D. *I like it* becomes literally "It pleases me" in Spanish: **Me gusta.** (*It* as subject is generally unexpressed in Spanish.) Similarly, *I like them* = "They please me" = **Me gustan.**

E. 1. The indirect object pronouns **le** and **les** have several possible meanings (see page 144). The following examples express what *Michael* likes (**lo que le gusta a Miguel**):

A Miguel le gusta **Le gusta a Miguel** } la película.	Michael likes the movie (film).
A Miguel le gusta. **Le gusta a Miguel.** }	Michael likes it.
Le gusta.	He likes it.
Le gustaría ir al cine.	He would like to go to the movies.

Le gusta mirar la televisión y tocar la guitarra.	He likes to watch television and play the guitar.
No le gustarán esos discos.	He won't like those records.
No le gustarán.	He won't like them.

Le may also refer to **usted:**

¿Le gustó la película?	Did you like (enjoy) the movie?
¿No le gustó?	Didn't you like (enjoy) it?

Les may refer to **ellos** or **ellas:**

No les gustó tampoco.	They didn't like it either.

2. To avoid confusion, a clarifying phrase may be used with **le** or **les** (see page 144, §12):

—¿No **le** gustó *a usted?*	"Didn't *you* like it?"
—Sí, *a mí* **me** gustó pero no **les** gustó *a ellos.*	"Yes, *I* liked it but *they* did not."

F. The verbs **faltar, importar, parecer, quedar,** and **tocar** are used like **gustar;** that is, the forms of the third person singular and plural are preceded by an indirect object pronoun:

Nos falta papel.	We need paper.
A los ricos no **les importa** el costo de vida.	The rich don't care about the cost of living. (The cost of living doesn't matter to . . .)
¿Les interesaría a Uds. el curso nuevo?	Would you be interested in the new course?
Me pareció que ellos no vendrían.	I thought they would not come. (It seemed to me that . . .)
—¿Qué **les pareció** la pieza a los críticos?	"What did the critics think of the play?"
—**Les pareció** bastante aburrida.	"They thought it was rather boring." ("It seemed rather boring to them.")
A la chica **le quedaron** sólo tres dólares.	The girl had only three dollars left.
Le tocará a Carlitos conseguir las entradas.	It will be Charlie's turn to get the tickets.

SPANISH-ENGLISH VOCABULARY

Note: (1) Verbs marked with an asterisk (*) have irregular forms that are listed in section III of the Verb Appendix. The number in parentheses indicates the verb's position in the list. For example, "***ir** (10)" shows that **ir** is verb #10 (see page 255). A number following an unstarred verb indicates that the verb is conjugated like the starred verb with that number. For example, "**detener** (18)" shows that the verb is conjugated like **tener,** which is #18 in the list.

(2) Stem-changing verbs are identified in parentheses by the type of stem change and a number indicating the appropriate group in section IV of the Verb Appendix. For example, "**divertir (ie, i)** (2)" shows that **divertir** belongs to Group 2, which comprises verbs in which stem vowel **e** change to **ie** in some forms, to **i** in others (see page 259).

(3) Verbs with spelling changes are identified in parentheses by the letter indicating the appropriate group in section V of the Verb Appendix. For example, "**conseguir** (B)" shows that **conseguir** belongs to Group B (see pages 262–263).

(4) Nouns that have both a masculine and a feminine form are displayed in the same style as adjectives. For example, **jugador -ra** represents the forms **jugador** *m.* and **jugadora** *f.* Similarly, **médico -a** indicates that a woman doctor is **una médica.**

a to, at

abajo down; **de abajo** below

abrazar (A) to embrace

abrigo *m.* overcoat

aburrido -a (with **ser**) boring, (with **estar**) bored

acabar to finish, end; **acabar de + inf.** to have just: **acabo de entrar** I have just entered; **acababa de llegar** he had just arrived

acaso perhaps

acerca de about, concerning

acercar (A): **acercarse a** to approach

acogedor -ra inviting

acordar (ue) (1): **acordarse de** to remember

acostar (ue) (1): **acostarse** to go to bed, lie down

actual present (time); **actualmente** at present, now

acuerdo *m.* agreement; **estar de acuerdo** to agree

adelante forward, ahead

además besides; **además de** besides, in addition to

¿adónde? (to) where?

afición *f.* fondness

aficionado -a fan, enthusiast

aficionado (-a) a fond of

afilado -a sharpened

afuera outside; **afueras** *f. pl.* outskirts

águila (el) *f.* eagle

agujero *m.* hole

ahí there

ahora now; **ahora mismo** right now

ahorrar to save (money)

ajedrez *m.* chess

ajeno -a alien, somebody else's

ala (el) *f.* wing; brim (of a hat)

alabar to praise

alambre *m.* wire

alcalde *m.* mayor; **alcaldesa** *f.* mayoress

alcanzar (A) to reach

alegrarse de + inf. to be glad to

alejar to take away, remove

Alemania *f.* Germany

alga (el) *f.* seaweed

algo something, anything; somewhat

alguien someone, anyone
alguno -a (algún) some
aliado -a ally
alimentación f. food, nourishment
alimentar to feed
alimento m. food
alma (el) f. soul
almacén m. department store
almirante m. & f. admiral
almorzar (ue) (1) (A) to have lunch
almuerzo m. lunch
alojarse to lodge, stay (at a hotel)
alpinista m. & f. mountain-climber
alrededor de around
altiplano m. high plateau
altura f. height, altitude
amabilidad f. kindness, friendliness
amable kind, nice
amanecer m. dawn
ambiente m. environment, surroundings, atmosphere
ambos -as both
amistad f. friendship
amistoso -a friendly
ancho -a wide; **tres metros de ancho** three meters wide
anchura f. width
andaluz -za Andalusian (from southern Spain)
*andar (1) to walk, go, progress
andén m. platform
anillo m. ring
anoche last night
antemano: de antemano in advance
antepasado -a ancestor
antes before(hand); (prep.) **antes de** before; (conj.) **antes de que** before; **lo más antes posible** as soon as possible
añadir to add
apagar (A) to turn off, put out, extinguish
aparecer (C) to appear
aparición f. appearance
apertura f. opening (of a store, etc.)
aplacar (A) to appease, placate, pacify
aplastar to crush, smash
apodo m. nickname
apoyar to support
aprendizaje m. apprenticeship, learning
aprovecharse de to take advantage of

apuntes: sacar apuntes to take notes
arena f. sand
armario m. closet
arrastrar to drag
arreglar to fix, repair; to arrange
arriesgar (A) to risk
arrojar to throw
arroz m. rice
ascenso m. ascent, climb
asegurar to assure
así so, thus, (in) this way; **así que** as soon as; **así como** as well as
asiento m. seat
asignatura f. (school) subject
asistir a to attend
asombrar to astonish; **asombrarse de** to be astonished at
astro m. star, heavenly body
astucia f. cunning, cleverness
asunto m. matter, subject
asustar to frighten; **asustarse** to become frightened
atraer (20) to attract
atrás back, behind
atreverse a + inf. to dare to
atropellar to run over
aun (aún) even, still
aunque although
autobús m. bus
avanzado -a advanced
ave (el) f. bird
avión m. airplane
ayer yesterday
ayudar to help
ayuntamiento m. city hall
azúcar m. sugar

bahía f. bay
bailar to dance
bailarín-ina dancer
bajar to go down; to take down
ballenero m. whaler
bañarse to bathe (oneself)
barba f. beard
barca f. boat
barco m. ship
barrio m. neighborhood
bastante enough; quite
bautizar (A) to baptise
bautizo m. baptism
beber to drink
bendición f. blessing
besar to kiss
billete m. ticket
bisonte m. bison
boda f. wedding
bolsa f. bag

bolsillo m. pocket
bombero -a firefighter
bondadoso -a kind
borracho -a drunk
borrador m. eraser
borrar to erase
bostezar to yawn
brazo m. arm
brillar to shine
brotar to gush forth
bufón m. clown
buque m. boat
burlón -ona teasing, mocking
buscar (A) to look for, seek
búsqueda f. search

caballero m. gentleman
caballo m. horse
cabellera f. head of hair
cabello m. hair
*caber (2) to fit
cabeza f. head
cacique m. chief
*caer (3) to fall
café m. coffee; cafe
calavera f. skull
calurosamente warmly
camarero -a waiter, waitress
cambio m. change
camino m. road, way; **camino de** on the way to
campana f. bell
campanada f. stroke (of a clock)
campesino -a peasant, farmer
canal m. TV channel
canción f. song
cancha f. court, field
cansado -a tired
cansancio m. tiredness, fatigue
cantante m. & f. singer
cantidad f. quantity, amount
cañón m. cannon
capaz capable
cara f. face
caracol m. snail
carbón m. coal, charcoal
carecer (C): **carecer de** to lack
carga f. burden, load
cargo m. duty, obligation
caricia f. caress, hug
cariño m. affection
cariñoso -a affectionate
caritativo -a charitable
caro -a expensive
carrera f. career; race (running, etc.)
carretera f. road, highway
carruaje m. carriage
carta f. letter

casarse con to get married to
casi almost
castigar (A) to punish
catarata *f.* waterfall
causa *f.* cause; **a causa de** because of
cazador -ra hunter
cena *f.* dinner, supper
ceniza *f.* ash
centenares *m. pl.* hundreds
centro *m.* center; **en el centro** downtown; **centro comercial** shopping center, mall
cercano -a nearby
cerrar (ie) (1) to close
cerveza *f.* beer
cesar de + *inf.* to stop (doing something)
cielo *m.* sky, heaven
científico -a scientific; (*noun*) scientist
ciervo *m.* deer
cinta *f.* tape
cita *f.* date, appointment
ciudad *f.* city
ciudadano -a citizen
ciudadela *f.* citadel
clase *f.* class; kind, type
clérigo *m.* clergyman
cobre *m.* copper
cocinero -a cook
coche *m.* car, automobile
coger (B) to take, catch, grab
cohete *m.* rocket
cola *f.* tail; queue, line (of people)
colegio *m.* school
colgar (ue) (1) (A) to hang
colocar (A) to place, put
comenzar (ie) (1) (A) to begin
comer to eat; **dar de comer,** to feed
comerciante *m. & f.* merchant
comestibles *m. pl.* groceries
cometa *f.* kite; *m.* comet
como as, like; **¿cómo?** how?
compañero -a companion; **compañero(-a) de clase** classmate
compartir to share
complejo -a complex
comportamiento *m.* behavior
compra *f.* purchase; *ir de compras* to go shopping
comprar to buy
computadora *f.* computer
con with
concurrido -a crowded

conducir (19) (C) to drive; **licencia de conducir** driver's license; **conducirse** to behave
confianza *f.* confidence, trust
conocer (C) to know (persons or places)
conseguir (i, i) (3) (B) to get, obtain
consistorial: casa consistorial *f.* town hall
construir (E) to build, construct
contar (ue) (1) to count; to tell, relate; **contar con** to count on
contestar to answer
contornos *m. pl.* surroundings
contra against
corazón *m.* heart
corregir (i, i) (3) (B) to correct
correo *m.* mail; post office
correr to run
corrida de toros bullfight
corriente *f.* current
cortaplumas *m., s. & pl.* penknife
cortar to cut
cortés courteous, polite
cortesía *f.* courtesy
corto -a short
costa *f.* coast
costar (ue) (1) to cost
crear to create
creencia *f.* belief
*creer (4) to believe
crucigrama *m.* crossword puzzle
cruzar (A) to cross
cuadrado -a square
cuadro *m.* square; picture; **a cuadros** checkered (design)
cual: el (la) cual, los (las) cuales which, who; **¿cuál? ¿cuáles?** which (one, ones)?
cualquier -ra any, whatever
cuando when; **¿cuándo?** when?
cuanto: en cuanto a as for
¿cuánto -a? how much?; **¿cuántos -as?** how many?
cuarto -a fourth; *m.* quarter, fourth; room
cuchillo *m.* knife
cuenta *f.* bill, check; account; **darse cuenta de** to realize
cuento *m.* story
cuerda *f.* cord, rope
cuero *m.* leather
cuerpo *m.* body
cuesta *f.* hill, slope
cueva *f.* cave
cuidado *m.* care; **con cuidado**

carefully; **tener cuidado** to be careful
cuidadoso -a careful
cuidar to take care of
cumbre *f.* top, summit
cumpleaños *m., s. & pl.* birthday
cura *m.* priest; *f.* cure
curva *f.* curve
cuyo -a whose
charlar to chat
chiste *m.* joke
chocar (A) to collide

daño *m.* harm, damage, injury; **hacer daño** to harm, hurt
*dar (5) to give
de of, from, in
deber to have to, ought to, must; to owe
debido(-a) a due to
*decir (6) to say, tell
defender (ie) (1) to defend
dejar to leave, let; **dejar de** + *inf.* to stop (doing something)
delante in front; **delante de** in front of
delfín *m.* dolphin
delgado -a thin, slender
demás: los (las) demás the others, the rest (of them)
demasiado (*adv.*) too
demasiado -a too much; **demasiados -as** too many
dentro de inside (of), within
dependiente -a sales clerk
deporte *m.* sport
derribar to throw down
derrotar to defeat
derrumbar to knock down
desarrollar(se) to develop
descansar to rest
descifrar to decipher
describir (*pp.* **descrito**) to describe
descubrir (*pp.* **descubierto**) to discover
desde from, since; (*conj.*) **desde que** since
desear to wish, want
desembocadura *f.* mouth (of a river)
desempeñar to play (a role), perform (a duty)
desfile *m.* parade
desgracia *f.* misfortune; **por desgracia** unfortunately
deslizarse (A) to slide

desmontar to knock down

despacio slowly

despedida f. good-bye, farewell

despedirse (i, i) (3): **despedirse de** to say good-bye to

despertarse (ie) (1) to wake up

despierto -a awake

después afterwards; **después de** after; (conj.) **después (de) que** after

destacarse (A) to stand out

destino m. destination

detalle m. detail

detener (18) to stop; to arrest; **detenerse** to stop

detrás de behind, in back of

devolver (ue) (1) to return give back

día m. day; **al día** a day, per day

dibujar to draw, sketch

dibujo m. drawing, sketch

difícil difficult

dificultad f. difficulty

difunto -a dead; **el Día de los Difuntos** All Soul's Day

dios m. god

discurso m. speech

discutir to discuss

diseñar to design

disminuir (E) to diminish, decrease

disparo m. shooting

disponible available

distinto -a different

disuadir to dissuade

divertido -a enjoyable, "fun"

divertir (ie, i) (2) to amuse, entertain; **divertirse** to enjoy oneself, have a good time

docena f. dozen

doler (ue) (1) to hurt: **le duele el brazo** her arm hurts her

doma f. taming

dominio m. rule

donde where; **¿dónde?** where?; **¿adónde?** (to) where?

dorado -a golden

dormir (ue, u) (2) to sleep; **dormirse** to fall asleep

dudar to doubt

dudoso -a doubtful

dulce sweet; m. piece of candy; pl. candy

duque m. duke

durante during

durar to last

duro -a hard

echar to throw; **echar de menos** to miss (someone)

edad f. age; **¿qué edad tiene?** how old is he?

edificio m. building

ejecutar to execute

ejército m. army

elegir (i, i) (3) (B) to elect

embargo: sin embargo however, nevertheless

emocionante exciting

empeñarse en + inf. to insist on (doing something)

emperador m. emperor

empezar (ie) (1) (A) to begin

emplear to employ, use

emprender to undertake

en in, on, at

encaminarse a to head towards

encantador -ra charming

encarcelar to imprison

encargar (A) to entrust

encender (ie) (1) to light up; to turn on (the light, radio, etc.)

encima (de) above

encontrar (ue) (1) to find; to meet; **encontrarse con,** to meet

encuentro m. encounter, clash

enemigo -a enemy

enfadado -a angry

enfermedad f. illness, disease

enfermero -a nurse; **de enfermero(-a)** as a nurse

enfermo -a sick, ill

enfrentar to face, confront

enfrente de in front of; **de enfrente** opposite

engordar to get fat

enlazar (A) to link

enredarse to get entangled

enseñar to teach; to show

entender (ie) (1) to understand

enterrar (ie) (1) to bury

entonces then

entrar (en) to enter

entre between, among

entrega f. delivery

entregar (A) to deliver, hand over; **entregarse a** to devote oneself to

entrenamiento m. training

entrenar to train

enviar (D) to send

envolver (ue) (1) to wrap

equipo m. team; equipment

equitación f. horseback riding

erigir (B) to erect

escalar to scale, climb

escalera f. staircase, stairs

escaparate m. store window

escarpado -a steep

escocés -esa Scottish

escoger (B) to choose

escolar (pertaining to) school

escombros m. pl. debris

esconder to hide

escuchar to listen (to)

esfuerzo m. effort

esmalte m. enamel

eso that; **por eso** therefore, for that reason

España Spain

espectáculo m. show

espeluznante hair-raising

esperar to wait (for); to hope; to expect

espeso -a thick

espuma f. foam

esquiar (D) to ski

esquina f. street corner

estación f. station; season

estacionar to park

estado m. state

estampilla f. stamp

estanque m. tank; pool, pond

estrecho -a narrow; m. strait

estrella f. star

estrenar to use or wear for the first time; to perform for the first time

evitar to avoid

exigencia f. demand

exigir (B) to demand

éxito m. success; **tener éxito** to be successful

explicar (A) to explain

explotar to explode; to exploit

exponer (13) to expose; to exhibit

extensión f. extent, expanse

extinguir (B) to extinguish, put out

extranjero -a foreign

extraño -a strange

extravagante odd, outlandish

extremo m. end

fábrica f. factory

fabricante m. manufacturer

fabricar (A) to manufacture

fácil easy

facilidad f. ease; **con facilidad** easily

falta f. mistake, error; lack

fallecer (C) to die, pass away

fascinar to fascinate

fase *f.* phase
fatigoso -a tiring
fecha *f.* date
feria *f.* fair
festejo *m.* festivity; *pl.* rejoicings, public festivities
fiar (D): **fiarse de** to trust
fiel faithful; *m. & f.* worshipper
fijar to fix; to set; **fijarse en** to notice
fin *m.* end; **por fin** finally; **a fin de** + *inf.* in order to
finca *f.* country estate, property
flaco -a skinny, thin
flor *f.* flower
florero *m.* flowerpot
flota *f.* fleet
fondo *m.* rear, bottom; fund
forastero -a stranger, person from another part of the country
fortaleza *f.* fortress; strength, toughness
frente *f.* forehead
fuego *m.* fire; **fuegos artificiales** fireworks
fuera outside, away; **fuera de** outside of, away from; **fuera borda** outboard
fuerte strong
fuerza strength, force
fui, fuiste, fue, etc. forms of the preterite tense of **ser** and **ir**
fumar to smoke
función *f.* performance
fundar to found, establish
fútbol *m.* soccer

gana *f.* desire; **tener ganas de** + *inf.* to feel like
ganadero *m.* cattle dealer
ganado *m.* cattle
ganar to win; to earn
ganga *f.* bargain
gaseosa *f.* soda
gastar to spend
gasto *m.* expense
gente *f.* people
giro *m.* turn
gobierno *m.* government
gordo -a fat
gorro *m.* cap
gozar (A): **gozar de** to enjoy
gozo *m.* enjoyment
grabadora *f.* tape recorder
graduarse (D) to graduate
grato -a pleasing
griego -a Greek
grueso -a thick

guapo -a handsome, beautiful
guerra *f.* war; **guerra mundial** world war
guerrero *m.* warrior
guiar (D) to guide; to drive
gustar to please; **me gusta(n)** I like it (them) (*see pages 274–275*)

haba (el) *f.* bean
***haber** (8), to have (*aux. verb*); for idioms with **haber,** see pages 272–273
había there was, there were
habitación *f.* room
habrá there will be
***hacer** (9) to do; to make; **hace un año** a year ago; **hacerse** to become; for idioms with **hacer,** see page 272
hacia towards
hallazgo *m.* finding
hambre (el) *f.* hunger; **tener hambre** to be hungry
hasta until; up to; even; **hasta que** + *verb* until
hay there is, there are; **hay que** + *inf.* one must, it is necessary
hazaña *f.* exploit, deed
hecho *m.* fact
helado *m.* ice cream
hembra *f.* female (of an animal)
herido -a wounded
herramienta *f.* tool
hielo *m.* ice
hilo *m.* thread, wire
hincar (A) to sink; to drive (in)
hoja *f.* leaf; blade
holgazán -ana lazy
hombro *m.* shoulder
hora *f.* hour, time; **horas pico** rush hours
hoy today; **hoy día** nowadays
huerta *f.* orchard
hueso *m.* bone
huésped *m.* guest
huevo *m.* egg
huida *f.* escape, flight
huir (E) to flee
humo *m.* smoke
hundirse to sink

idioma *m.* language
iglesia *f.* church
igual equal
igualar to equal
imperio *m.* empire
imponente imposing
imponer (13) to impose

inacabado -a incomplete, unfinished
incendio *m.* fire
indígena *m. & f.* native
informe *m.* report; piece of information; **informe semestral** term paper
ingenuamente naively
Inglaterra *f.* England
inglés -esa English
ingreso *m.* entrance
inquieto -a worried, upset
insoportable unbearable
***ir** (10) to go; **ir a** + *inf.* to be going to: **van a salir** they are going to leave; **irse** to go away, leave
izquierdo -a left; **a la izquierda** to (at) the left

jabón *m.* soap
jamás never, ever
jefe *m.* chief, boss
jinete *m.* horseman
joven (*pl.* **jóvenes**) young; *m.* young man, *f.* young woman
joya *f.* jewel
juego *m.* game; **salón de juegos** game room
jugador -ra player
jugar (ue) (1) (A) to play; **jugar al tenis** to play tennis
juguete *m.* toy
junto a next to
juntos -as together
jurar to swear

kilo *m.* kilogram (= 2.2 pounds)
kilómetro *m.* kilometer (about $\frac{5}{8}$ mile)

lado *m.* side
lago *m.* lake
lanzar (A) to throw, hurl
largo -a long; **a lo largo de** along
lástima *f.* pity; **es lástima** it's a pity
latido *m.* beat (of the heart)
lavar to wash; **lavarse** to get washed, to wash up
lazo *m.* bond, tie
leal loyal, faithful
lealtad *f.* loyalty
lectura *f.* reading
legar (A) to bequeath
lejano -a distant, remote
lejos (de) far (from)
lentitud *f.* slowness

lento -a slow
levantarse to get up, rise
ley *f.* law
leyenda *f.* legend
libra *f.* pound
libre free
ligero -a light (in weight)
limpiar to clean
listo -a (with **estar**) ready; (with **ser**) clever
lograr + *inf.* to succeed in, manage to
lo que what (= that which), which
luchar to fight, struggle
luego then; **luego que** as soon as
lugar *m.* place; **tener lugar** to take place
lujo *m.* luxury
lujoso -a luxurious
lujuriante lush, luxuriant
luto *m.* mourning; **de luto** in mourning
luna *f.* moon
luz (*pl.* **luces**) *f.* light

llamar to call; **llamarse** to be called, named
llanto *m.* sob, sobbing
llegada *f.* arrival
llegar (A) to arrive; **llegar a** to reach, arrive at; **llegar a ser** to become
llenar to fill
lleno -a full
llevar to wear; to carry; to take (someone somewhere); **llevar a cabo** to carry out
llorar to cry, weep
llover (ue) (1) to rain
lluvia *f.* rain

madrugada *f.* early morning (between midnight and dawn)
maduro -a (with **ser**) mature, (with **estar**) ripe
mal badly, ill, sick
maldito -a accursed
maleta *f.* suitcase
maletín *m.* small suitcase
maltrato *m.* mistreatment, bad treatment
manada *f.* herd
mancha *f.* stain
mandar to send; to order
mando *m.* command
manejar to manage; to operate; to drive (a car)
manera *f.* way, manner

manta *f.* blanket
manzana *f.* apple
mañana tomorrow; *f.* morning
máquina *f.* machine; **escribir a máquina** to typewrite
mar *m.* sea
maravilla *f.* wonder, marvel
marcha: estar en marcha to be on one's way
marroquí Moroccan
más more, most
máscara *f.* mask
matar to kill
maya Mayan (Indian)
mayor older, oldest; greater, greatest
mediados: hasta mediados de till the middle of
médico -a doctor
medio -a half; average; *m.* means
medir (i, i) (3) to measure
mejor better, best
menor younger, youngest
menos less, fewer, least; except; **al menos** at least; **por lo menos** at least
mensaje *m.* message
mente *f.* mind
mentir (ie, i) (2) to lie
mentira *f.* lie
menudo: a menudo often
merecer (C) to deserve
meridional southern
meseta *f.* plateau
meteorólogo *m.* weather forecaster
meter to put in(to), insert; **meterse** to meddle
metro *m.* subway; meter (= 3.3 feet)
miedo *m.* fear; **tener miedo** to be afraid
mientras while; **mientras tanto** meanwhile
milagroso -a miraculous
miles *m. pl.* thousands
milla *f.* mile
mirar to look (at)
mismo -a (*before noun*) same; (*after noun*) self: **Ud. mismo(-a)** you yourself; **lo mismo** the same (thing)
modo *m.* way, manner; **de todos modos** anyway, at any rate
mole *f.* mass; **mole pétrea** rocky mass
molestar to bother, disturb
moneda *f.* coin

monstruoso -a monstrous
montaña *f.* mountain
montar to mount; **montar a caballo** to go horseback riding
moreno -a dark-complexioned; *f.* brunette
morir(se) (ue, u) (2) to die (*pp.* **muerto**)
mosquete *m.* musket
mostrar (ue) (1) to show
motora *f.* motor boat
muchedumbre *f.* crowd
muchísimo -a very much; *pl.* very many
mueble *m.* piece of furniture; *pl.* furniture
muerte *f.* death
muerto -a dead
muralla *f.* wall
muro *m.* wall
museo *m.* museum
música *f.* music
músico *m.* musician
muy very

nacer (C) to be born
nacimiento *m.* birth; source (of a river)
nada nothing, (not) anything
nadie no one, nobody; (not) anybody
narrador -ra narrator
natural natural; native
naturaleza *f.* nature
naufragar (A) to be shipwrecked
nave *f.* ship; nave (of a church)
navío *m.* ship
negar (ie) (1) (A) to deny; **negarse a** + *inf.* to refuse to
negocio *m.* business
nene -a baby
neoyorquino -a New Yorker
nevar (ie) (1) to snow
nevera *f.* icebox, refrigerator
niebla *f.* fog, mist
nieto -a *m.* grandson, *f.* granddaughter, *pl.* grandchildren
nivel *m.* level; **nivel del mar** sea level
noche *f.* night, evening; **esta noche** tonight; **por la noche** in the evening; **de la noche** in the evening, P.M. (*when clock time is expressed*)
nombre *m.* name
nordeste *m.* northeast
noroeste *m.* northwest
norte *m.* north

nota *f.* note; grade, mark; **sacar buenas (malas) notas** to get good (bad) marks
noticia *f.* news item, piece of news; *pl.* news
novedoso -a novel (= new)
noveno -a ninth
nube *f.* cloud
nuera *f.* daughter-in-law
nuestro -a our
nuevo -a new; **de nuevo** again
número *m.* number
nunca never, (not) ever

o or
obedecer (C) to obey
obra *f.* work (of art, literature, etc.); **obra teatral** play
obrero -a worker
obstante: no obstante nevertheless
obtener (18) to obtain, get
occidental western
ocio *m.* leisure
ocultar to hide
odio *m.* hatred
oeste *m.* west
ofrecer (C) to offer
***oír** (11) to hear
oler (huelo) (1) to smell
olvidar, olvidarse de to forget
onda *f.* wave
oración *f.* sentence
ordenador *m.* computer
ordinario ordinary; **de ordinario** ordinarily
orilla *f.* bank (of a river); **a orillas de** on the banks of
oro *m.* gold
otro -a other, another
oveja *f.* sheep

pabellón *m.* pavilion
pagar (1) to pay (for)
país *m.* country, nation
paisaje *m.* landscape, countryside
paja *f.* straw
pájaro *m.* bird
pálido -a pale
palo *m.* stick
pan *m.* bread
panadería *f.* bakery
papel *m.* paper; **hacer un papel** to play a role
para for; by; + *inf.* in order to; **para que** + *subjunctive* in order that

parada *f.* stop; **parada de autobuses** bus stop
paraguas *m., s. & pl.* umbrella
paraíso *m.* paradise
parar(se) to stop
pardoamarillento -a, yellowish brown
parecer (C) to seem; **parecerse a** to resemble, look like
parecido -a similar, alike
pared *f.* wall
pareja *f.* couple, partner
pariente *m. & f.* relative
parque *m.* park; **parque zoológico** zoo
párrafo *m.* paragraph
parroquia *f.* parish
particular private
partido *m.* game, match; (political) party
partir to leave, depart; **a partir de,** starting on (at, from)
pasado -a past, last; **la semana pasada** last week
pasar to pass; to happen; to spend (time)
pasatiempo *m.* pastime, hobby
Pascua *f.* Easter; **Pascua Florida** Easter
paseo *m.* walk, stroll, ride; **dar un paseo** to take a walk (ride); **salir de paseo** to go out for a walk
pasillo *m.* passageway, aisle, corridor
paso *m.* step
pastel *m.* pie, cake, pastry
pata *f.* paw, foot (of an animal)
patinar to skate
pavo *m.* turkey
paz, *f.* peace; **hacer las paces** to make up, "bury the hatchet"
peatonal *m.* pedestrian walkway
pedazo *m.* piece
pedir (i, i) (3) to ask (for), request
película *f.* film, movie
peligro *m.* danger
peligroso -a dangerous
pelo *m.* hair
peluquería *f.* barber shop (hairdresser's)
peluquero -a barber, hairdresser
pena *f.* trouble, effort; **valer la pena** to be worthwhile
pensar (ie) (1) to think; **pensar** + *inf.* to intend to; **pensar en** to think of (about)
perder (ie) (1) to lose; to miss (a train, etc.); **perderse** to get lost

peregrino -a pilgrim
permanecer (C) to stay, remain
pero but
pertenecer (C) to belong
pesado -a heavy
pesar to weigh; **a pesar de** in spite of
pescador *m.* fisherman
peso *m.* weight
pez *m.* fish (alive and still in the water)
pico *m.* (mountain) peak
piel *f.* skin, fur
pieza *f.* piece
pila *f.* battery
pintura *f.* painting
pisar to step on
piscina *f.* pool
piso *m.* floor, apartment
placer *m.* pleasure
planeador *m.* glider
plano *m.* blueprint
plata *f.* silver
playa *f.* beach
poco (*adv.*) little; **poco -a** little (in quantity); **pocos -as** few; **hace poco** a short while ago
***poder** (12) to be able, can, could
poderoso -a powerful
poetisa *f.* poetess
político *m.* politician
pollo *m.* chicken
***poner** (13) to put; to turn on (the radio, TV, etc.); **ponerse** to put on (clothing); to become; **ponerse a** + *inf.* to begin to
por through, by, for, in, along
poro *m.* pore
¿por qué? why?
porque because
portarse to behave
posada *f.* inn
postre *m.* dessert
precio *m.* price
precipitarse to rush, dart
pregunta *f.* question; **hacer una pregunta** to ask a question
preguntar to ask
premio *m.* prize, award, reward; **premio gordo** first prize (in a lottery)
prender to take root
presentimiento *m.* premonition
prestar to lend
primero -a (primer) first
primo -a cousin
príncipe *m.* prince

principio *m.* beginning; **al principio** at first

prisa: de prisa fast; **tener prisa** to be in a hurry; **darse prisa** to hurry

probar (ue) (1) to test, try (on); **probarse** to try on (clothes)

prodigioso -a prodigious, marvelous

prometer to promise

pronosticar (A) to forecast

pronto soon; **de pronto** suddenly

pronunciar to pronounce

propietario -a owner

propina *f.* tip, gratuity

propio -a own, self

proporcionar to provide

propósito *m.* purpose

proteger (B) to protect

provisional temporary

próximo -a next

proyectar to project

puente *m.* bridge; **puente colgante** suspension bridge

pues well, then, well then

puesto *m.* job, position; stand *or* booth (in a market, fair, etc.)

pulgada *f.* inch

pulular to swarm, abound

puntiagudo -a pointed

punto *m.* point; **en punto** (*with clock time*) sharp, exactly

que who, which, that; than; **¿qué?** what? which?

quejarse to complain

quemar to burn

*****querer** (14) to want, wish; to love; **querer decir** to mean

querido -a dear

queso *m.* cheese

quien -es who; **¿quién -es?** who?; **¿a quién -es?** (to) whom?; **¿de quién -es?** whose?

quitar to take away, remove; **quitarse** to take off (clothes)

raíz *f.* root

ramo *m.* branch; **Domingo de Ramos** Palm Sunday

rapidez *f.* rapidity; **con rapidez** rapidly

rascacielos *m., s. & pl.* skyscraper

rasgo *m.* trait

rato *m.* while; **al poco rato** after a while

razón *f.* reason; **tener razón** to be right

rebajar to lower

recetar to prescribe

recién (*used before past participles*) recently; **recién llegado** recently arrived

recientemente recently

recobrar to recover

recoger (B) to pick up

reconocer (C) to recognize

recordar (ue) (1) to remember

recorrer to tour, go through, cross (a city, country, region)

recorrido *m.* course, distance covered, route

recurso *m.* resource

regalar to give as a gift

regalo *m.* gift, present

regañar to scold

reglamento *m.* regulations

regresar to return, go back

reina *f.* queen

reír (i, i) (3) to laugh; **reírse de** to laugh at, make fun of

reloj *m.* watch, clock

remontar to go up (a river)

renacentista (of the) Renaissance

renovar (ue) (1) to renew

reparación *f.* repair

reparar to repair

repetir (i, i) (3) to repeat

reponerse (13) to recover

requisito *m.* requirement

resfriar (D): **resfriarse** to catch cold

responder to answer

respuesta *f.* answer, reply

restaurar to restore

restos *m. pl.* remains

Resurrección: Domingo de Resurrección Easter Sunday

retirar to withdraw

retrato *m.* portrait

reunir(se) (reúno) to gather

revista *f.* magazine

rey *m.* king; **los Reyes Magos** the Three Wise Men

rezar (A) to pray

riachuelo *m.* brook, stream

rico -a (with **ser**) rich; (with **estar**) delicious

rincón *m.* corner

riqueza *f.* wealth, riches

rodear to surround

romper (*pp.* **roto**) to break; to tear (up)

ropa *f.* clothes, clothing

rostro *m.* face

roto -a broken, torn (see *pp.* of **romper**)

rueda *f.* wheel

ruido *m.* noise

rumbo a headed for

ruta *f.* route

*****saber** (15) to know; **saber + *inf.*** to know how; *preterite:* found out, learned

sabio -a wise, learned; (*noun*) wise person, scholar, scientist

sacar (A) to take out; **sacar apuntes** to take notes; **sacar buenas (malas) notas** to get good (bad) marks; **sacar fotos** to take pictures (*with a camera*)

sacudida *f.* shaking, jolt

sagrado -a sacred

sal *f.* salt

salado -a salty

*****salir** (16): **salir (de)** to leave, go out, come out; **salir bien (mal) en un examen** to pass (fail) a test

salón *m.* meeting room

saltar to jump

salud *f.* health

saludar to greet

salvar to save (= rescue)

sangre *f.* blood

santuario *m.* sanctuary

satisfecho -a satisfied

sé I know (1st pers. sing., present indicative, of **saber**)

secuaz *m.* follower

sed *f.* thirst; **tener sed** to be thirsty

seguida: en seguida at once, immediately

seguir (i, i) (B) to follow; to continue, keep on: **siguen hablando** they continue to talk, keep on talking

según according to

seguridad *f.* safety, security

seguro -a sure, safe

selva *f.* jungle

sello *m.* stamp

semáforo *m.* traffic light

semana *f.* week; **día de entre semana** week day; **la semana pasada** last week

semejante similar

semestre *m.* term, semester

semilla *f.* seed

sencillo -a simple

sendero *m.* path

sentado -a seated

sentarse (ie) (1) to sit down

sentir (ie, i) (2) to regret, be sorry; **sentirse** to feel (sick, well, etc.)

señal *f.* sign, signal

*ser (17) to be; *m.* being

servir (i, i) (3) to serve; **servir de** to serve as

si if

sí yes

sí (*reflexive pronoun used after a prep.*) oneself, himself, herself, itself, yourself (-selves), themselves: **lo guardó para sí** he kept it for himself

siempre always; **para siempre** forever

siglo *m.* century

siguiente following

sillón *m.* armchair

sin without; **sin que** + *subjunctive* without: **lo hizo sin que yo lo supiera** he did it without my knowing it

sino (*used after a negative phrase or clause*) but: **no es gordo sino bastante bajo para su peso** he is not fat but rather short for his weight

sitio *m.* place

situado -a situated, located

sobre on, above, on top of, over; about (= concerning); **sobre todo** especially

sobredicho -a aforementioned

sobrevivir to survive

sol *m.* sun; **tomar el sol** to sunbathe, "get some sun"

solamente only

soler (ue) (1): **soler** + *inf.* to be accustomed to, in the habit of, to generally . . . : **suelo estudiar por la tarde** I generally study in the afternoon

solo -a alone

sólo only

soltar (ue) (1) to loosen, release

soltera *f.* unmarried woman; **soltero** *m.* bachelor

someter to submit

sonar (ue) (1) to ring, sound

sonreír (i, i) (3) to smile

soñar (ue) (1) to dream; **soñar con** to dream of

sorprendente surprising

sorprender to surprise

sosiego *m.* calm, quiet, peacefulness

sótano *m.* basement, cellar

subir to go up, climb, rise; **subir a** to get into (a vehicle)

subrayar to underline

suceder to happen

sudar to sweat

suegro -a *m.* father-in-law, *f.* mother-in-law; *m. pl.* in-laws

sueldo *m.* salary

suelo *m.* ground; floor

suelto -a loose

sueño *m.* sleep; **tener sueño** to be sleepy

suerte *f.* luck; fate; **tener suerte** to be lucky

sufrir to suffer

sugerir (ie, i) (2) to suggest

sumamente very, extremely

sumergir (B) to submerge

superar to surpass

superficie *f.* surface

suponer (13) (*pp.* **supuesto**) to suppose

surgir (B) to rise

sustantivo *m.* noun

sustento *m.* sustenance, food

tabla *f.* board

tacaño -a stingy

tal such; **con tal de** + *inf.* provided that one . . . : **con tal de estudiar** provided that he (she, etc.) studies; **con tal que** + *subjunctive* provided that

tallar to carve

taller *m.* workshop

tamaño *m.* size

también also, too

tampoco neither, (not) either

tan so, as

tanto -a so much, as much; **tantos -as** so many, as many; **tanto . . . como** both . . . and

tardar en + *inf.* to take (+ time interval): **tardé una hora en llegar allí** it took me an hour to get there

tarde late; **más tarde** later; *f.* afternoon

tarea *f.* task, assignment

tarjeta *f.* card; **tarjeta postal** postcard

techo *m.* ceiling; roof

tema *m.* theme, subject

temblor *m.* trembling; **temblor de tierra** earthquake

temer to fear, be afraid

tempestad *f.* storm

temprano early

tenedor *m.* fork

*tener (18) to have; for idioms with **tener,** see page 271

tentativa *f.* attempt

terremoto *m.* earthquake

tesoro *m.* treasure

tiburón *m.* shark

tiempo *m.* time; weather; tense; **a tiempo** on time; **tiempo compuesto** compound tense; for idioms with **tiempo,** see page 272

tienda *f.* store

tierno -a tender

tierra *f.* land, earth

tipo *m.* kind, type

tirar to pull; to shoot

tocadiscos *m., s. & pl.* record player, phonograph

tocar (A) to play (*an instrument*); to touch; to ring (a bell)

todavía still, yet

todo -a all, every; **todos** everybody; **del todo** at all

tomar to take; to have (= to eat or drink)

tonelada *f.* ton

tontería *f.* foolishness, nonsense

torcer (ue) (1) (C) to twist

toro *m.* bull

torre *f.* tower

trabajador -ra worker

trabajar to work

*traducir (19) (C) to translate

traductor -ra translator

*traer (20) to bring

traje *m.* suit, dress; **traje de baño** swimsuit

trastornar to upset

tratar to treat; **tratar de** to deal with, be about: **el cuento trata de los negocios** the story deals with (is about) business; **tratar de** + *inf.* to try to; **tratarse** to be a question of: **se trata de dinero** it's a question of money

través: a través de across, through

travieso -a mischievous, naughty

trayecto *m.* journey, route

trazar to trace

tribu *f.* tribe

tripulante *m. & f.* crew member

triste sad

tristeza *f.* sadness

trono *m.* throne

tropezar (ie) (1) (A): **tropezar con** to bump into, stumble upon, come across

último -a last
único -a only
útil useful
uva *f.* grape

va, vas, vamos, vais, van forms of the present tense of **ir**
vaca *f.* cow
vacilar to hesitate
vacío -a empty
valentía *f.* bravery
***valer** (21) to be worth; **valer la pena** to be worthwhile
valiente brave, valiant
vasco -a Basque
vecindario *m.* neighborhood
velocidad *f.* speed, velocity
vencer (C) to conquer, beat, defeat
vendar to bandage; **vendar los ojos** to blindfold
vender to sell
vengar (A): **vengarse (de)** to avenge oneself, take revenge (for)
***venir** (22) to come
venta *f.* sale
ventaja *f.* advantage
***ver** (23) to see

veraniego -a (pertaining to) summer
verdad *f.* truth; **es verdad** it is true, that's right; **¿verdad? (¿no es verdad?)** right? isn't it so? isn't she? don't they? etc.
verdadero -a true, real
vestido *m.* dress
vestir (i, i) (3) to dress; **vestirse** to get dressed
vez (*pl.* **veces**) *f.* time; **a la vez** at the same time; **tal vez** perhaps; **una vez** once; **dos veces** twice; **otra vez** again; **en vez de** instead of; **de vez en cuando** from time to time
viajar to travel
viaje *m.* trip, journey; **hacer un viaje** to take a trip
viajero -a traveler
vicio *m.* vice
vida *f.* life
viejo -a old; *m.* old man, *f.* old woman
viento *m.* wind; **hace viento** it is windy
villancico *m.* Christmas carol
vino *m.* wine
vislumbrar to glimpse, catch sight of
víspera *f.* eve

vista *f.* view, sight; **hasta la vista,** see you again
visto: por lo visto apparently
viuda *f.* widow
vivo -a (with **estar**) alive; (with **ser**) lively
volador -ra flying
volante flying; *m.* steering wheel; **platillo volante** flying saucer
volar (ue) (1) to fly
volcán *m.* volcano
volcar (ue) (1) to overturn
voluntad *f.* will
volver (ue) (1) to return, go back
voy I am going (see **ir**)
voz (*pl.* **voces**) *f.* voice; **en voz baja** in a low voice; **en voz alta** aloud
vuelo *m.* flight
vuelta *f.* turn; **dar una vuelta** to make a turn

y and
ya already; **ya no** no longer, not . . . anymore
yate *m.* yacht

zapato *m.* shoe
zoológico: parque zoológico zoo

ENGLISH-SPANISH VOCABULARY

Concerning the Spanish verbs marked with an asterisk (*) and the indications in parentheses, see the first three notes on page 276.

The personal pronouns are not included here since they are covered in chapter 15.

able: to be able *poder

about (*concerning*) acerca de, sobre; (*approximately*) alrededor de, unos -as; **at about** + *clock time* a eso de

absent ausente

accept aceptar

accident el accidente

activity la actividad

actor el actor

actress la actriz

Adam Adán

addicted adicto -a

address la dirección

advice (*piece of advice*) el consejo; (*generally*) los consejos

affection el cariño

after después (de); **afterward** después, luego

afternoon la tarde; **in the afternoon** por la tarde; (*with clock time*) de la tarde

again otra vez, volver a + *inf.*: **he will write again** volverá a escribir

ago: ten days ago hace diez días

agree *estar de acuerdo; **to agree (to do something)** convenir en (hacer algo): **they agreed to meet** convinieron en reunirse

aisle el pasillo

all todo -a, todos -as; **all night** toda la noche; **all the money** todo el dinero; **all the books** todos los libros

already ya

although aunque

always siempre

amusing divertido -a

angry enfadado -a, enojado -a; **to get angry** enfadarse, enojarse

announce anunciar

annoy molestar, fastidiar

another otro -a

answer la respuesta; contestar, responder

anybody (see **anyone**)

anymore más, ya no: **he does not come anymore** no viene más, ya no viene

anyone alguien, nadie; **did they see anyone?** ¿vieron a alguien?; **we did not see anyone** no vimos a nadie

anything algo, nada; **do they have anything?** ¿tienen algo?; **she does not see anything** no ve nada

anyway de todos modos, de todas maneras

apply aplicar (A); **to apply for** solicitar; **to apply for admission (to a college, etc.)** solicitar ingreso

around alrededor (de)

arrive llegar (A); **arrive at** llegar a (en)

art el arte (*pl.* las artes)

article el artículo

artistic artístico -a

ask, preguntar; **ask for (request)** pedir (i, i) (3)

asleep dormido -a; **to fall asleep** dormirse

astronaut el (la) astronauta

at a; (= *in*) en

attend asistir a

attentive atento -a

automobile el automóvil, el coche, el carro

average medio -a

award el premio

bad malo -a (mal)

badly, mal

bank el banco

barbecue la barbacoa

baseball el béibol

basketball el básquetbol, el baloncesto

be *estar (7), *ser (17)

beach la playa

beautiful hermoso -a, bello -a

because porque; **because of** a causa de

bed la cama; **to go to bed** acostarse (ue) (1)

before (*prep.*) antes de, (*conj.*) antes (de) que + *subj*; (= *beforehand*) antes

begin comenzar (ie) (1), empezar (ie) (1)

bell la campana; (*electric*) el timbre

best el (la) mejor, los (las) mejores; **I like ice cream best** me gusta más el helado

better mejor, mejores

bill la cuenta

birthday el cumpleaños; (*pl.*) los cumpleaños

blouse la blusa

bookshelf el estante

bookshop la librería

bored: to be bored estar aburrido(-a); **to get bored** aburrirse

boring aburrido -a (with *ser*)

box office la taquilla

break romper (*pp.* roto); **break down** descomponerse (13)

bring *traer (20)

broken roto -a

brother el hermano

build construir (E)

building el edificio

bull el toro

bus el autobús; (*in Cuba and Puerto Rico*) la guagua; **bus stop** la parada de autobuses

buy comprar; **buy tickets** (*to a show, etc.*) sacar entradas

by por; (*by a certain time*) para

calculator la calculadora
call llamar
can (=be able) *poder (12)
candidate el candidato, la candidata
car el coche, el carro, el auto
card la tarjeta
care el cuidado
careful cuidadoso -a; **to be careful** *tener (18) cuidado
case: in case en caso de que + subj.
catch coger (B)
certain cierto -a
change el cambio; cambiar; **change one's mind** cambiar de parecer
Charles Carlos
chat charlar
chess el ajedrez
chicken el pollo; **chicken with rice** arroz con pollo
cigarette el cigarrillo
citizen el ciudadano, la ciudadana
city la ciudad
clarinet el clarinete
clarity la claridad
clean limpio -a; limpiar
close cerrar (ie) (1)
clothes la ropa
club el club
coat el abrigo
coin la moneda
cold frío -a; (*noun*) el frío; **to have a cold** tener un resfriado (catarro); for idioms with frío, see pages 271–272
collection la colección
college la universidad
come *venir (22); **come in** entrar (en)
comfortable cómodo, -a
company la compañía
competition (*sports*) la competición
complain quejarse
computer la computadora, el ordenador
concert el concierto; **rock concert** el concierto de rock
conference la conferencia
continue continuar (D), seguir (i, i) (3) (B); **he continues studying (to study)** continúa (sigue) estudiando
contribute contribuir (E)
corner (*of a room*) el rincón, (*street corner*) la esquina

correct correcto -a; corregir (i, i) (3) (B)
cost costar (ue) (1)
cough toser
could use the appropr. form of *poder (12): **he could** (*past tense*) pudo *or* podía; (*conditional*) podría; (*imperf. subj.*) pudiera
count contar (ue) (1); **count on** contar con
country (*nation*) el país; (*opposite of the city*) el campo
courteous cortés
cousin el primo, la prima
cup la taza
custom la costumbre

dance el baile; bailar
danger el peligro
dangerous peligroso -a
day el día; **these days (nowadays)** hoy día
decide decidir, decidirse a
Democrat demócrata, *m. & f.*
deserve merecer (C)
destroy destruir (E)
detail el detalle
die morir (ue, u) (2) (*pp.* muerto), morirse
different diferente, distinto -a; (= *another*) otro -a
difficult difícil
difficulty la dificultad
dinner la cena
direct dirigir (B)
discotheque la discoteca
discussion la discusión
dish el plato
distinguished distinguido -a
do *hacer (9)
dollar el dólar
doubt dudar
doubtful dudoso -a
downtown: to be downtown estar en el centro; **to go downtown** ir al centro
dream el sueño; soñar; **dream of** soñar con
dress el vestido; vestir(se) (i, i) (3)
drive conducir (C), manejar, guiar (guío)
driver el chofer, el conductor
duchess la duquesa
during durante

early temprano -a
educational educativo -a

election la elección, (*for candidates*) las elecciones
electric eléctrico -a
elephant el elefante
empress la emperatriz
end el fin; terminar, acabar; **by the end of** para finales de
engineer el ingeniero, la ingeniera
enjoy gozar (A) de; **I enjoyed the game** me gustó el partido; **he enjoys life** goza de la vida; **to enjoy oneself** divertirse (ie, i) (2)
enjoyable divertido -a
enough bastante, suficiente
enter entrar en
error la falta, el error
escape escaparse
even: even if aunque; **even more** aun más
evening la noche; **in the evening** por la noche; (*with clock time*) de la noche; **this evening** esta noche
every cada, todos los, todas las
examination el examen (*pl.* exámenes)
exceedingly sumamente
exceptional excepcional
exciting emocionante
exhibit la exhibición; exhibir
exist existir
expect esperar
expensive caro -a
explain explicar
explosion explosión
eyeglasses las gafas, los anteojos

fall *caer(se) (3); **fall asleep** dormirse (ue, u) (2)
far (from) lejos (de)
fast (*adj.*) rápido, -a; (*adv.*) rápidamente, de prisa
feel sentirse (ie, i) (2): **they don't feel well** no se sienten bien
few pocos, -as; **fewer** menos; **a few** algunos -as, unos, -as
film la película
finally por fin, al fin
find encontrar (ue) (1), hallar
find out averiguar (D); **I found out the truth**, supe la verdad
finish terminar, acabar
fire el fuego; (*in a building*) el incendio
fireman (firefighter) el bombero, la bombera
first primero -a (primer)

fit *caber (2)
flat llano -a; (*surface*) plano -a
flee huir (E)
flood el diluvio, la inundación
Florida la Florida
flunk (*to fail someone*) suspender; (*to fail an exam or a course*) ser suspendido(-a) en un examen (curso)
follow seguir (i, i) (3) (B)
food el alimento, la comida
for para, por (*see pages 273–274*)
foreign extranjero -a
forget olvidar, olvidarse de
former antiguo -a (*before noun*)
fortune la fortuna
Frank, Francisco
free libre; (= *free of charge*) gratis
friendly amable
friendship la amistad
from de
fun: to be fun ser divertido (-a)
function funcionar
future (*adj.*) futuro -a; (*noun*) el futuro, el porvenir

game el juego; (*match*) el partido; **electronic game** juego electrónico; **Olympic Games** los Juegos Olímpicos; **video games** los juegos de vídeo
general general; **generally** generalmente, por lo general
gentleman el caballero, el señor
George Jorge
German alemán -ana; (*language*) el alemán
get conseguir (i, i) (3) (B), obtener (18); **get to** (= *arrive at*) llegar a (en); **get up** levantarse; **get used to** acostumbrarse a
give *dar (5)
glad: to be glad to alegrarse de + *inf.*
glove el guante
go *ir (10); **go away** *irse, marcharse; **go out** *salir (16) de; **go up** subir
government el gobierno
governor el gobernador
grandparents los abuelos
greet saludar
group el grupo; (*rock combo, etc.*) el conjunto
guest el invitado, la invitada
guitar la guitarra

habit la costumbre

half medio -a; *half hour* media hora; **at half past four** a las cuatro y media
happen pasar, ocurrir, suceder
happy (with *ser*) feliz; (with *estar*) contento -a, alegre
hard-working trabajador -ra
have *tener (18); (*a meal or drink*) tomar; **have a good time** divertirse (ie, i) (2), pasar un buen rato; **have to** (*obligation*) deber + *inf.*, (*necessity*) tener que + *inf.*
hear *oír (11)
heat el calor; (*in a building*) la calefacción
help la ayuda; ayudar
here aquí
high alto -a
home: at home en casa; **to go (return) home** *ir (regresar) a casa; **to leave home** *salir de casa
homework las tareas, el trabajo escolar
hope esperar
hospital el hospital
house la casa; **publishing house** la casa editorial
how? ¿cómo?; **how many?** ¿cuántos -as?; **how much?** ¿cuánto -a?
however sin embargo
human humano -a
hurricane el huracán
hurry: to be in a hurry *tener prisa; **to hurry** darse prisa, apresurarse
hurt herir (ie, i) (2), hacer daño a

ice el hielo
ideal ideal
illness la enfermedad
illusion: optical illusion la ilusión (de) óptica
incredible increíble
independent independiente
ingredient el ingrediente
inhabitant el (la) habitante
innocence la inocencia
intend pensar (ie) (1) + *inf.*
interview la entrevista
invent inventar
it *as subject, usually not expressed;* (*direct object*) lo, la; (*indirect object*) le; (*object of preposition*) él, ella; **we like it** nos gusta

jacket la chaqueta
Jane Juana
jewel la joya
job el empleo, el puesto; (*task*) el trabajo, la tarea
John Juan
just: to have just acabar de + *inf.*: **I have just arrived** acabo de llegar; **they had just left** acababan de salir

keep guardar; **to keep a promise** cumplir una promesa; **to keep on —ing** seguir (i, i) (3) (B) + *gerundio*: **keep on working** siga Ud. trabajando; (= *to continue*) seguir: **they continued to read,** siguieron leyendo
kind el tipo, la clase; (*adj.*) amable
king el rey
know (*facts*) *saber (15); (*persons and places*) conocer (C)

landlord el dueño
language la lengua, el idioma
last (*final*) último -a; (*past*) pasado -a: **the last train** el último tren; **last year** el año pasado; (*verb*) durar
late tarde
lateness la tardanza
later más tarde
lawyer el abogado, la abogada
lazy perezoso -a
least menos; **at least** por lo menos
leave *salir (16) (de), partir; (*to go away*) *irse (10); **to leave for** salir para; **to leave (an object somewhere)** dejar
lecture la conferencia
lend prestar
less menos
let (= *allow*) dejar, permitir
let us (let's) vamos a + *inf.*, *or use present subjunctive, 1st pers. pl.*: **let's dance** vamos a bailar, bailemos; **let's not . . .** *use present subjunctive, 1st pers. pl.*: **let's not do the work,** no hagamos el trabajo
license la licencia; **driver's license** la licencia (el permiso) de conducir
lie la mentira; mentir (ie, i) (2); **lie down** acostarse
light la luz (*pl.* luces); claro -a
like, see *gustar*, pages 274–275

line (*of people*) la cola, la fila; **to wait in line** *hacer cola

lion el león

listen (to) escuchar

lively vivo -a

living room la sala

long largo -a; **a long time** mucho tiempo; **how long?** ¿cuánto tiempo?

look (at) mirar; **look for** buscar (A); (= *to seem*) parecer: **it looks good** parece bueno

lose perder (ie) (1)

lost: to get lost perderse (ie) (1)

lottery la lotería

Louis Luis

low bajo -a

lunch al almuerzo; **to eat lunch** almorzar (ue) (1) (A), tomar el almuerzo

magazine la revista

magnificent magnífico -a

main principal

make *hacer (9)

male (*of an animal*) el macho

mall (= *shopping center*) el centro comercial

manage: to manage to lograr + inf.

marathon el (la) maratón

mark (= *school grade*) la nota

married casado -a

marry casarse con

mayor el alcalde, la alcaldesa

meal la comida

measure medir (i, i) (3)

meet encontrar (ue) (1), encontrarse con; (= *to get together*) reunirse (me reúno); (= *to make the acquaintance of*) conocer (C)

meeting la reunión

member el miembro (*no feminine form*), el socio, la socia

mention mencionar

Michael Miguel

microphone el micrófono

midnight la medianoche

mind la mente; **to make up one's mind** decidirse; **to change one's mind** cambiar de parecer

mix mezclar

mom mamá

moon la luna

more más

morning la mañana; **in the**

morning por la mañana; (*with clock time*) de la mañana; **yesterday morning** ayer por la mañana

most más; **most of** la mayoría de, la mayor parte de

motorcycle la moto(cicleta)

movie la película; **movie theater** el cine; **movies** el cine

museum el museo

must (*obligation*) deber + inf., (*necessity*) tener que + inf., (*probability*) deber de + inf.

myself: I myself yo mismo -a

near cerca de; **nearby,** cercano -a, próximo -a

need necesitar; (= *to lack*) faltarle (hacerle falta) a uno: **we need books** nos faltan (nos hacen falta) libros

never nunca, jamás

new nuevo -a

next próximo -a; **the next day** al día siguiente

nice (= *likeable*) simpático, -a; (= *kind, obliging*) amable; (*weather*) bueno

night la noche; **at night** por la noche, de noche; **last night** anoche; **tonight** esta noche

nobody nadie

no one nadie

nothing nada

now ahora

nowadays hoy día

nuisance (*person*) pesado -a

obtain obtener (18), conseguir (i, i) (3) (B)

obvious obvio -a, evidente

offer ofrecer (C)

office la oficina; (*private office*) el despacho

often a menudo; **how often?** ¿cuántas veces?

old viejo -a; (= *ancient*) antiguo -a; **how old is he?** ¿cuántos años tiene él? **I am ten years old** tengo diez años; **the oldest** el (la) mayor, los (las) mayores

on en; **on Friday** el viernes; **on Mondays** los lunes; **on May 15** el quince de mayo; **on . . . -ing** al + inf.: **on leaving** al salir

once una vez; **at once** en seguida

only (*adv.*) sólo, solamente; (*adj.*) único -a; **I have only five**

books tengo sólo (solamente) cinco libros, no tengo más que cinco libros; **my only friend** mi único amigo

open abrir (*pp.* abierto)

opera glasses los gemelos de teatro

orchestra la orquesta

order la orden, (*arrangement*) el orden; (*to give orders*) mandar; (*from a menu*) pedir (i, i) (3); **in order to** para + inf.; **in order for (that)** para que + *subjunctive*: **in order for you to go,** para que tú vayas

other otro -a

outside fuera, afuera; (*prep*) fuera de

own propio -a: **my own house** mi propia casa

package el paquete

painting la pintura

pair el par

parents los padres

park el parque

part la parte; **to take part** tomar parte, participar

party la fiesta; (*political party*) el partido

pass pasar; **to pass a test** *salir bien en un examen, aprobar (ue) (1) un examen

patience la paciencia

patient paciente

pay (for) pagar (A); **I paid for the shirt** pagué la camisa; **I paid ten dollars for the shirt** pagué diez dólares por la camisa

people (*as a group*) la gente; (*as individuals*) las personas; (*nation or race*) el pueblo

permit permitir

personal personal

phone el teléfono

photo la foto(grafía)

photocopy la fotocopia

piano el piano

pick up recoger (B)

picture (*movie*) la película; (*photo*) la foto(grafía); (*in a book*) la imagen

pity la lástima; **it is a pity** es lástima

place el lugar, el sitio; **to take place** *tener lugar

play (*theater*) la pieza, la comedia;

jugar (ue) (1) (A); (*a musical instrument*) tocar (A); **to play cards** jugar a las cartas

player el jugador, la jugadora

please, (*with command*) por favor; (*with inf.*) haga Ud. el favor de; **please sit down:** siéntese, por favor, haga Ud. el favor de sentarse

poet el poeta, la poetisa

policeman el policía

politician el político

polluted contaminado -a

possibility la posibilidad

prefer preferir (ie, i) (2)

prepare preparar; **to prepare for something** prepararse para algo

present (*adj.*) actual; (*gift*) el regalo

pretty bonito -a

princess la princesa

principal (*of a school*) el director, la directora

prison la cárcel

prize el premio; (*lottery*) **the grand prize** el premio gordo

program el programa

prohibit prohibir (prohíbo)

promise prometer; la promesa

properly correctamente

propose proponer (13)

public público -a

publish publicar (A); **publishing house** la casa editorial

put *poner (13); **to put on** (*radio, TV*) poner; (*clothes*) ponerse; **to put out (extinguish)** apagar (A)

quality (*characteristic*) la cualidad; (*degree of excellence*) la calidad

quick rápido -a

quite bastante

racquet la raqueta

radio la radio; (*radio set*) el radio

rain la lluvia; llover (ue) (1)

raise (*lift*) levantar; (*increase*) aumentar

rapid rápido -a

read leer (4)

ready: to be ready *estar listo(-a)

real verdadero -a

realize (*to make happen*) realizar; (*to become aware of*) *darse cuenta de: **I realized my dreams** realicé mis sueños; **she realized he had left** se dio cuenta de que había salido

record el disco; **record player** el tocadiscos

refreshed refrescado -a

refreshments los refrescos

refuse negarse (ie) (1) (A); **to refuse to (do something)** negarse a (hacer algo)

relations las relaciones

relative el (la) pariente

remain quedarse, permanecer (C)

remember recordar (ue) (1); acordarse (ue) (1) de

rent el alquiler; alquilar

repeat repetir (i, i) (3)

report el informe

Republican republicano -a

rescue salvar

respect respetar

rest (*the remainer*) el resto; descansar

result resultar

return (*go back*) regresar, volver (ue) (1) (*pp.* vuelto); (*give back*) devolver (ue) (1) (*pp.* devuelto)

rice el arroz

ride: to go for a ride (in a car) dar un paseo (en coche)

right el derecho; (*opposite of left*) derecho -a; **on the right (side)** a la derecha; **to be right** tener razón; **right now** ahora mismo

ring sonar (ue) (1), tocar (A); **the bell is ringing** suena el timbre; **he rang the bell** tocó el timbre

road el camino, la carretera

room el cuarto, la habitación; **to be room (space) for** *caber (2): **there is no room for me in the car** no quepo en el coche

route la ruta

run correr

sad triste

sadness la tristeza

safe seguro -a

salad la ensalada

same mismo -a

saucer: flying saucer el platillo volante

save (*money*) ahorrar; (*rescue*) salvar

say *decir (6)

school la escuela; **to school** a la escuela; **in (at) school** en la escuela

season la estación

seat el asiento

secret el secreto

section la sección; **front section** la sección delantera

see *ver (23)

seem parecer (C)

sell vender

send mandar, enviar (D)

serious serio -a, grave

serve servir (i, i) (3)

several varios -as

severe grave, severo -a

shape: in good shape en buena forma

shopping: to go shopping *ir de compras

should deber + *inf.*: **you should study** tú debes estudiar

show el espectáculo, la función; mostrar (ue) (1), enseñar

sick enfermo -a

silent silencioso -a

since (= *because*) como, puesto que

sing cantar

singer el (la) cantante

single (*unmarried*) soltero -a

sit (*to be seated*) *estar sentado(-a); (*to sit down*) sentarse (ie) (1)

skate el patín; patinar

ski el esquí; esquiar (D); **to go skiing** *ir a esquiar

sleep dormir (ue, u) (2)

sleepy: to be sleepy *tener sueño

slide la diapositiva

slow lento -a; **slowly** despacio, lentamente

slowness la lentitud

smile la sonrisa; sonreír (i, i) (3)

smoke fumar; el humo

snow la nieve; nevar (ie) (1)

soccer el fútbol, el balompié

soda la gaseosa

sofa el sofá

some alguno -a (algún)

somebody, someone alguien; **someone else,** otra persona

something algo

sometimes algunas veces

son el hijo

son-in-law el yerno

soon pronto; **as soon as** así que, luego que; **as soon as possible** lo más pronto posible, cuanto antes

sorry: to be sorry sentir (ie, i) (2): **I'm sorry** lo siento

spectator el espectador, la espectadora

speech el discurso
speed la velocidad
spend (*time*) pasar; (*money*) gastar
sport el deporte
stadium el estadio
stage la escena
stamp el sello, la estampilla
stand: to stand up ponerse en pie; **to be standing** estar de pie
star la estrella
start empezar (ie) (1), comenzar (ie) (1); **to start to** empezar a, comenzar a,*ponerse a (*all three followed by inf.*)
state el estado; **the United States** los Estados Unidos
statue la estatua
stay quedarse; (*in a hotel*) parar, alojarse
steal robar
stereophonic estereofónico -a; **stereophonic components** los componentes estereofónicos, el equipo estereofónico
still (= *yet*) todavía, aún
stop parar; **stop . . . -ing** cesar (dejar) de + *inf.*
story el cuento
street la calle; **along (through) the street** por la calle
strong fuerte
such tal; **such small portions** raciones tan pequeñas
suffer sufrir
suit el traje
sunbathe tomar un baño de sol
sunglasses las gafas de sol
support apoyar
supposed to deber + *inf.*
Susan Susana
swim nadar
system el sistema

take tomar; (*take someone or something somewhere*) llevar; **take a ride** *dar un paseo (en coche, en bicicleta, etc.); **take away** llevarse; **take off** (*clothes*) quitarse; **take out** sacar (A); **take (long, three days, etc.) to** tardar en + *inf.*: **it took me two hours to get there** tardé dos horas en llegar allí; **take a walk** *dar un paseo (una vuelta)
talent el talento
tall alto -a
tape la cinta; (= *record on tape*) grabar en cinta

tape recorder la grabadora
task la tarea, el trabajo
taste el gusto, el sabor
teach enseñar; **to teach someone to** enseñar a alguien a + *inf.*: **I taught her to read** le enseñé a leer
team el equipo
telephone el teléfono; telefonear, llamar por teléfono
television la televisión; **television set** el televisor; **color TV** la televisión (el televisor) en colores; **black-and-white TV** la televisión (el televisor) en blanco y negro
tell *decir (6); (= *to narrate*) contar (ue) (1)
temperature la temperatura
tennis el tenis; **tennis match** el partido de tenis
tense el tiempo
term (*school*) el semestre
terrible terrible
test el examen (*pl.* exámenes)
than que, de; **I am taller than you** soy más alto(-a) que tú; **there are more than ten books** hay más de diez libros (see chapter 12)
thank *dar las gracias, agradecer (C): **I thanked him for his kindness** le di las gracias por su bondad, le agradecí su bondad
that (*conj. & rel. pron.*) que; (*dem. adj.*) ese, esa, aquel, aquella; **that one** ése, ésa, aquél, aquélla: **this house and that one** esta casa y ésa; **what is that?** ¿qué es eso (aquello)?; **I know that he is coming** sé que viene; **the girl that I saw** la chica que vi
theater el teatro
then (= *afterward*) luego, después; (= *at that time*) entonces
there allí, allá
there is, there are hay (see pages 272–273)
these (*adj.*) estos, estas; (*pron.*) éstos, éstas: **those pictures and these** esos cuadros y éstos
thief el ladrón, la ladrona
thing la cosa
think pensar (ie) (1); **to think of** pensar en: **I am thinking of my friend** pienso en mi amigo; **what do you think of her?**

¿qué piensas de ella?; (= *believe*) *creer (4)
this (*adj.*) este, esta; **this one** éste, ésta; **that house and this one** esa casa y ésta; **what is this?** ¿qué es esto?
those (*adj.*) esos, esas, aquellos, aquellas; (*pron.*) ésos -as, aquéllos -as: **these boys and those (over there)** estos chicos y aquéllos
threaten amenazar (A); **to threaten to** amenazar con + *inf.*
ticket el billete, el boleto; (= *to a show*) la entrada: **to buy tickets** sacar (A) entradas
time el tiempo; (*time of day*) la hora; (*in succession*) la vez; (*short while*) el rato; **on time** a tiempo; **from time to time** de vez en cuando; **a long time** mucho tiempo; **at what time?** ¿a qué hora?; **three times** tres veces; **at this time (of day)** a estas horas; **to have a good time** divertirse (ie, i) (2), pasar un buen rato
tired: to be tired *estar cansado(-a)
to a; (= *in order to*) para + *inf.*
today hoy
together juntos -as
tomorrow mañana; **tomorrow morning** mañana por la mañana
tonight esta noche
too (= *also*) también; **too late** demasiado tarde
too much (*adv.*) demasiado; (*adj.*) demasiado -a; **too many** demasiados -as
towards hacia
town el pueblo
train el tren
travel viajar
trial el juicio
trip el viaje; **to take a trip** *hacer un viaje
trust fiarse (D) de
truth la verdad
try tratar de + *inf.*; (*to taste*) probar (ue) (1); **to try on (a garment)** probarse
typewriter la máquina de escribir

ugly feo -a
umbrella el paraguas (*pl.* los paraguas)
uncle el tío

understand comprender, entender (ie) (1)
unique único (*follows noun*)
university la universidad
until (*prep.*) hasta; (*conj.*) hasta que
use usar
used to *use the imperfect tense*; **she used to dance well,** ella bailaba bien
useful útil

valuable valioso -a, de valor
vary variar (D)
very muy; **very much** muchísimo; expressed by *mucho* in idioms with *hacer* and *tener* (see pages 271–272)
video el vídeo
visit visitar, la visita; **to pay a visit** *hacer una visita

wait (for) esperar
wake up despertar(se) (ie) (1)
walk *andar, caminar; (*instead of ride*) *ir a pie; **to take a walk** pasearse, *dar un paseo
want desear, *querer
war la guerra; **nuclear war** la guerra nuclear
warm: to be warm (*weather*) *hacer calor, (*persons*) *tener calor, (*things*) *estar caliente; **it is very warm today** hoy hace mucho calor; **we are (= feel) very warm** tenemos mucho calor; **the soup is very warm** la sopa está muy caliente
watch (*wristwatch*) el reloj; **to watch TV** mirar la televisión; **to**

watch a program (film, etc.) ver un programa (una película, etc.)
water el agua (*f*); **the cold water** el agua fría; **the waters** las aguas
weak débil
wear llevar, usar
weather el tiempo (see page 272)
wedding la boda
week la semana
weird extraño -a
well bien
what? ¿qué?
what (= that which) lo que
when cuando; **when?** ¿cuándo?
where donde; **where?** ¿dónde?; (= *to where?*) ¿adónde?
whether si
which (*rel. pron.*) que, el cual, etc. (see chapter 18); **which?** (= *which one(s)?*) ¿cuál, cuáles? (see chapter 18)
who (*rel. pron.*) que, quien, -es, el cual, etc. (see chapter 18); **who?** ¿quién, -es?
whom (*rel. pron.*) a quien, -es, que (see chapter 18); **whom?** ¿a quién, -es?
why? ¿por qué?; (= *for what reason?*) ¿para qué?
wide ancho -a
wife la esposa
will: auxiliary verb of future tense (see chapter 4)
win ganar
windy: it is windy hace viento
wish desear, *querer

with con; **with me** conmigo; **with you** (*fam.*) contigo
within dentro de
without (*prep.*) sin; (*conj.*) sin que + *subjunctive*: **he left without my seeing him** salió sin que yo lo viera
witness el testigo, la testigo
wonder: use future or conditional of probability (see chapter 4): **I wonder where he is** ¿dónde estará él? **I wonder where he was** ¿dónde estaría él?
wonderful maravilloso -a
word la palabra
work el trabajo; trabajar; (*work of art*) la obra; (= *to function*) funcionar
worth: to be worth *valer (21)
would: auxiliary verb of conditional (see chapter 4)
would like: I would like to see it me gustaría verlo
wreck destruir (E), estropear

year el año
yesterday ayer; **yesterday morning** ayer por la mañana
yet todavía
young joven (*pl.* jóvenes); **young man (woman)** el (la) joven; **younger** menor, más joven; **the youngest** el (la) menor, el (la) más joven, los (las) menores, los (las) más jóvenes
youngster el (la) joven

zoo el parque zoológico, el zoológico, el zoo

Index